2004

...ther Praise for

MONEYBALL

"Ebullient, invigorating. . . . Provides plenty of action, both numerical and athletic, on the field and in the draft-day war room." —Lev Grossman, *Time*

"By playing Boswell to Beane's Samuel Johnson, Lewis has given us one of the most enjoyable baseball books in years." —Lawrence S. Ritter, *New York Times Book Review*

"A journalistic tour de force." —Richard J. Tofel, *Wall Street Journal*

"A brilliantly told tale. . . . Michael Lewis's beautiful obsession with the idea of value has once again yielded gold. . . . *Moneyball* explains baseball's startling new insight; that for all our dreams of blasts to the bleachers, the sport's hidden glory lies in not getting out." —Garry Trudeau

"Amazing anecdotes . . . an entertaining, enlightening read." —Will Lingo, *Baseball America*

"This delightfully written, lesson-laden book deserves a place of its own in the Baseball Hall of Fame." —Rich Karlgaard, *Forbes*

"An extraordinary job of reporting and writing." —Mark Emmons, *San Jose Mercury News*

"Anyone who cares about baseball must read it." —Cathleen McGuigan, *Newsweek*

"Michael Lewis has written what might be the best book ever about baseball." —Steve Weinberg, *Orlando Sentinel*

"Lewis has a wonderful story to tell, and he tells it wonderfully." —Richard H. Thaler and Cass R. Sunstein, *The New Republic*

"[Lewis's] descriptive writing allows Beane and the others in the lively cast of baseball characters to come alive." —*Publishers Weekly*

"Lewis's book is a thoroughly modern, entertaining . . . even revolutionary look at the way the game has changed and is changing . . . guaranteed to ruffle a lot of feathers." —Brad Zellar, *Minneapolis Star Tribune*

"This book is as much for people who take joy in new ideas as in games." —Brian O'Neill, *Pittsburgh Post-Gazette*

"Engaging, informative and deliciously contrarian." —Jonathan Yardley, *Washington Post*

"Lewis is a five-tool reporter: He can think, joke, characterize, write for average readers and write for powerful decision makers." —David Kipen, *San Francisco Chronicle*

"Lewis has managed to put together a compelling inside-baseball book that skewers many of the sport's longstanding sacred cows." —Carol Knopes, *USA Today*

"Lewis's glee about the depth of baseball's irrationality has plenty to say to anyone who's human. . . . He rises to Jamesean heights in describing the difference between Beane's view of baseball talent and the rest of baseball's." —Marta Salij, *Detroit Free Press*

"This insightful volume refutes the conventional wisdom of veteran baseball men and celebrates an underdog."
                    —David Lieberfarb, *Newark Star Ledger*

"I understood about one in four words of *Moneyball*, and it's still the best and most engrossing sports book I've read for years. If you know anything about baseball, you will enjoy it four times as much as I did, which means that you might explode."
                    —Nick Hornby, *The Believer*

"Fantastically informative and entertaining . . . bound to excite extreme envy."   —Josh Benson, *New York Observer*

"Open this book . . . and your mind."
                    —Nat Newell, Columbia, South Carolina, *State*

MONEYBALL

The Art of Winning an Unfair Game

MICHAEL LEWIS

W. W. NORTON & COMPANY

NEW YORK LONDON

For information about permission to reproduce selections from this
book, write to Permissions, W. W. Norton & Company, Inc.,
500 Fifth Avenue, New York, NY 10110

Manufacturing by RR Donnelley, Harrisonburg
Book design by Chris Welch
Production manager: Julia Druskin

Library of Congress Cataloging-in-Publication Data

Lewis, Michael (Michael M.)
Moneyball : the art of winning an unfair game / by Michael Lewis.—
1st ed.
p. cm.
ISBN 0-393-05765-8 (hardcover)
1. Baseball—Economic aspects—United States. 2. Baseball—Scouting—
United States. 3. Baseball players—Salaries, etc.—United States. I. Title.
GV880.L49 2003
796.357'06'91
2003005089

ISBN-13: 978-0-393-33839-3 pbk.

W. W. Norton & Company, Inc.
500 Fifth Avenue, New York, N.Y. 10110
www.wwnorton.com

W. W. Norton & Company Ltd.
Castle House, 75/76 Wells Street, London W1T 3QT

2 3 4 5 6 7 8 9 0

For Billy Fitzgerald
I can still hear him shouting at me

CONTENTS

Lately in a wreck of a Californian ship, one of the passengers fastened a belt about him with two hundred pounds of gold in it, with which he was found afterwards at the bottom. Now, as he was sinking—had he the gold? or the gold him?

—John Ruskin, *Unto This Last*

PREFACE

I WROTE THIS BOOK because I fell in love with a story. The story concerned a small group of undervalued professional baseball players and executives, many of whom had been rejected as unfit for the big leagues, who had turned themselves into one of the most successful franchises in Major League Baseball. But the idea for the book came well before I had good reason to write it—before I had a story to fall in love with. It began, really, with an innocent question: how did one of the poorest teams in baseball, the Oakland Athletics, win so many games?

For more than a decade the people who run professional baseball have argued that the game was ceasing to be an athletic competition and becoming a financial one. The gap between rich and poor in baseball was far greater than in any other professional sport, and widening rapidly. At the opening of the 2002 season, the richest team, the New York Yankees, had a payroll of $126 million while the two poorest teams, the Oakland A's and the Tampa Bay Devil Rays, had payrolls of less than a third of that, about $40 million. A decade before, the highest payroll team, the New York Mets, had spent about $44 million on baseball players and the lowest payroll team, the Cleveland Indians, a bit more than $8 million. The raw disparities meant that only the rich teams could afford the best players. A poor team could afford only the maimed and the inept, and was almost certain to fail. Or so argued the people who ran baseball.

And I was inclined to concede the point. The people with the most money often win. But when you looked at what actually had happened over the past few years, you had to wonder. The bottom of each division was littered with teams—the Rangers, the Orioles, the Dodgers, the Mets—that had spent huge sums and failed spectacularly. On the other end of the spectrum was Oakland. For the past several years, working with either the lowest or next to lowest payroll in the game, the Oakland A's had won more regular season games than any other team, except the Atlanta Braves. They'd been to the play-offs three years in a row and in the previous two taken the richest team in baseball, the Yankees, to within a few outs of elimination. How on earth had they done that? The Yankees, after all, were the most egregious example of financial determinism. The Yankees understood what New York understood, that there was no shame in buying success, and maybe because of their lack of shame they did what they did better than anyone in the business.

As early as 1999, Major League Baseball Commissioner Allan H. ("Bud") Selig had taken to calling the Oakland A's success "an aberration," but that was less an explanation than an excuse not to grapple with the question: how'd they do it? What was their secret? How did the second poorest team in baseball, opposing ever greater mountains of cash, stand even the faintest chance of success, much less the ability to win more regular season games than all but one of the other twenty-nine teams? For that matter, what was it about baseball success that resisted so many rich

men's attempt to buy it? These were the questions that first interested me, and this book seeks to answer.

That answer begins with an obvious point: in professional baseball it still matters less how much money you have than how well
you spend it. When I first stumbled into the Oakland front office,
they were coming off a season in which they had spent $34 mil-
lion and won an astonishing 102 games; the year before that, 2000,
they'd spent $26 million and won 91 games, and their division. A
leading independent authority on baseball finance, a Manhattan
lawyer named Doug Pappas, pointed out a quantifiable distinction
between Oakland and the rest of baseball. The least you could
spend on a twenty-five-man team was $5 million, plus another $2
million more for players on the disabled list and the remainder of
the forty-man roster. The huge role of luck in any baseball game,
and the relatively small difference in ability between most major
leaguers and the rookies who might work for the minimum wage,
meant that the fewest games a minimum-wage baseball team
would win during a 162-game season is something like 49. The
Pappas measure of financial efficiency was: how many dollars over
the minimum $7 million does each team pay for each win over its
forty-ninth? How many marginal dollars does a team spend for
each marginal win?

Over the past three years the Oakland A's had paid about half a
million dollars per win. The only other team in six figures was the
Minnesota Twins, at $675,000 per win. The most profligate rich
franchises—the Baltimore Orioles, for instance, or the Texas
Rangers—paid nearly $3 million for each win, or more than six
times what Oakland paid. Oakland seemed to be playing a different game than everyone else. In any ordinary industry the Oakland A's would have long since acquired most other baseball
teams, and built an empire. But this was baseball, so they could
only embarrass other, richer teams on the field, and leave it at
that.

At the bottom of the Oakland experiment was a willingness to rethink baseball: how it is managed, how it is played, who is best suited to play it, and why. Understanding that he would never have a Yankee-sized checkbook, the Oakland A's general manager, Billy Beane, had set about looking for inefficiencies in the game. Looking for, in essence, new baseball knowledge. In what amounted to a systematic scientific investigation of their sport, the Oakland front office had reexamined everything from the market price of foot speed to the inherent difference between the average major league player and the superior Triple-A one. That's how they found their bargains. Many of the players drafted or acquired by the Oakland A's had been the victims of an unthinking prejudice rooted in baseball's traditions. The research and development department in the Oakland front office liberated them from this prejudice, and allowed them to demonstrate their true worth. A baseball team, of all things, was at the center of a story about the possibilities—and the limits—of reason in human affairs. Baseball—of all things—was an example of how an unscientific culture responds, or fails to respond, to the scientific method.

As I say, I fell in love with a story. The story is about professional baseball and the people who play it. At its center is a man whose life was turned upside down by professional baseball, and who, miraculously, found a way to return the favor. In an effort to learn more about that man, and the revolution he was inspiring, I spent a few days with J. P. Ricciardi, the general manager of the Toronto Blue Jays. Ricciardi had worked with Billy Beane in Oakland, and was now having a ball tearing down and rebuilding his new team along the same radical lines as the Oakland A's. Ridiculed at first, Ricciardi had, by the time I met him, earned the respect of even the crustiest of the old baseball writers. By the end of the 2002 season, the big fear in Toronto was that he would bolt town for the job that had been offered to him to run the Boston

Red Sox, who now said that they, too, wished to reinvent their organization in the image of the Oakland A's.

It was at a Red Sox game that I tried to tempt Ricciardi into a self-serving conversation. Months before he had said to me, and with some insistence, that there was a truly astonishing discrepancy between Billy Beane and every other general manager in the game. He'd raised one hand as high as he could and lowered the other as low as he could and said, "Billy is up here and everyone else is down here." Now, as we sat watching the Boston Red Sox lose to his brand-new Blue Jays, I asked Ricciardi if he was willing to entertain the possibility that he was as good at this strange business of running a baseball team as the man he'd left behind in Oakland. He just laughed at me. There was no question that Billy was the best in the game. The question was why.

MONEYBALL

Chapter One

THE CURSE OF TALENT

Whom the gods wish to destroy they first call promising.
—Cyril Connolly, *Enemies of Promise*

THE FIRST THING they always did was run you. When big league scouts road-tested a group of elite amateur prospects, foot speed was the first item they checked off their lists. The scouts actually carried around checklists. "Tools" is what they called the talents they were checking for in a kid. There were five tools: the abilities to run, throw, field, hit, and hit with power. A guy who could run had "wheels"; a guy with a strong arm had "a hose." Scouts spoke the language of auto mechanics. You could be forgiven, if you listened to them, for thinking they were discussing sports cars and not young men.

On this late spring day in San Diego several big league teams were putting a group of prospects through their paces. If the feeling in the air was a bit more tense than it used to be, that was because it was 1980. The risks in drafting baseball players had just risen. A few years earlier, professional baseball players had been granted free agency by a court of law, and, after about two seconds of foot-shuffling, baseball owners put prices on players that defied the old commonsensical notions of what a baseball player should be paid. Inside of four years, the average big league salary had nearly tripled, from about $52,000 to almost $150,000 a year. The new owner of the New York Yankees, George Steinbrenner, had paid $10 million for the entire team in 1973; in 1975, he paid $3.75 million for baseball's first modern free agent, Catfish Hunter. A few years ago no one thought twice about bad calls on prospects. But what used to be a thousand-dollar mistake was rapidly becoming a million-dollar one.

Anyway, the first thing they always did was run you. Five young men stretch and canter on the outfield crabgrass: Darnell Coles. Cecil Espy. Erik Erickson. Garry Harris. Billy Beane. They're still boys, really; all of them have had to produce letters from their mothers saying that it is okay for them to be here. No one outside their hometowns would ever have heard of them, but to the scouts they already feel like household names. All five are legitimate first-round picks, among the thirty or so most promising prospects in the country. They've been culled from the nation's richest trove of baseball talent, Southern California, and invited to the baseball field at San Diego's Herbert Hoover High to answer a question: who is the best of the best?

As the boys get loose, a few scouts chitchat on the infield grass. In the outfield Pat Gillick, the general manager of the Toronto Blue Jays, stands with a stopwatch in the palm of his hand. Clustered around Gillick are five or six more scouts, each with his own stopwatch. One of them paces off sixty yards and marks the finish line with his foot. The boys line up along the left field foul line. To their left is the outfield wall off which Ted Williams, as a high school player, smacked opposite field doubles. Herbert Hoover High is Ted Williams's alma mater. The fact means nothing to the boys. They are indifferent to their surroundings. Numb. During the past few months they have been so thoroughly examined by so many older men that they don't even think about where they are performing, or for whom. They feel more like sports cars being taken out for a spin than they do like young men being tested. Paul Weaver, the Padres scout, is here. He's struck by the kids' cool. Weaver has seen new kids panic when they work out for scouts. Mark McLemore, the same Mark McLemore who will one day be a $3-million-a-year outfielder for the Seattle Mariners, will vomit on the field before one of Weaver's workouts. These kids aren't like that. They've all been too good for too long.

Darnell Coles. Cecil Espy. Erik Erickson. Garry Harris. Billy Beane. One of the scouts turns to another and says: *I'll take the three black kids [Coles, Harris, Espy]. They'll dust the white kids. And Espy will dust everyone, even Coles.* Coles is a sprinter who has already signed a football scholarship to play wide receiver at UCLA. That's how fast Espy is: the scouts are certain that even Coles can't keep up with him.

Gillick drops his hand. Five born athletes lift up and push off. They're at full tilt after just a few steps. It's all over inside of seven seconds. Billy Beane has made all the others look slow. Espy finished second, three full strides behind him.

And as straightforward as it seems—what ambiguity could there possibly be in a sixty-yard dash?—Gillick is troubled. He hollers at one of the scouts to walk off the track again, and make certain that the distance is exactly sixty yards. Then he tells the five boys to return to the starting line. The boys don't understand; they run you first but they usually only run you once. They think maybe Gillick wants to test their endurance, but that's not what's on Gillick's mind. Gillick's job is to believe what he sees and disbelieve what he doesn't and yet he cannot bring himself to believe what he's just seen. Just for starters, he doesn't believe that Billy Beane outran Cecil Espy and Darnell Coles, fair and square. Nor does he believe the time on his stopwatch. It reads 6.4 seconds— you'd expect that from a sprinter, not a big kid like this one.

Not quite understanding why they are being asked to do it, the boys walk back to the starting line, and run their race all over again. Nothing important changes. "Billy just flat-out smoked 'em all," says Paul Weaver.

WHEN HE WAS a young man Billy Beane could beat anyone at anything. He was so naturally superior to whomever he happened to be playing against, in whatever sport they happened to be playing, that he appeared to be in a different, easier game. By the time he was a sophomore in high school, Billy was the quarterback on the football team and the high scorer on the basketball team. He found talents in himself almost before his body was ready to exploit them: he could dunk a basketball before his hands were big enough to palm it.

Billy's father, no athlete himself, had taught his son baseball from manuals. A career naval officer, he'd spend nine months on end at sea. When he was home, in the family's naval housing, he was intent on teaching his son something. He taught him how to pitch: pitching was something you could study and learn. Whatever the season he'd take his son and his dog-eared baseball books to empty Little League diamonds. These sessions weren't simple fun. Billy's father was a perfectionist. He ran their pitching drills with military efficiency and boot camp intensity.

Billy still felt lucky. He knew that he wanted to play catch every day, and that every day, his father would play catch with him.

By the time Billy was fourteen, he was six inches taller than his father and doing things that his father's books failed to describe. As a freshman in high school he was brought up by his coach, over the angry objections of the older players, to pitch the last varsity game of the season. He threw a shutout with ten strikeouts, and went two for four at the plate. As a fifteen-year-old sophomore, he hit over .500 in one of the toughest high school baseball leagues in the country. By his junior year he was six foot four, 180 pounds and still growing, and his high school diamond was infested with major league scouts, who watched him hit over .500 again. In the first big game after Billy had come to the scouts' attention, Billy pitched a two-hitter, stole four bases, and hit three triples. Twenty-two years later the triples would remain a California schoolboy record, but it was the way he'd hit them that stuck in the mind. The ballpark that day had no fences; it was just an endless hot tundra in the San Diego suburbs. After Billy hit the first triple over the heads of the opposing outfielders, the outfielders played him deeper. When he hit it over their heads the second time, the outfielders moved back again, and played him roughly where the parking lot would have been outside a big league stadium. Whereupon Billy hit it over their heads a third time. The crowd had actually laughed the last time he'd done it. That's how it was with Billy when he played anything, but especially when he played baseball: blink and you might miss something you'd never see again.

He encouraged strong feelings in the older men who were paid to imagine what kind of pro ballplayer a young man might become. The boy had a body you could dream on. Ramrod-straight and lean but not so lean you couldn't imagine him filling out. And that face! Beneath an unruly mop of dark brown hair the boy had the sharp features the scouts loved. Some of the scouts still believed they could tell by the structure of a young man's face not only his character but his future in pro ball. They had a phrase they used: "the Good Face." Billy had the Good Face.

Billy's coach, Sam Blalock, didn't know what to make of the scouts. "I've got this first-round draft pick," he says, "and fifteen and twenty scouts showing up every time we *scrimmage*. And I didn't know what to do. I'd never played pro ball." Twenty years later Sam Blalock would be selected by his peers as the best high school baseball coach in the country. His teams at Rancho Bernardo High School in San Diego would produce so many big league prospects that the school would come to be known, in baseball circles, as "The Factory." But in 1979 Blalock was only a few years into his job, and he was still in awe of Major League Baseball, and its many representatives who turned up at his practices. Each and every one of them, it seemed, wanted to get to know Billy Beane personally. It got so that Billy would run from practice straight to some friend's house to avoid their incessant phone calls to his home. With the scouts, Billy was cool. With his coaches, Billy was cool. The only one who ever got to Billy where he lived was an English teacher who yanked him out of class one day and told him he was too bright to get by on his athletic gifts and his charm. For her, Billy wanted to be better than he was. For the scouts—well, the scouts he could take or leave.

What Sam Blalock now thinks he should have done is to herd the scouts into a corner and tell them to just sit there until such time as they were called upon. What he did, instead, was whatever they wanted him to do; and what they wanted him to do was trot his star out for inspection. They'd ask to see Billy run. Sam would have Billy run sprints for them. They'd ask to see Billy throw and Billy would proceed to the outfield and fire rockets to Sam at the plate. They'd want to see Billy hit and Sam would throw batting practice with no one there but Billy and the scouts. ("Me throwing, Billy hitting, and twenty big league scouts in the outfield shagging flies," recalls Blalock.) Each time the scouts saw Billy they saw only what they wanted to see: a future big league star.

As for Billy—Sam just let him be. Baseball, to Blalock's way of thinking, at least at the beginning of his career, was more of an individual than a team sport, and more of an instinctive athletic event than a learned skill. Handed an athlete of Billy's gifts, Blalock assumed, a coach should just let him loose. "I was young and a little bit scared," Blalock says, "and I didn't want to screw him up." He'd later change his mind about what baseball was, but he'd never change his mind about Billy's talent. Twenty-two years later, after more than sixty of his players, and two of his nephews, had been drafted to play pro baseball, Blalock would say that he had yet to see another athlete of Billy's caliber.

They all missed the clues. They didn't notice, for instance, that Billy's batting average collapsed from over .500 in his junior year to just over .300 in his senior year. It was hard to say why. Maybe it was the pressure of the scouts. Maybe it was that the other teams found different ways to pitch to him, and Billy failed to adapt. Or maybe it was plain bad luck. The point is: no one even noticed the drop-off. "I never looked at a single statistic of Billy's," admits one of the scouts. "It wouldn't have crossed my mind. Billy was a five-tool guy. He had it all." Roger Jongewaard, the Mets' head scout, says, "You have to understand: we don't just look at performance. We were looking at talent." But in Billy's case, talent was a mask. Things went so well for him so often that no one ever needed to worry about how he behaved when they didn't go well. Blalock worried, though. Blalock lived with it. The moment Billy failed, he went looking for something to break. One time after Billy struck out, he whacked his aluminum bat against a wall with such violence that he bent it at a right angle. The next time he came to the plate he was still so furious with himself that he insisted on hitting with the crooked bat. Another time he threw such a tantrum that Blalock tossed him off the team. "You have some guys that when they strike out and come back to the bench all the other guys move down to the other end of the bench," says Blalock. "That was Billy."

When things did not go well for Billy on the playing field, a wall came down between him and his talent, and he didn't know any other way to get through the wall than to try to smash a hole in it. It wasn't merely that he didn't like to fail; it was as if he didn't know how to fail.

The scouts never considered this. By the end of Billy's senior year the only question they had about Billy was: Can I get him? And as the 1980 major league draft approached, they were given reason to think not. The first bad sign was that the head scout from the New York Mets, Roger Jongewaard, took a more than usual interest in Billy. The Mets held the first overall pick in the 1980 draft, and so Billy was theirs for the taking. Word was that the Mets had winnowed their short list to two players, Billy and a Los Angeles high school player named Darryl Strawberry. Word also was that Jongewaard preferred Billy to Strawberry. (He wasn't alone.) "There are good guys and there are premium guys," says Jongewaard. "And Billy was a premium premium guy. He had the size, the speed, the arm, the whole package. He could play other sports. He was a true athlete. And then, on top of all that, he had good grades in school and he was going with all the prettiest girls. He had charm. He could have been anything."

The other bad sign was that Billy kept saying he didn't want to play pro baseball. He wanted to go to college. Specifically, he wanted to attend Stanford University on a joint baseball and football scholarship. He was at least as interested in the school as the sports. The baseball recruiter from the University of Southern California had tried to talk Billy out of Stanford. "They'll make you take a whole week off for final exams," he'd said. To which Billy had replied, "That's the idea, isn't it?" A few of the scouts had tried to point out that Billy didn't actually play football—he'd quit after his sophomore year in high school, to avoid an injury that might end his baseball career. Stanford didn't care. The university was in the market for a quarterback to succeed its current star, a sophomore named John Elway. The baseball team didn't have the pull that the football team had with the Stanford admissions office, and so the baseball coach asked the football coach to have a look at Billy. A few hours on the practice field and the football coach endorsed Billy Beane as the man to take over after John Elway left. All Billy had to do was get his B in math. The Stanford athletic department would take care of the rest. And it had.

By the day of the draft every big league scout had pretty much written off Billy as unobtainable. "Billy just scared a lot of people away," recalls scout Paul Weaver. "No one thought he was going to sign." It was insane for a team to waste its only first-round draft choice on a kid who didn't want to play.

The only one who refused to be scared off was Roger Jongewaard. The Mets had three first-round picks in the 1980 draft and so, Jongewaard figured, the front office might be willing to risk one of them on a player who might not sign. Plus there was this other thing. In the months leading up to the draft the Mets front office had allowed themselves to become part of a strange experiment. *Sports Illustrated* had asked the Mets' general manager, Frank Cashen, if one of the magazine's reporters could follow the team as it decided who would become the first overall draft pick in the country. The Mets had shown the magazine their short list of prospects, and the magazine had said it would be convenient, journalistically, if the team selected Darryl Strawberry.

Strawberry was just a great story: a poor kid from the inner-city of Los Angeles who didn't know he was about to become rich and famous. Jongewaard, who preferred Billy to Strawberry, argued against letting the magazine become involved at all because, as he put it later, "we'd be creating a monster. It'd cost us a lot of money." The club overruled him. The Mets front office felt that the benefits of the national publicity outweighed the costs of raising Darryl Strawberry's expectations, or even of picking the wrong guy. The Mets took Strawberry with the first pick and paid him a then fantastic signing bonus of $210,000. The Blue Jays took Garry Harris with the second pick of the draft. Darnell Coles went to the Mariners with the sixth pick, and Cecil Espy to the White Sox with the eighth pick. With their second first-round draft pick, the twenty-third overall, the Mets let Roger Jongewaard do what he wanted, and Jongewaard selected Billy Beane.

Jongewaard had seen kids say they were going to college only to change their minds the minute the money hit the table. But in the weeks following the draft he had laid a hundred grand in front of Billy's parents and it had done nothing to improve the tone of the

discussion. He began to worry that Billy was serious. To the cha-
grin of Billy's mother, who was intent on her son going to Stanford, Jongewaard planted himself in the Beane household. That
didn't work either. "I wasn't getting the vibes I would like," Jongewaard now says. "And so I took Billy to see the big club."

It was 1980. The Beane family was military middle class. Billy
had hardly been outside of San Diego, much less to New York
City. To him the New York Mets were not so much a baseball
team as a remote idea. But that summer, when the Mets came to
San Diego to play the Padres, Jongewaard escorted Billy into the
visitors' clubhouse. There Billy found waiting for him a Mets uniform with his name on the back, and a receiving party of players:
Lee Mazzilli, Mookie Wilson, Wally Backman. The players knew
who he was; they came up to him and joked about how they
needed him to hurry up and get his ass to the big leagues. Even the
Mets' manager, Joe Torre, took an interest. "I think that's what
turned Billy," says Jongewaard. "He met the big league team and
he thought: I can play with these guys." "It was such a sacred
place," says Billy, "and it was closed off to so many people. And I
was inside. It became real."

The decision was Billy's to make. A year or so earlier, Billy's
father had sat him down at a table and challenged him to arm-
wrestle. The gesture struck Billy as strange, unlike his father. His
father was intense but never physically aggressive. Father and son
wrestled: Billy won. Afterward, his father told Billy that if he was
man enough to beat his father in arm-wrestling, he was man
enough to make his own decisions in life. The offer from the Mets
was Billy's first big life decision. Billy told Roger Jongewaard he'd
sign.

What happened next was odd. Years later Billy couldn't be sure
if he dreamed it, or it actually happened. After he told the Mets he
planned to sign their contract, but before he'd actually done it, he
changed his mind. When he told his father that he was having sec-

ond thoughts, that he wasn't sure he wanted to play pro ball, his father said, "You made your decision, you're signing."

In any case, Billy took the $125,000 offered by the Mets. He appeased his mother (and his conscience) by telling her (and himself) he would attend classes at Stanford during the off-season. Stanford disagreed. When the admissions office learned that Billy wouldn't be playing sports for Stanford, they told him that he was no longer welcome in Stanford's classrooms. "Dear Mrs. Beane," read the letter from the Stanford dean of admissions, Fred A. Hargadon, "we are withdrawing Billy's admission . . . I do wish him every success, both with his professional career in baseball and with his alternate plans for continuing his education."

Just like that, a life changed. One day Billy Beane could have been anything; the next he was just another minor league baseball player, and not even a rich one. On the advice of a family friend, Billy's parents invested on their son's behalf his entire $125,000 bonus in a real estate partnership that promptly went bust. It was many years before Billy's mother would speak to Roger Jongewaard.

Chapter Two

HOW TO FIND A BALLPLAYER

YEARS LATER he would say that when he'd decided to become a professional baseball player, it was the only time he'd done something just for the money, and that he'd never do something just for the money ever again. He would never again let the market dictate the direction of his life. The funny thing about that, now he was running a poor major league baseball team, was that his job was almost entirely about money: where to find it, how to spend it, whom to spend it on. There was no more intensely financial period in his life than the few weeks, just after the regular season opened, leading up to the amateur draft. There was also no time that he found more enjoyable. He didn't mind living with money at the center of his life, so long as he was using it on other people, and not having it used on him.

He began that day in the summer of 2002 facing a roomful of his scouts. Billy Beane, now in his fortieth year on earth and his fifth as the Oakland A's general manager, had changed. He'd lost the ramrod posture of his youth. The brown mop of hair had thinned, and been trained, poorly, to part. Otherwise the saggings and crin-klings of middle age were barely discernable on him. The differ-ence in Billy wasn't what had happened to him, but what hadn't. He had a life he hadn't led, and he knew it. He just hoped nobody else noticed.

The men in this room were the spiritual descendants of the older men who had identified Billy Beane, as a boy of sixteen, as a future baseball superstar. Invisible to the ordinary fan, they were nevertheless the heart of the game. They decide who gets to play and, therefore, how it is played. For the first time in his career Billy was about to start an argument about how they did what they did. Calling them in from the field and stuffing them into a dank room in the bowels of the Coliseum for the seven days before the draft had become something of an Oakland custom. It was the point of the exercise that was about to change.

A year ago, before the 2001 draft, the goal had been for the gen-eral manager of the Oakland A's and his scouts to come to some mutually satisfying decision about who to select with the top picks. Billy had allowed the scouts to lead the discussion and influence his decisions. He had even let the scouts choose a lot of their own guys in higher rounds. That changed about five seconds after the 2001 draft, which had been an expensive disaster. The elite players that Billy and the scouts had discussed in advance had been snapped up by other teams before the A's turn came to make their second and final first-round draft pick. All that remained were guys the scouts loved and Billy knew next to noth-ing about. In the confusion, Grady Fuson, the A's soon to be for-mer head of scouting, had taken a high school pitcher named Jeremy Bonderman. The kid had a 94-mile-per-hour fastball, a clean delivery, and a body that looked as if it had been created to wear a baseball uniform. He was, in short, precisely the kind of pitcher Billy thought he had trained his scouting department to avoid.

It was impossible to say whether Jeremy Bonderman would

make it to the big leagues, but that wasn't the point. The odds were against him, just as they were against any high school player. The scouts adored high school players, and they especially adored high school pitchers. High school pitchers were so far away from being who they would be when they grew up that you could imagine them becoming almost anything. High school pitchers also had brand-new arms, and brand-new arms were able to generate the one asset scouts could measure: a fastball's velocity. The most important quality in a pitcher was not his brute strength but his ability to deceive, and deception took many forms.

In any case, you had only to study the history of the draft to see that high school pitchers were twice less likely than college pitchers, and four times less likely than college position players, to make it to the big leagues. Taking a high school pitcher in the first round—and spending 1.2 million bucks to sign him—was exactly the sort of thing that happened when you let scouts have their way. It defied the odds; it defied reason. Reason, even science, was what Billy Beane was intent on bringing to baseball. He used many unreasonable means—anger, passion, even physical intimidation—to do it. "My deep-down belief about how to build a baseball team is at odds with my day-to-day personality," he said. "It's a constant struggle for me."

It was hard to know what Grady Fuson imagined would happen after he took a high school pitcher with the first pick. On draft day the Oakland draft room was a ceremonial place. Wives, owners, friends of the owners—all these people who made you think twice before saying "fuck"—gathered politely along the back wall of the room to watch the Oakland team determine its future. Grady, a soft five foot eight next to Billy's still dangerous-looking six foot four, might have thought that their presence would buffer Billy's fury. It didn't. Professional baseball had violently detached Billy Beane from his youthful self, but Billy was still the guy whose anger after striking out caused the rest of the team to gather on the other end of the bench. When Grady leaned into the phone to take

Bonderman, Billy, in a single motion, erupted from his chair, grabbed it, and hurled it right through the wall. When the chair hit the wall it didn't bang and clang; it exploded. Until they saw the hole Billy had made in it, the scouts had assumed that the wall was, like their futures, solid.

Up till then, Grady had every reason to feel secure in his job. Other teams, when they sought to explain to themselves why the Oakland A's had won so many games with so little money, and excuse themselves for winning so few with so much, usually invoked the A's scouting. Certainly, Grady could never have imagined that his scouting department was on the brink of total overhaul, and that his job was on the line. But that was the direction Billy's mind was heading. He couldn't help but notice that his scouting department was the one part of his organization that most resembled the rest of baseball. From that it followed that it was most in need of change. "The draft has never been anything but a fucking crapshoot," Billy had taken to saying, "We take fifty guys and we celebrate if two of them make it. In what other business is two for fifty a success? If you did that in the stock market, you'd go broke." Grady had no way of knowing how much Billy disapproved of Grady's most deeply ingrained attitudes—that Billy had come to believe that baseball scouting was at roughly the same stage of development in the twenty-first century as professional medicine had been in the eighteenth. Or that all of Billy's beliefs, at the moment of Jeremy Bonderman's selection, acquired a new intensity.

On the other hand, Grady wasn't entirely oblivious to Billy's hostility. He had known enough to be uncomfortable the week before the draft, when Billy's assistant, Paul DePodesta, had turned up in the draft room with his laptop. Paul hadn't played pro ball. Paul was a Harvard graduate. Paul looked and sounded more like a Harvard graduate than a baseball man. Maybe more to the point, Paul shouldn't have even been in the draft room. The draft room was for scouts, not assistant general managers.

It was Paul's computer that Grady dwelled upon. "What do you need that for?" Grady asked Paul after the meeting, as if he sensed the machine somehow challenged his authority. "You're sitting over there with your computer and I don't know what you're doing."

"I'm just looking at stats," said Paul. "It's easier than printing them all out."

Paul wanted to look at stats because the stats offered him new ways of understanding amateur players. He had graduated from college with distinction in economics, but his interest, discouraged by the Harvard economics department, had been on the uneasy border between psychology and economics. He was fascinated by irrationality, and the opportunities it created in human affairs for anyone who resisted it. He was just the sort of person who might have made an easy fortune in finance, but the market for baseball players, in Paul's view, was far more interesting than anything Wall Street offered. There was, for starters, the tendency of everyone who actually played the game to generalize wildly from his own experience. People always thought their own experience was typical when it wasn't. There was also a tendency to be overly influenced by a guy's most recent performance: what he did last was not necessarily what he would do next. Thirdly—but not lastly—there was the bias toward what people saw with their own eyes, or thought they had seen. The human mind played tricks on itself when it relied exclusively on what it saw, and every trick it played was a financial opportunity for someone who saw through the illusion to the reality. There was a lot you couldn't see when you watched a baseball game.

For Billy Beane, it was a little different, a little less cerebral and a little more visceral. Billy intended to rip away from the scouts the power to decide who would be a pro baseball player and who would not, and Paul was his weapon for doing it.

Grady did not know about that. Grady had ignored Paul's prodding to scout the players his computer flushed out. Paul had said the scouts ought to go have a look at a college kid named Kevin Youkilis. Youkilis was a fat third baseman who couldn't run, throw, or field. What was the point of going to see *that*? (Because, Paul would be able to say three months later, Kevin Youkilis has the second highest on-base percentage in all of professional baseball, after Barry Bonds. To Paul, he'd become Euclis: the Greek god of walks.) Grady and his scouts had ignored Paul when he said they ought to check out a college pitcher named Kirk Saarloos. Saarloos was a short right-hander with an 88-mile-per-hour fastball. Why waste time on a short right-hander? (Because, Paul would be able to say less than a year later, Saarloos is one of only two players from the 2001 draft pitching in the big leagues.)

Raw violence had gotten Grady's attention. It was only baseball tradition that allowed scouting directors and scouts to go off and find the ballplayers on their own without worrying too much about the GM looking over their shoulders. And if there was one thing Grady knew about Billy, it was that he could give a fuck about baseball tradition. All Billy cared about was winning. A few days after the 2001 draft—with Billy away and still not speaking to him—Grady crept into Paul's' office. In conciliatory tones, he allowed as how he still needed to sign a pitcher to fill out the A's rookie league roster in Arizona. There was this kid Paul had mentioned who, along with Youkilis and Saarloos, Grady had ignored. David Beck was his name. Beck had gone completely undrafted. Thirty big league teams, each with fifty draft picks, had passed on him. Oddly enough, Paul's computer had spit out Beck's name only because one of Beck's teammates at Cumberland University in Tennessee, a big kid with a 98-mile-per-hour fastball, had made everyone's list as a potential first-round draft pick. Paul had noticed that on the same pitching staff as this consensus first-round pick was this complete unknown, a six foot four left-hander, who had even better numbers than the first rounder. A lower earned run average, fewer home runs allowed, more strike-outs, and fewer walks per nine innings. And Paul just wondered:

maybe the kid had something going for him that the scouts were missing.

He was left wondering. Months passed without any word of Beck from the scouting department. Paul finally asked Grady about him. And Grady said, "Oh yeah, I forgot, I'll have one of the scouts go have a look." But he didn't do it, at least not seriously. When Paul asked again, Billy Owens, the A's scout responsible for covering Tennessee grudgingly came back to him with the word that Beck was "a soft tosser." Soft tosser was scouting code for not worth my time. Paul still had the impression that no one had bothered to scout David Beck.

When he came to see Paul after the draft, Grady was in a different mood about David Beck. Should we sign your guy? he asked.

What guy? asked Paul. He'd forgotten about Beck.

Beck, said Grady.

Grady, he's not *my* guy, said Paul. I just asked you to check him out.

Grady was eager to make peace with the front office, and he thought he could do it by throwing Paul a bone. He ran off and signed David Beck, sight unseen. A few days later, Beck reported for duty at the A's training facility in Scottsdale, Arizona. Most of the scouts, and Paul, happened to be there when Beck warmed up in the A's bullpen. It was one of the most bizarre sights any of them ever had seen on a pitcher's mound. When the kid drew back his left arm to throw, his left hand flopped and twirled maniacally. His wrist might as well not exist: at any moment, it seemed, his hand might disengage itself and fly away. The kid was double-jointed, maybe even crippled. At that moment David Beck ceased to be known to the scouts as David Beck and became, simply, "The Creature." A scout from another organization came right up to Billy Owens, chuckling, and asked how he came to sign The Creature. Billy O pointed over to Paul and said, "I didn't sign him. Paul made me do it."

Whereupon The Creature went out and dominated the Arizona

rookie league. He and his Halloween hand and his 84-mph fastball shut down the opposition so completely that the opposition never knew what happened. In the short season The Creature pitched eighteen innings in relief, struck out thirty-two batters, and finished with an earned run average of an even 1.00. He was named the closer on the rookie league All-Star team.

The Creature was the first thing to come out of Paul's computer that the A's scouting department signed. There were about to be a lot more. The 2002 draft was to be the first science experiment Billy Beane performed upon amateur players.

It wasn't quite ten in the morning and everyone in the draft room except the Harvard graduates had a lipful of chewing tobacco. The snuff rearranged their features into masks of grim determination. Anyone whose name wasn't two syllables, or didn't end in a vowel or a spitable consonant, has had it changed for the benefit of baseball conversation. Ron Hopkins is "Hoppy," Chris Pittaro is "Pitter," Dick Bogard is "Bogie." Most were former infielders who had topped out someplace in the minor leagues. A handful actually made it to the big leagues, but so briefly that it almost hadn't happened at all. John Poloni had pitched seven innings in 1977 with the Texas Rangers. Kelly Heath had played second base in the Royals organization, and had exactly one major league at bat, in 1982, after the Royals regular second baseman, Frank White, decided in the middle of a game that his hemorrhoids were bothering him. As one of the other scouts put it, Kelly was the only player in history whose entire big league career was made possible by a single asshole. Chris Pittaro had played second base for the Tigers and Twins. Back in 1985, during Pitter's rookie year, Detroit's manager Sparky Andersen was quoted saying Pitter "has a chance to become the greatest second baseman who ever lived." It hadn't turned out that way.

All of them had lived different versions of the same story. They

were uncoiled springs, firecrackers that had failed to explode. The
only bona fide big league regular in the room was Matt Keough,
who'd won sixteen games for the A's in 1980. In his rookie year,
1978, he'd pitched in the All-Star Game. Matty, as he is known,
easily was the most detached of the group. He had the air of a man
taking a break from some perpetual Hawaiian vacation of the soul
to stop by and chat with his old buddies. The rest of them weren't
like that.

There was no avoiding just how important the 2002 amateur
draft was for the future of the Oakland A's. The Oakland A's survived by finding cheap labor. The treatment of amateur players is
the most glaring of the many violations of free market principles
in Major League Baseball. A team that drafts and signs a player
holds the rights to his first seven years in the minor leagues and
his first six in the majors. It also enjoys the right to pay the player
far less than he is worth. For instance, the Oakland A's were able
to pay their All-Star pitcher Barry Zito $200,000 in 2000, $240,000
in 2001, and $500,000 in 2002 (when he would win the Cy Young
Award as the best pitcher in the American League) because they
had drafted him in 1999. For his first three years of big league ball,
Zito was stuck; for his next three years he could apply for salary
arbitration, which would bump him up to maybe a few million a
year but would still keep him millions below the $10–$15 million
a year he could get for himself on the open market. Not until
2007, after he had been in the big leagues for six years, would
Barry Zito, like any other citizen of the republic, be allowed to
auction his services to the highest bidder. At which point, of
course, the Oakland A's would no longer be able to afford Barry
Zito. That's why it was important to find Barry Zito here, in the
draft room, and obtain him for the period of his career when he
could be paid the baseball equivalent of slave's wages.

This year was the best chance they might ever have to find several Barry Zito's. In 2001, the A's had lost all three of their top free
agents to richer teams. First baseman Jason Giambi had left for the

Yankees for $120 million over seven years. Outfielder Johnny Damon had gone to the Red Sox for $32 million over four years. Closer Jason Isringhausen had signed with the Cardinals for $28 million over four years. The $33 million the three players would make each year was just $5 million less than the entire Oakland team. The rules of the game granted the A's the first-round draft picks of the three teams that had poached their top talent, plus three more "compensation" picks at the end of the first round. Together with their own first round pick the A's had, in effect, seven first-round draft picks. In the history of the draft going back to 1965 no team had ever held seven first-round picks. The question for Billy Beane was what to do with them. What he *wasn't* going to do with them was what Grady had done last year, or what old baseball men had done with them for the past thirty-seven years. "You know what?" Billy said to Paul, before the draft-room meetings. "However we do it we're never going to be more wrong than the way we did it before."

Already the scouts had whittled, or thought they had whittled, the vast universe of North American amateur baseball down to 680 players. They'd pasted all the names onto little magnetic strips. They now had one week to reduce that pile of magnetic nameplates to some kind of order. They would do this, more or less, by a process of elimination. Erik would read a kid's name off a sheet. The scout who knew the kid then offered up a brief, dispassionate description of him. Anyone else who had seen the kid play might then chime in. Then the floor was open for general discussion, until everyone was satisfied that enough had been said.

They begin that first morning by weeding out the pile. Some large number of amateur ballplayers were, for one reason or another, unworthy of serious consideration.

"Lark," says Erik, for instance. Erik is Erik Kubota, the new young scouting director Billy hired to replace Grady. Erik used a giant wad of Copenhagen to disguise the fact that he was a brainy graduate of the University of California Berkeley, whose first job with the Oakland A's had been as a public relations intern. That Erik had never played even high school ball was, in Billy Beane's mind, a point in his favor. At least he hasn't learned the wrong lessons. Billy had played pro ball, and regarded it as an experience he needed to overcome if he wanted to do his job well. "A reformed alcoholic," is how he described himself.

Lark is a high school pitcher with a blazing fastball. He's a favorite of one of the older scouts, who introduces him in a language only faintly resembling English. "Good body, big arm. Good fastball, playable slider, so-so change," he says. "A little funk on the backside but nothing you can't clean up. I saw him good one day and not so good another."

"Any risk he'll go to college?" asks Erik.

"He's not a student type," says the older scout. "I'm not sure he's even signed with a college."

"So is this guy a rockhead?" asks Pitter. Pitter (Chris Pittaro) is a graduate of the University of North Carolina who roomed with Billy when they both played for the Minnesota Twins and who Billy had long ago identified as a person willing to rethink everything he learned, or thought he had learned, playing baseball.

"Ah," says the older scout, thinking about how to address the question. It's possible for a baseball player to be too stupid for the job. It's also possible for him to be too smart. "He may be too smart," is a phrase that will recur several times over the next week.

"He's a confident kid. But—"

"But," says Erik.

"There might be some, uh, family issues here," says the old scout. "I heard the dad had spent some time in prison. Porno or something."

No one on either side of the room seems to know what to make of that. You can see thirty men thinking: *is porno a crime?*

"Can he bring it?" someone finally asks. The air clears.

"I can see this guy in somebody's pen throwing aspirin tablets someday," says the older scout. "The guy has a cannon." This old scout is pushing fifty-five but still has a lean quickness about him, as if he hadn't completely abandoned the hope that he might one day play the game. The old scout likes high school kids and refuses to apologize for that fact.

"I'm worried about the makeup," says someone.

"What does his profile say?" asks someone else.

A young man sits quietly off to one side at the room's lone desktop computer. He punches a few keys. He's looking for Lark's results on the psychological test given by Major League Baseball to all prospects.

"Not good," he says, at length. "Competitive drive: one out of ten. Leadership: one out of ten. Conscientiousness: one out of ten." He keeps on reading down the list, but no matter what the category the kid's score is always the same.

"Shit," Bogie finally says, "does he even have a *two* in anything?" Bogie is the oldest scout. In 1972, scouting for the Houston Astros, Bogie administered what he believes to have been the first ever baseball psychological test, to a pitcher named Dick Ruthven. (He passed.)

"Bad makeup," says someone else and no one disagrees.

The scouts used several catch phrases to describe what they need to avoid. "Rockhead" clearly isn't a good thing to be, but the quality can be overcome. "Soft" is also fairly damning—it connotes both "out of shape" and "wimp"—but it, too, is inconclusive. "Bad makeup" is a death sentence. "Bad makeup" means "this kid's got problems we can't afford to solve." The phrase signaled anything from jail time to drinking problems to severe personality disorders. Whenever a player is convicted of "bad make-up" another young man reaches into a cardboard box for a tiny magnetized photograph of a former A's employee named Phil Milo. Milo had worked as one of Billy Beane's assistants for a brief spell and in that time offended pretty much everyone in the organization. When I ask Paul how it was possible for one man to personify so many different personality disorders, Paul says, "Put it this way. On the day I was hired, Milo came over to meet me. The first thing out of his mouth was, 'I got to be honest with you. I'm really not pleased we hired you.'" Milo was just that kind of guy.

During the first few days of the draft meetings the tiny photos of Phil Milo fly like confetti. And the conversations that ended with Milo's picture plastered beside a prospect's name told you something: not just what baseball men distrusted in a player's character, but how little they really knew the people they were about to rain money on.

A high school pitcher:

"Where's he going to college?" asks Billy, idly.

"He's not," says the scout who knows him best. "He's a Christian kid and he was given a free ride to UC Irvine. Coach set him up with a couple of his players. Took him to a party and all it was was drinking. Kid was offended and he left and said, 'I'm not going to school.'"

"Oh, then he'll fit right into pro ball, won't he?" says Billy.

"Put a Milo on him," says Erik.

A collegiate right-handed pitcher:

"He's a cocky guy," says Matt Keough, who is arguing on the pitcher's behalf. "He'd shove it up your ass. And taunt you. So you hate the guy. He's had a couple of ejections."

"But no drugs?" asks Erik.

"No drugs," says Matty, then thinks about it. "There are rumors of some hash."

An old scout laughs. "Corned beef hash?"

"It's unsubstantiated," Matty protests.

"Where there's smoke, there's fire," says another old scout.

Erik looks up: "Is he the guy who was selling wacky tobacky in high school?"

"Hell," says Matty, now genuinely indignant. "That was three years ago!"

Everyone groans. "Put a Milo on him," says Erik, and spits tobacco juice.

A power-hitting outfielder:

"I'm not sure he wants to sign. He said he'd like to go to law school."

"Law school?"

"He's getting pressure from his girlfriend, I think."

"He's looking for love, it sounds like."

"Put a Milo on him."

Another collegiate left-handed pitcher:

"The guy's got no grades," says a scout.

"You mean bad grades?" asks another.

"No, I mean no grades," says the first.

"How can a guy have no grades at Chico State?" asks the other.

"He really has no desire at all to be in college," says the first scout, almost admiringly. "This guy was designed to play ball."

"I'm not really jazzed about a guy who has no desire whatsoever to go to college," says Billy. "That's not a badge of honor."

"Put a Milo on him."

Billy doesn't interfere much in the search for bad makeup, and Paul says nothing at all. The meetings, from their point of view, are all about minimizing risk. They can't afford to have guys not work out. There's no point in taking risks on players temperamentally, or legally, unsuited to pro ball. At one point Billy looks up and asks, "Who's that fucking guy we took last year we had to release because he robbed a bank?" The others are too absorbed in weeding out the bad makeup to reply, or to even consider how remarkable the question is.

Most of the first few days were devoted to culling the original pile of 680 players. Other than an excessive affection for one's girl-friend, or a criminal record, or other signs of bad makeup, there were just two reasons why the Oakland A's did not waste further time on a player. One was age: with rare exceptions the new scout-ing directors toss all high school players immediately onto the dumping ground, leaving the younger scouts who spent their days following them wondering why they bothered. The other is what is delicately known in the draft room as "expectations."

"What are his expectations?" Erik Kubota asks, of a promising college pitcher.

The scout who knows him best says, "His dad said, and I quote, '$4.2 million is a good place to start.'"

"Put him over there," Erik will say. When his name is tossed onto the dump heap nobody in the front office cares.

B Y THE END of the third day the scouts have organized the play-ers into two groups: the prospects not worth considering further, and everyone else. The second group, maybe four hundred players, they parse further by position. They'll rank 120 right-handed pitchers; they'll list 37 catchers, 1 through 37, and 94 outfielders, 1 through 94. But before they do, they turn their attention from eliminating players to selecting them. Billy's already made it clear that this year he has only a secondary interest in pitchers. The past few years he has stocked up on arms. It's the bats he needs. On the white board closest to Billy, the "Big Board," there was space for sixty players. Only one slot had been filled, the first:

SWISHER

Nick Swisher, a center fielder from Ohio State. For the past six months, Billy's been sure about Swisher, and he knows he won't get the slightest disagreement from his scouts. Swisher is a rare point of agreement between Paul's computer and the internal compass of an old baseball guy. He has the raw athletic ability the scouts adore; but he also has the stats Billy and Paul have decided matter more than anything: he's proven he can hit, and hit with power; he drew more than his share of walks.

Oddly enough, Billy has never actually seen Swisher play. He had wanted to fly across the country to watch a few of Swisher's games, but his scouting department told him that if he did, word would quickly spread to the rest of Major League Baseball that Billy Beane was onto Nick Swisher, Swisher's stock would rise, and the odds that he'd still be around when the A's made this first pick—the sixteenth of the draft—would plummet. "Operation Shutdown," the scouts called their project to keep Billy as far away from Swisher as they could.

Operation Shutdown has had some perverse effects. One of them is to lead Billy to speak of Swisher in the needy tone of a man who has been restrained for too long from seeing his beloved. Swisher is his picture bride.

"Swisher is noticeable, isn't he?" says Billy, hoping to hear more about what Swisher *looks* like. How Swisher *really is*.

"Oh, he's noticeable," says an old scout. "From the moment he gets off the bus he doesn't shut up."

"His background is interesting," says Billy. "His dad was a major league player. That's huge. A great chip in his favor. Those guys succeed." (Swisher's dad is Steve Swisher, who caught for the Cubs, Cardinals, and Padres.)

"He does have a presence," agrees an old scout.

"Did Operation Shutdown work?" asks Billy.

"Too well," says an old scout. "Guy from the White Sox called me yesterday and said he knows you must be in love with Swisher because you haven't been to see him."

Billy laughs. "Out of this room, Swisher is hush-hush," he says.

The conversation turns from Nick Swisher, and the moment it does it becomes contentious. Not violently so—these are people with an interest in getting along. The tone of the conversation is that of a meeting in a big company that has just decided to drop a product line, or shift resources from marketing to R&D. Still, it's a dispute with two sides riven by some fundamental difference. The two sides are, on the one hand, the old scouts and, on the other, Billy Beane. The old scouts are like a Greek chorus; it is their job to underscore the eternal themes of baseball. The eternal themes are precisely what Billy Beane wants to exploit for profit— by ignoring them.

One by one Billy takes the names of the players the old scouts have fallen in love with, and picks apart their flaws. The first time he does this an old scout protests.

"The guy's an athlete, Billy," the old scout says. "There's a lot of upside there."

"He can't hit," says Billy.

"He's not that bad a hitter," says the old scout.

"Yeah, what happens when he doesn't know a fastball is coming?" says Billy.

"He's a tools guy," says the old scout, defensively. The old scouts aren't built to argue; they are built to *agree*. They are part of a tightly woven class of former baseball players. The scout looks left and right for support. It doesn't arrive.

"But can he *hit*?" asks Billy.

"He can hit," says the old scout, unconvincingly.

Paul reads the player's college batting statistics. They contain a conspicuous lack of extra base hits and walks.

"My only question is," says Billy, "if he's that good a hitter why doesn't he hit better?"

"The swing needs some work. You have to reinvent him. But he can hit."

"Pro baseball's not real good at reinventing guys," says Billy.

Whatever happened when an older man who failed to become a big league star looks at a younger man with a view to imagining whether he might become a big league star, Billy wanted nothing more to do with it. He'd been on the receiving end of the dreams of older men and he knew what they were worth. Over and over the old scouts will say, "The guy has a great body," or, "This guy may be the best body in the draft." And every time they do, Billy will say, "We're not selling jeans here," and deposit yet another highly touted player, beloved by the scouts, onto his shit list. One after another of the players the scouts rated highly vanish from the white board, until it's empty. If the Oakland A's aren't going to use their seven first-round draft picks to take the players their scouts loved, who on earth are they going to take? That question begins to be answered when Billy Beane, after tossing another name on the slag heap, inserts a new one:

TEAHEN

The older scouts lean back in their chairs, spittoons in hand. Paul leans forward into a laptop and quietly pulls up statistics from college Web sites. Erik Kubota, scouting director, holds a ranked list of all the amateur baseball players in the country. He turns many pages, and passes hundreds and hundreds of names, before he finds Teahen. "Tell us about Teahen," says Billy.

Mark Teahen, says Erik, is a third baseman from St. Mary's College just down the road in Moraga, California. "Teahen," says Erik. "Six three. Two ten. Left right. Good approach to hitting. Not a lot of power right now. Our kind of guy. He takes pitches."

"Why haven't we talked about this guy before?" asks the old scout.

"It's because Teahen doesn't project," says Erik. "He's a corner guy who doesn't hit a lot of home runs."

"Power is something that can be acquired," says Billy quickly. "Good hitters develop power. Power hitters don't become good hitters."

"Do you see him at third base or shortstop?" asks another old scout, like a prosecuting attorney leading a witness.

"Let's forget about positions and just ask: who is the best hitter?" says Billy.

Paul looks up from his computer. "Teahen: .493 on base; .624 slug. Thirty walks and only seventeen strikeouts in one hundred ninety-four at bats." It's hard to tell what the scouts make of these numbers. Scouts from other teams would almost surely say: who gives a shit about a guy's numbers? It's college ball. You need to *look* at the guy. *Imagine* what he might become.

Everyone stares silently at Teahen's name for about thirty seconds. Erik says, "I hate to say it but if you want to talk about another Jason Giambi, this guy could be it." Giambi was a natural hitter who developed power only after the Oakland A's drafted him. In the second round. Over the objections of scouts who said he couldn't run, throw, field, or hit with power. Jason Giambi: MVP of the American League in 2000.

More silence. Decades of scouting experience are being rendered meaningless. "I hate to piss on the campfire," one of the scouts finally says, "but I haven't heard Teahen's name *once* all year. I haven't heard other teams talking about him. I haven't heard his name *around here* all year. It wasn't like this guy was a fifty-five we all liked." The scouts put numbers on players. The numbers are one of the little tricks that lend scouting an air of precision. A player who receives a "55" is a player they think will one day be a regular big league player.

"Who do you like better?" asks Billy.

The old scout leans back in his chair and folds his arms. "What about Perry?" he says. "When you see him do something right on a swing, it's impressive. There's some work that needs to be done. He needs to be reworked a bit."

"You don't change guys," says Billy. "They are who they are."

"That's just my opinion," says the old scout, and folds his arms.

Once Teahen has found his slot high up on the Big Board, Billy Beane takes out a Magic Marker and writes another name:

BROWN

The four scouts across from him either wince or laugh. Brown? *Brown?* Billy can't be serious.

"Let's talk about Jeremy Brown," Billy says.

In moving from Mark Teahen, whoever he is, to Jeremy Brown, whoever *he* is, Billy Beane, in the scouting mind, had gone from the remotely plausible to the ridiculous. Jeremy Brown made the scouting lists, just. His name appears on the last page; he is a lesser member of the rabble regarded by the scouts as, at best, low-level minor league players. He's a senior catcher at the University of Alabama. Only three of the old scouts saw him and none of them rated him even close to a big leaguer. Each of them has about a thousand players ranked above him.

"Jeremy Brown is a bad body catcher," says the most vocal of the old scouts.

"A bad body who owns the Alabama record books," says Pitter.

"He's the only player in the history of the SEC with three hundred hits and two hundred walks," says Paul, looking up from his computer.

It's what he doesn't say that is interesting. No one in big league baseball cares how often a college players walks; Paul cares about it more than just about anything else. He doesn't explain why walks are important. He doesn't explain that he has gone back and studied which amateur hitters made it to the big leagues, and which did not, and why. He doesn't explain that the important traits in a baseball player were not all equally important. That foot speed, fielding ability, even raw power tended to be dramatically overpriced. That the ability to control the strike zone was the greatest indicator of future success. That the number of walks a hitter drew was the best indicator of whether he understood how to control the strike zone. Paul doesn't say that if a guy has a keen eye at the plate in college, he'll likely keep that keen eye in the pros. He doesn't explain that plate discipline might be an innate trait, rather than something a free-swinging amateur can be taught in the pros. He doesn't talk about all the other statistically based insights—the overwhelming importance of on-base percentage, the significance of pitches seen per plate appearance—that he uses to value precisely a hitter's contribution to a baseball offense. He doesn't stress the importance of generalizing from a large body of evidence as opposed to a small one. He doesn't explain anything because Billy doesn't want him to. Billy was forever telling Paul that when you try to explain probability theory to baseball guys, you just end up confusing them.

"This kid wears a large pair of underwear," says another old scout. It's the first time in two days that this old scout has spoken. He enjoys, briefly, the unusual attention accorded the silent man in a big meeting. The others in the room can only assume that if the scout was moved to speak it must be because he had something earth-shatteringly important to say. He doesn't.

"Okay," says Billy.

"It's soft body," says the most vocal old scout. "A fleshy kind of a body."

"Oh, you mean like Babe Ruth?" says Billy. Everyone laughs, the guys on Billy's side of the room more happily than the older scouts across from him.

"I don't know," says the scout. "A body like that can be low energy."

"Sometimes low energy is just being cool," says Billy.

"Yeah," says the scout. "Well, in this case low energy is because when he walks, his thighs stick together."

"I repeat: we're not selling jeans here," says Billy.

"That's good," says the scout. "Because if you put him in corduroys, he'd start a fire."

Clutching Jeremy Brown's yellow nameplate, Billy inches

toward the Big Board with the "Top 60" names on it. The scouts shift and spit. The leading scouting publication, *Baseball America*, has just published its special issue devoted to the 2002 draft, and in it a list of the top twenty-five amateur catchers in the country. Jeremy Brown's name is not on the list. *Baseball America* has more or less said that Jeremy Brown will be lucky to get drafted. Billy Beane is walking Jeremy Brown into the first five rounds of the draft.

"Billy, does he really belong in that group?" asks the old scout plaintively. "He went in the nineteenth round last year and he'll be lucky to go there this year." The Red Sox had drafted Brown the year before, and Brown had turned down the peanuts they'd offered and returned to the University of Alabama for his senior year. It was beginning to look like a wise move.

The older scouts all share their brother's incredulity. One of them, the fat scout, when he returned from the trip Billy made him take to the University of Alabama, called Billy and told him that he couldn't recommend drafting Jeremy Brown. Period. There were fifteen hundred draft-eligible players in North America alone that he would rather own than this misshapen catcher. Like all the scouts, the fat scout had the overriding impression that Brown was fat and growing fatter. He had the further impression that Brown didn't look all that good when he did anything but hit. "Behind the plate he's not mobile," the fat scout now says. "His throws are all slingshot throws." Throws from catchers with a slinging motion tend not to follow a straight line but to tail off toward the first-base side of second base.

Billy takes a step toward the Big Board, sticks Brown's name onto the top of the Big Board's second column, the seventeenth slot, and says, "All right, push him down, guys." Jeremy Brown is now a high second-round, or even low first-round, draft pick. If baseball scouts were capable of gasping, these men would have gasped. Instead, they spit tobacco juice into their cups. That was the moment when the scouts realized just how far Billy Beane was willing to go to push his supposedly rational and objective view of things.

"Come on, Billy," the vocal scout says.

"Finding a catcher who can hit—there's not one of them out there who can hit," says Billy. "This guy can hit."

Erik looks across the table and says, "This guy's a senior with, like, a huge history."

The scouts don't see the point of history. In their view history isn't terribly relevant when you're talking about kids who haven't become who they will be.

"Come on," says Erik, "you guys have all played with guys who were bad bodies and good baseball players."

"Yeah," says Billy. "I played with Pitter." Everyone laughs, even Pitter. "Another thing about Brown," says Billy; "he walks his ass off."

"He's leading the country in walks," says Paul. Walks!

"He better walk because he can't run," says one of the scouts.

"That body, Billy," says the most vocal old scout. "It's not natural." He's pleading now.

"He's got big thighs," says the fat scout, thoughtfully munching another jumbo-sized chocolate chip cookie. "A big butt. He's *huge* in the ass."

"Every year that body has just gotten worse and worse and worse," says a third.

"Can he hit, though?" asks Billy Beane.

"Wanna hear something," says Paul, gazing into his computer screen at the University of Alabama Web site. "In the past two years: 390 at bats; 98 walks; 38 Ks. Those numbers are better than *anyone's* in minor league baseball. Oh yeah, 21 jacks." Jacks are home runs. So are dongs, bombs, and big flies. Baseball people express their fondness for a thing by thinking up lots of different ways to say it.

The fat scout looks up from his giant chocolate chip cookie and seeks to find a way to get across just how unimpressed he is. "Well," he says, exaggerating his natural drawl, "I musta severely unnerestimated Jeremy Brown's hittin' ability."

"I just don't see it," says the vocal scout.

"That's all right," says Billy. "We're blending what we see but we aren't allowing ourselves to be victimized by what we see."

This argument had nothing to do with Jeremy Brown. It was about how to find a big league ballplayer. In the scouts' view, you found a big league ballplayer by driving sixty thousand miles, staying in a hundred crappy motels, and eating god knows how many meals at Denny's all so you could watch 200 high school and college baseball games inside of four months, 199 of which were completely meaningless to you. Most of your worth derived from your membership in the fraternity of old scouts who did this for a living. The other little part came from the one time out of two hundred when you would walk into the ballpark, find a seat on the aluminum plank in the fourth row directly behind the catcher, and see something no one else had seen—at least no one who knew the meaning of it. You only had to see him once. "If you see it once, it's there," says Erik. "There's always been that belief in scouting." And if you saw it once, you, and only you, would know the meaning of what you saw. You had found the boy who was going to make you famous.

Billy had his own idea about where to find future major league baseball players: inside Paul's computer. He'd flirted with the idea of firing all the scouts and just drafting the kids straight from Paul's laptop. The Internet now served up just about every statistic you could want about every college player in the country, and Paul knew them all. Paul's laptop didn't have a tiny red bell on top that whirled and whistled whenever a college player's on-base percentage climbed above .450, but it might as well have. From Paul's point of view, that was the great thing about college players: they had meaningful stats. They played a lot more games, against stiffer competition, than high school players. The sample size of their relevant statistics was larger, and therefore a more accurate reflection of some underlying reality. You could project college players with greater certainty than you could project high school players. The statistics enabled you to find your way past all sorts of sight-based scouting prejudices: the scouting dislike of short right-handed pitchers, for instance, or the scouting distrust of skinny little guys who get on base. Or the scouting distaste for fat catchers.

That was the source of this conflict. For Billy and Paul and, to a slightly lesser extent, Erik and Chris, a young player is not what he looks like, or what he might become, but *what he has done.* As elementary as that might sound to someone who knew nothing about professional baseball, it counts as heresy here. The scouts even have a catch phrase for what Billy and Paul are up to: "performance scouting." "Performance scouting," in scouting circles, is an insult. It directly contradicts the baseball man's view that a young player is what you can see him doing in your mind's eye. It argues that most of what's important about a baseball player, maybe even including his character, can be found in his statistics.

After Billy said what he had to say about being "victimized by what we see," no one knew what to say. Everyone stared at Jeremy Brown's name. Maybe then they all understood that they weren't here to make decisions. They were here to learn about the new way that decisions were going to be made.

"This is a cutting-edge approach we're taking this year," says Erik, whose job, it is increasingly clear, is to stand between Billy and the old scouts, and reconcile the one to the other. "Five years from now everyone might be doing it this way."

"I hope not," says Paul. He doesn't mean this in the way that the old scouts would like him to mean it.

"Bogie," says Erik, calling across the table on the vast moral authority of the oldest scout of all, Dick Bogard. "Does this make sense to you?" Erik adores Bogie, though of course he'd never put it that way. When Erik announced he wanted to leave the A's advertising department and get into the baseball end of things, even though he himself had never played, Bogie not only did not laugh at him; he encouraged him. "My baseball father," Erik called Bogie.

Bogie is not merely the oldest of the scouts; he is the scout who has worked for the most other teams. He is a walking map of his own little world. In spite of his age, or maybe because of it, he knows when an old thing has died.

"Oh definitely," says Bogie, motioning to Paul's computer. "It's a new game. Years ago we didn't have these stats to look up. We had to go with what we saw."

"Years ago it only cost a hundred grand to sign them," says Erik. The other older scouts are unmoved. "Look," says Erik, "Pitter and I are the ones that people are going to say, 'What the hell were you doing? How the hell could you take Brown in the first round?'"

No one says anything.

"The hardest thing," says Billy, "is there is a certain pride, or lack of pride, required to do this right. You take a guy high no one else likes and it makes you uncomfortable. But I mean, really, who gives a fuck where guys are taken? Remember Zito? Everyone said we were nuts to take Zito with the ninth pick of the draft. And we *knew* everyone was going to say that. One fucking month later it's clear we kicked everyone's ass. Nobody remembers that now. But understand, when we stop trying to figure out the perception of guys, we've done better."

"Jeremy Brown isn't Zito," says one of the scouts. But he is. A lot of people in the room have forgotten that the scouting department hadn't wanted to take Barry Zito because Barry Zito threw an 88-mph fastball. They preferred a flamethrower named Ben Sheets. "Billy made us take Zito," Bogie later confesses.

"Let me ask you this," says Billy. "If Jeremy Brown looked as good in a uniform as Majewski [a Greek Kouros who played out-field for the University of Texas], where on this board would you put him?"

The scouts pretend to consider this. Nobody says anything so Pitter says it for them: "He'd be in that first column." A first-round pick.

"You guys really are trying to sell jeans, aren't you?" says Billy. And on that note of affectionate disgust, he ends the debate. He simply takes Jeremy Brown's nameplate and moves him from the top of the second column on the Big Board to the bottom of the first, from #17 to #15. Jeremy Brown, whose name had some-how failed to turn up on *Baseball America*'s list of the top twenty-five amateur catchers, who serious scouts believed should never be a pro baseball player, is now a first-round draft choice of the Oakland A's.

"Since we're talking about Brown anyway," says Paul, which wasn't exactly true, since the scouts were now distinctly *not* talk-ing about Brown, "there's a list of hitters I want to talk about. All of these guys share certain qualities. They are the eight guys we definitely want. And we want *all* eight of these guys" He reads a list:

Jeremy Brown
Stephen Stanley
John Baker
Mark Kiger
Shaun Larkin
John McCurdy
Brant Colamarino
Brian Stavisky

All eight are college players. Most of them are guys the scouts either did not particularly like, or, in a few cases, don't really know. A young man rises to put their names on the board. Paul quickly organizes them, like a dinner guest who has spilled his wine and hopes to clean it up before the host notices. When he's finished, the board is a market but from a particular point of view, that of a trader who possesses, or believes he possesses, superior knowledge.

With that, the coup was complete. Paul's list of hitters were distinctly not guys the scouts found driving around. They were guys Paul found surfing the Internet. Some of the names the older scouts do not even recognize. The evaluation of young baseball players had been taken out of the hands of old baseball men and placed in the hands of people who had what Billy valued most (and what Billy didn't have), a degree in something other than baseball.

"There's some serious on-base percentage up there," says Billy. No one else says anything. The room is filled with silence.

"We got three guys at the top of the board that no one has ever heard of," Pitter finally says, with just a trace of pride.

"There isn't a board in the game that looks like this one," agrees Bogie.

Bogie brought into the draft room something unique: vast experience to which he had no visceral attachment. He'd been in the game for nearly fifty years. He'd seen a lot, perhaps everything, and he was willing to forget it, if asked. As it happened, one of the things he had seen, back in 1980, was a high school game in San Diego. That was the year that the Mets took Darryl Strawberry with the first overall pick in the draft. But that year there was another high school player, who, in his ability to conjure fantasies in the baseball scouting mind, rivaled Strawberry. Bogie had gone to see him at the behest of the Houston Astros. Great body, plus wheels, plus arm, good instincts, and the ability to hit the ball over light towers. To top it off, he'd scored higher than any other prospect on the psychological tests. Bogie had phoned Houston and told the front office that he had found a better prospect than Darryl Strawberry: Billy Beane.

When asked which player, on the Oakland A's draft board, most resembled the young Billy Beane, Bogie said, "Shit, man. There *is* no Billy Beane. Not up there." When asked why, he'd said, "Billy was a guy you could dream on," and left it to you to understand that Billy Beane, the general manager, had just systematically· eliminated guys "you could dream on." But when asked what became of those still unforgotten dreams, Bogie hesitated. He looked over and met the eye of the grown-up Billy Beane.

"That's enough!" said Billy. He'd only been pretending not to listen. Bogie just smiled, shrugged, and said no more.

Chapter Three

THE ENLIGHTENMENT

THE METS had had only the greatest expectations of him. They'd wanted to hold a big press conference in Dodger Stadium to announce his signing. Billy asked them not to. He had a claustrophobic unease with ceremony of any kind, and a press conference was nothing but a ceremonial event. It'd make him feel trapped. Plus he didn't want to make a big deal about becoming a pro baseball player. It was less a decision to celebrate than a vaguely uncomfortable fact to get his mind around. The Mets failed to consider the cause or implications of his reticence. In the belief that Billy was more ready for pro ball than Darryl Strawberry, they sent Strawberry to the low-level rookie team with the other high school kids and Billy to the high-level rookie team, in Little Falls, New York, with the college players. Little Falls, New York, could not have felt farther from San Diego, California. His teammates might as well have been a different species than the high school kids he was used to playing with. They had hair on their backs and fat on their stomachs. They smoked before games and drank after them. A few had wives. And all of the pitchers had sliders.

The Mets were betting that Billy was better equipped than Strawberry to deal with the pressures, and inevitable frustrations, that went with playing against much older players. Roger Jongewaard, the Mets' head scout, fully expected Billy to rocket through the minors and into the big leagues well ahead of Strawberry. The Mets scouting department had badly misjudged Billy's nature. They had set him up to fail. If there was one thing Billy was not equipped for, it was failure. He didn't even begin to know what to make of a stat sheet at the end of his first short season in high-level rookie ball that showed him hitting .210. He didn't know how to think of himself if he couldn't think of himself as a success. When the season ended he returned home, enrolled in classes at the University of California at San Diego, and forgot that he played baseball for a living. He didn't so much as pick up a bat or a glove until spring training the following March. That in itself should have been an ominous sign, but no one was looking for ominous signs.

The next year went well enough for him—he was, after all, Billy Beane—and by the summer of 1982 he had been promoted to the Mets' Double-A team in Jackson, Mississippi. He played left, Strawberry played right, and the whole team played the field. For a lot of the players it was their first exposure to the Southern female—the most flagrant cheater in the mutual disarmament pact known as feminism. Lipstick! Hairdos! Submissiveness! Baseball was a game but chasing women was a business, in which Billy Beane was designed to succeed without even trying. Billy had the rap. Billy, said his old teammate J. P. Ricciardi, "could talk a dog off a meat wagon." Billy was forever having to explain to another teammate of his, Steve Springer, that when you'd just met some girl, what you didn't do was tell her you played pro ball. It wasn't fair to her; you had to give the girl a chance to turn you down. Billy's way of giving her a chance was to tell her that what he did for a living was collect roadkill off local highways. Springer didn't have Billy's awesome God-given ability with women; he thought he needed the Mets to stand a chance; and this need of his led to one of those great little moments that make even the most dismal minor league baseball careers worth remembering. They were leaving one of the local burger joints when two pretty girls called after them, in their fetching drawls: "You boys Yankees?" Springer turned around and said, "No, we're the Mets."

Off the field Billy was Billy; on the field Billy was crumbling. The only thing worse than an ambivalent minor league baseball player was an ambivalent minor league baseball player with a terror of failure, forced to compare himself every afternoon to Darryl Strawberry. "People would look at Billy and Darryl and think about the untapped potential that might be brought out of them," recalls Jeff Bittiger, who was the ace of the staff on the same team. "They weren't just supposed to be big leaguers. They were supposed to be big league all-stars." That year Strawberry would be named the most valuable player in the Texas League. Billy would hit only .220. Often they'd hit third and fourth in the lineup, and so Billy spent a lot of hours in the outfield dwelling on Strawberry's heroics and his own failure. "That was the first year I really questioned if I'd made the right decision to sign," Billy said.

Darryl Strawberry presented one kind of problem for Billy; Lenny Dykstra presented another, perhaps even more serious one. Billy and Lenny lived together and played side by side in minor league outfields for nearly two years, beginning in 1984. In the spring of that year both were invited to the Mets' big league spring training camp. With Strawberry now a fixture in the Mets' right field, the talk in the minors was that Billy was being groomed to replace George Foster in left, and Lenny was supposed to replace Mookie Wilson in center. Lenny thought of himself and Billy as two buddies racing together down the same track, but Billy sensed fundamental differences between himself and Lenny. Physically, Lenny didn't belong in the same league with him. He was half

Billy's size, and had a fraction of Billy's promise—which is why
the Mets hadn't drafted him until the thirteenth round. Mentally,
Lenny was superior, which was odd considering Lenny wasn't
what you'd call a student of the game. Billy remembers sitting
with Lenny in a Mets dugout watching the opposing pitcher warm
up. "Lenny says, 'So who's that big dumb ass out there on the
hill?' And I say, 'Lenny, you're kidding me, right? That's Steve
Carlton. He's maybe the greatest left-hander in the history of the
game.' Lenny says, 'Oh yeah! I knew that!' He sits there for a
minute and says, "So, what's he got?' And I say, 'Lenny, come on.
Steve Carlton. He's got heat and also maybe the nastiest slider
ever.' And Lenny sits there for a while longer as if he's taking that
in. Finally he just says, 'Shit, I'll stick him.' I'm sitting there
thinking, that's a *magazine cover* out there on the hill and all
Lenny can think is that he'll stick him."

The point about Lenny, at least to Billy, was clear: Lenny didn't
let his mind screw him up. The physical gifts required to play pro
ball were, in some ways, less extraordinary than the mental ones.
Only a psychological freak could approach a 100-mph fastball
aimed not all that far from his head with total confidence. "Lenny
was so perfectly designed, emotionally, to play the game of baseball," said Billy. "He was able to instantly forget any failure and
draw strength from every success. He had no concept of failure.
And he had no idea of where he was. And I was the opposite."

Living with Lenny, Billy became even less sure that he was destined to be the star everyone told him he would be. He began, in
the private casino of his mind, to hedge his bets. He told teammates he might quit baseball and go back to college and play football. He might enter politics; everyone said he'd be good at it. He
took to reading some nights—a radical idea for a minor league
baseball player—to compensate for the formal education he now
realized he wasn't getting. Lenny would come home and find Billy
curled up in a chair with a book. "He'd look at me," recalls Billy,

"and say, 'Dude, you shouldn't be doing that. That shit'll ruin your eyes.' Lenny's attitude was: I'm going to do nothing that will interfere with getting to the big leagues, including learning." Maybe more to the point, Lenny—a thirteenth-round draft pick!— hadn't the slightest doubt that he was going to make it to the big leagues and make it big. "I started to get a sense of what a baseball player was," Billy said, "and I could see it wasn't me. It was Lenny."

That thought led to another: *I'm not sure I like it here.* Before Billy was sent back to the minor leagues in the first cuts of 1984 spring training, he was confronted by the Mets' big league manager, Davey Johnson. Johnson told Billy that he didn't think he, Billy, really wanted to play baseball. "I didn't take it as a criticism," said Billy. "I took it as 'I think he's right.' I was so geared to going to college. I was sort of half in and half out."

The half that was in stayed in. He didn't quit baseball. He kept grinding his way up through the minor leagues, propelled by his private fears and other people's dreams. The difference between who he was, and who other people thought he should be, grew by the day. A lot of people who watched Billy Beane play still thought what J. P. Ricciardi thought when he played with Billy that first year in Little Falls. "He was so physically gifted that I thought he would overcome everything," said Ricciardi. "I remember coming home from that first season and telling my friends, 'I just played with this guy who you gotta see to believe. He isn't like other animals.'" Teammates would look at Billy and see the future of the New York Mets. Scouts would look at him and see what they had always seen. The hose. The wheels. The body. The Good Face.

Billy was smart enough to fake his way through his assigned role: young man of promise. "Billy *never* looked bad, even when he struggled," recalls the scout who had signed him, Roger Jongewaard. "He was the most talented player I ever played with," says Chris Pittaro, who made it to the big leagues with the Tigers and won a World Series with the Twins. "He had the ability to do things in a game that ninety-five percent of the people in the big leagues could not do in practice because they didn't have the physical ability. There aren't many plays I remember from fifteen years ago but I remember some of Billy's. We were in Albuquerque in '87 [in Triple-A ball] and Billy made this play in right field. He had to run up and down over the bullpen mound to make a catch, and then throw a tagging runner out at the plate. I remember being astonished—first of all, that he even got to the ball. Second, that he ran up and down a pitcher's mound at full speed without breaking stride. Third, that he even thought to make that throw. Speed. Balance. Presence of mind. I think that the runner when he found the ball waiting for him was more surprised than anybody."

Billy could run and Billy could throw and Billy could catch and Billy even had presence of mind in the field. Billy was quick-witted and charming and perceptive about other people, if not about himself. He had a bravado, increasingly false, that no one in a fifty-mile radius was ever going to see through. He looked more like a superstar than any actual superstar. He was a natural leader of young men. Billy's weakness was simple: he couldn't hit.

Or, rather, he hit sometimes but not others; and when he didn't hit, he unraveled. "Billy was of the opinion that he should never make an out," said Pittaro. "Relief pitchers used to come down from the bullpen to watch Billy hit, just to see what he did when he struck out." He busted so many bats against so many walls that his teammates lost count. One time he destroyed the dugout toilet; another time, in a Triple-A game in Tacoma, he went after a fan in the stands, and proved, to everyone's satisfaction, that fans, no matter what challenges they hollered from the safety of their seats, were better off not getting into fistfights with ballplayers. From the moment Billy entered a batter's box he set about devouring himself from the inside until, fully self-consumed, he went looking around him for something else to feed his rage. "He didn't have a baseball mentality," said Jeff Bittiger. "He was more like a basketball or a football player. Emotions were always such a big part of whatever he did. A bad at bat or two and he was done for the third and fourth at bats of the game."

Yet even inside the batter's box, where he came unglued in a matter of a few seconds, Billy enjoyed sensational success. In 1983, in response to his special inconsistency against right-handed pitching, Billy played around with switch-hitting. Who tried hitting from the wrong side of the plate for the first time in his life in Double-A ball? Nobody. And yet by the middle of the Double-A season, against pitchers with big league stuff, Billy was hitting .300 left-handed. Then he slumped, and lost his nerve. He went back to hitting exclusively right-handed.

In late 1984, Billy and Lenny both came up for a few weeks at the end of the season. Billy got his first big league hit off Jerry Koosman—who immediately picked him off first base. It was funny; it was also sad. Just as the game seemed willing to bend to his talent, it snapped back, and took whatever it had just given him away. In late 1985, Lenny was brought up for good to the big league team—for which Darryl Strawberry already had hit more than seventy home runs. Lenny played center, Strawberry played right, Billy played the guy who never made it out to left field. The next year Lenny hit critical home runs in the NLCS and the World Series, and wrote a book about them, in which he mentioned that it should have been Billy Beane, not he, who became the big league star. (Lenny didn't read books; he wrote them.)

Rather than make Billy a big leaguer, the Mets traded him to the Minnesota Twins. The Twins in 1986 had a new manager, Ray Miller, who announced that Billy Beane would be his starting left fielder. Billy immediately went out and hurt himself in spring training, but when he came back he was, for the first time in his big league career, sent out to left field as a regular rather than a substitute. That day the Twins were in Yankee Stadium facing

Ron Guidry. Billy went five for five off Guidry, with a home run. Then he went hitless the next two nights and found himself written out of the Twins' starting lineup—for good, as it turned out. Billy understood, or said he did. The team was losing and Ray Miller was new, and feeling pressure to play veterans.

For the next three and a half seasons Billy was up and down between Triple-A and the big leagues, with the Twins, the Detroit Tigers, and, finally, the Oakland A's. Inside the batter's box he struggled to adapt, but every change he made was aimed more at preventing embarrassment than at achieving success. To reduce his strikeouts, he shortened his swing, and traded the possibility of hitting a home run for a greater likelihood of simply putting the ball in play. He crouched and hunched in an attempt to hit like a smaller man. He might have struck out less than he otherwise would have done, but at the cost of crippling his natural powers. Eight years into his professional baseball career he was, in some ways, a weaker hitter than when he was seventeen years old.

At least, when it counted. When it didn't count—when he didn't think about it—anything could happen. One afternoon during Billy's one-month stint with the Detroit Tigers, he was asked by the general manager, Bill Lajoie, to come out to Tiger Stadium on an off-day. Lajoie called in a few scrubs to help with the rehabilitation of a pitcher named Walt Terrell. Terrell, who had been injured, was about to reenter the Tigers' starting rotation. Before that happened the pitching coach wanted Terrell to throw a simulated game. Billy was expected to stand in the box, as a foil.

Once they'd taken the field there was just one thought on everyone's mind: *was Terrell his old self?* Billy sat and watched Terrell dispatch a couple of hitters. He was indeed his old self. When Billy's turn came to hit, nobody was paying him any attention. All eyes were on Terrell. Nobody much cared whether Billy Beane struck out or hooted at the moon. He couldn't fail. He became, for a moment, a boy playing a game. While the coaches and the GM scrutinized their precious pitcher, Billy took the first pitch he liked and launched a major league fastball into the upper deck of Tiger Stadium.

There was a new thought on everyone's mind: *who the fuck did that?*

Billy was no longer ignorable. The GM, Lajoie, came over to him. *Billy, you looked like a different guy. The stance, the attitude—everything was different. Why don't you do that all the time?* By now everyone knew that Billy was the guy destined for the Hall of Fame who never panned out. "He was still at an age where he might have developed further as a player," said Lajoie. The GM thought there was hope; the GM really didn't understand. Nobody understood. Inside a batter's box, during a baseball game, Billy was no longer able to be himself. Billy was built to move: inside a batter's box he had to be perfectly still. Inside a batter's box he experienced a kind of claustrophobia. The batter's box was a cage designed to crush his spirit.

In his last three and a half years of pro ball Billy watched a lot more baseball than he played, and demonstrated an odd knack for being near the center of other people's action. "The Forrest Gump of baseball," he later called himself. He was on the bench when the Twins won the 1987 World Series and also when the A's won the 1989 World Series. He was forever finding himself next to people who were about to become stars. He'd played outfield with Lenny Dykstra and Darryl Strawberry. He'd subbed for Mark McGwire and Jose Canseco. He'd lockered beside Rickey Henderson. In his slivers of five years in the big leagues he played for four famous managers: Sparky Andersen, Tom Kelly, Davey Johnson, and Tony La Russa. But by the end of 1989 his career stat line (301 at bats, .219 batting average, .246 on-base percentage, .296 slugging percentage, and 11 walks against 80 strikeouts) told an eloquent tale of suffering. You didn't need to know Billy Beane at all—you only needed to read his stats—to sense that he left every on-deck circle in trouble. That he had developed neither discipline nor composure. That he had never learned to lay off a bad pitch. That he was easily fooled. That, fooled so often, he came to expect that he would be fooled. That he hit with fear. That his fear masqueraded as aggression. That the aggression enabled him to exit the batter's box as quickly as possible. One season in the big leagues he came to the plate seventy-nine times and failed to draw a single walk. Not many players do that.

Billy's failure was less interesting than the many attempts to explain it. His teammate and friend, Chris Pittaro, said, "Billy was as competitive and intense as anyone I ever played with. He never let his talent dictate. He fought himself too hard." Billy's high school coach, Sam Blalock, said that "he would have made it if he'd had the intangibles—if he would have had a better self-image. I think he would have been a big star in the big leagues. No. I *know*. He was amazing. If he'd wanted to, he could even have made it as a pitcher." The scouts who had been so high on Billy when he was seventeen years old still spoke of him in odd tones when he was twenty-five, as if he'd become exactly what they all said he would be and it was only by some piece of sorcery that he didn't have the numbers to prove it. Paul Weaver: "The guy had it all. But some guys just never figure it out. Whatever it is that allows you to perform day in, day out, and to make adjustments, he didn't have it. The game is that way." Roger Jongewaard: "He had the talent to be a superstar. A Mike Schmidt–type player. His problem was makeup. I thought Billy had makeup on his side. But he tried too hard. He tried to force it. He couldn't stay loose."

Inside baseball, among the older men, that was the general consensus: Billy Beane's failure was not physical but mental. His mind had shoved his talent to one side. He hadn't allowed nature to take its course. It was hardly surprising that it occurred to the older men that what Billy really needed was a shrink.

That, briefly, is what he got. The whole idea of a baseball shrink
had been reinvented by the Oakland A's in the early 1980s.*

The first of the new breed was a charismatic former prep school
teacher with some academic training in psychology named Harvey Dorfman. The A's minor league coordinator Karl Kuehl, with
whom Dorfman wrote the seminal book, *The Mental Game of
Baseball*, had actually put Dorfman in uniform and let him sit in
the dugout during games, so he could deal with the players'
assorted brain screams in real time. Kuehl had no time for a
player's loss of composure during a game. "If you were throwing
equipment or whatever, you were going to spend time with Harvey, whether you wanted to or not," said Kuehl. One of the most
efficient destroyers of baseball equipment his teammates had ever
seen, Billy was destined to spend time with Harvey. Harvey's main
impression of Billy was that Billy had played hide-and-seek with
his demons, and that professional baseball had helped him to win.
"Baseball organizations don't understand that with a certain kind
of highly talented player who has trouble with failure, they need
to suck it up and let the kid develop," Dorfman said. "You don't
push him along too fast. Take it slow, so his failure is not public
exposure and humiliation. Teach him perspective—that baseball
matters but it doesn't matter too much. Teach him that what matters isn't whether I just struck out. What matters is that I behave
impeccably when I compete. The guy believes in his talent. What

* There'd been some flirtation with shrinking players back in the late 1940s.
The old St. Louis Browns hired a psychologist named David Tracy who specialized
in hypnotic therapy. Tracy wrote a book about his experience called *Psychologist
At Bat*, which, if nothing else, gives you some idea why baseball didn't rush to
embrace the psychiatric profession. Here's Tracy describing his technique: "I had
[a Browns' pitcher] lie down on the couch and I stood behind him. I held up my
finger about six inches above his eyes and told him to look at it steadily as I talked:
'Your legs are growing heavy, v-e-r-y heavy. Your arms are growing heavy, v-e-r-y
heavy. You are going deep, d-e-e-p asleep.'"

he doesn't believe in is himself. He sees himself exclusively in his statistics. If his stats are bad, he has zero self-worth. He's never developed a coping mechanism because he's never had anything to cope with."

Billy's view of himself was radically different. Baseball hadn't yielded itself to his character. He thought it was just bullshit to say that his character—or more exactly, his emotional predisposition—might be changed. "You know what?" he said. "If it doesn't happen, it never was going to happen. If you never did it, it wasn't there to begin with." All these attempts to manipulate his psyche he regarded as so much crap. "Sports psychologists are a crutch," he said. "An excuse for why you are not doing it rather than a solution. If somebody needs them, there is a weakness in them that will prevent them from succeeding. It's not a character flaw; it's just a character flaw when it comes to baseball." He was who he was. Baseball was what it was. And they were a bad match. "It wasn't anyone's fault," he said. "I just didn't have it in me."

During spring training of 1990 he finally capitulated to this realization. He no longer was a boy. He was a man. He had married his high school girlfriend and she was seven months pregnant with their first child. He had responsibilities and no real future to cover them. He had gone from promising to disappointing without ever quite figuring out how or why: but he wasn't blind. All he had to do was look around to see that something had changed. "The luster and the shine came off because there was a whole new crop of guys coming in," he said. "I was twenty-seven years old and by and large you are what you are when you're twenty-seven." He had blossomed into the physical specimen the scouts had dreamed he would become. And yet, somehow, the game had shrunk him.

The game had also rendered him unfit for anything but itself. The people on the big club assumed that Billy would break camp in 1990 with them, and spend another season shuttling between the bench and Triple-A. Billy did something else instead. He walked out of the Oakland A's dugout and into their front office, and said he wanted a job as an advance scout. An advance scout traveled ahead of the big league team and analyzed the strengths and weaknesses of future opponents. Billy was entering what was meant to be his prime as a baseball player, and he'd decided he'd rather watch than play. "I always say that I loved playing the game but I'm not sure that I really did," he said. "I never felt comfortable."

When their fifth outfielder turned up looking for a desk job, the A's front office didn't know what to make of it. It was as unlikely as some successful politician quitting a campaign and saying he wanted to be a staffer, or a movie actor walking off the set and taking a job as key grip. None of the staff had played big league baseball and all of them wished they had. Most would have given their glove hands, or at least a few fingers, for a year in a big league uniform. The A's general manager Sandy Alderson was maybe the most perplexed of all. "Nobody does that," he said. "Nobody says, 'I quit as a player. I want to be an advance scout.'" He hired Billy anyway. "I didn't think there was much risk in making him an advance scout," Alderson said, "because I didn't think an advance scout did anything." Chris Pittaro had gone into scouting after an injury ended his playing career. When Billy called to tell him what he'd done, Pittaro was incredulous. "When you're in the game you always think something is going to break for you. *No one* gives up on that. I didn't. I was forced to retire. Billy chose to retire. And that was something I couldn't imagine." In the end Billy Beane proved what he had been trying to say at least since he was seventeen years old: he didn't want to play ball.

With that, he concluded his fruitless argument with his talent. He decided that his talent was beside the point: how could you call it talent if it didn't lead to success? Baseball was a skill, or maybe it was a trick: whatever it was he hadn't played it very well. In his own mind he ceased to be a guy who should have made it and became a guy upon whom had been heaped a lot of irrational

hopes and dreams. He had reason to feel some distaste for baseball's mystical nature. He would soon be handed a weapon to
destroy it.

SANDY ALDERSON has a clear memory from earlier that spring of
1990, of Billy Beane taking batting practice. He didn't know much
about Billy and wondered what kind of player he was. "He was
very undisciplined at the plate," Alderson said. "Not a lot of
power. I remember after I watched him very specifically asking:
why is this guy even on the team?" Not that it mattered. Tony La
Russa was the A's manager and, in the great tradition of big-shot
baseball managers, he paid only faint attention to what the GM
had to say.

That was one of the many things about baseball Alderson was
determined to change. When Billy came to work inside the A's
front office in 1993, he walked into the early stages of a fitful science experiment. When Alderson had been hired as the A's general
manager a decade earlier, he'd been a complete outsider to baseball. This was rare. Most GMs start out as scouts and rise up
through the baseball establishment. Alderson was an expensively
educated San Francisco lawyer (Dartmouth College, Harvard Law
School) with no experience of the game, outside of a bit of time on
school playing fields. He was also a former Marine Corps officer,
and his self-presentation was much closer to "former Marine
Corps officer" than "fancy-pants lawyer." "Sandy didn't know
shit about baseball," says Harvey Dorfman, the baseball psychologist Alderson more or less invented. "He was a neophyte. But he
was a progressive thinker. And he wanted to understand how the
game worked. He also had the capacity to instill fear in others."

When Alderson entered the game he wanted to get his mind
around it, and he did. He concluded that everything from on-field
strategies to player evaluation was better conducted by scientific
investigation—hypotheses tested by analysis of historical statisti-

cal baseball data—than by reference to the collective wisdom of old baseball men. By analyzing baseball statistics you could see through a lot of baseball nonsense. For instance, when baseball managers talked about scoring runs, they tended to focus on team batting average, but if you ran the analysis you could see that the number of runs a team scored bore little relation to that team's batting average. It correlated much more exactly with a team's on-base and slugging percentages. A lot of the offensive tactics that made baseball managers famous—the bunt, the steal, the hit and run—could be proven to have been, in most situations, either pointless or self-defeating. "I figured out that managers do all this shit because it is safe," said Alderson. "They don't get criticized for it." He wasn't particularly facile with numbers, but he could understand them well enough to use their conclusions. "I couldn't do a regressions analysis," he said, "but I knew what one was. And the results of them made sense to me."

Alderson hadn't set out to reexamine the premises of professional baseball but he wound up doing it anyway. For a long stretch, his investigations were largely academic. "You have to remember," he said, "that there wasn't any evidence that any of this shit worked. And I had credibility problems. I didn't have a baseball background." The high payroll Oakland teams managed by Tony La Russa had done well enough in the late 1980s and early 1990s that Alderson felt he should "defer to success." For more than a decade he could afford to do this. Since the late 1970s the A's had been owned by Walter A. Haas, Jr., who was, by instinct, more of a philanthropist than a businessman. Haas viewed professional baseball ownership as a kind of public trust and spent money on it accordingly. In 1991, the Oakland A's actually had the highest payroll in all of baseball. Haas was willing to lose millions to field a competitive team that would do Oakland proud, and he did. The A's had gone to the World Series three straight seasons from 1988 to 1990.

Deferring to success became an untenable strategy in 1995,

when Walter Haas died. His estate sold the team to a pair of Bay Area real estate developers, Steve Schott and Ken Hofmann, who were, by instinct, more businessmen than philanthropists. Schott and Hofmann wanted Alderson to continue running the team but on a much tighter budget. "We had new owners who weren't going to spend any money," said Alderson. "They made it clear that this had to be a business. And so we suddenly were put in the position of: we can only afford a one-tool player. Which tool is it going to be?" What—and this is what the question amounted to—was the efficient way to spend money on baseball players? The first, short answer, according to a pamphlet commissioned by Alderson, was to spend it on hitters. The pamphlet was written by a former aerospace engineer turned baseball writer, Eric Walker. Fielding, Walker wrote, was "at most five percent of the game." The rest was pitching and offense, and while "good pitchers are usually valued properly, good batters often are not." In Walker's words:

> Analyzing baseball yields many numbers of interest and value. Yet far and away—far, far and away—the most critical number in all of baseball is 3: the three outs that define an inning. Until the third out, anything is possible; after it, nothing is. Anything that increases the offense's chances of making an out is bad; anything that decreases it is good. And what is on-base percentage? Simply yet exactly put, it is the probability that the batter will not make an out. When we state it that way, it becomes, or should become, crystal clear that the most important isolated (one-dimensional) offensive statistic is the on-base percentage. It measures the probability that the batter will not be another step toward the end of the inning.

Alderson's reference point for running an organization was the time he'd spent as an officer in the Marine Corps. He approached the A's farm teams the way the Marine Corps approached its boot camps. The individual star was less important than the organization as a whole, and the organization as a whole functioned well only if it was uniformly disciplined. Once he decided that hitting was the most important tool and everything else was secondary, Alderson set about implementing throughout the organization, with Marine Corps rigor, a uniform approach to hitting. The approach had three rules:

1. Every batter needs to behave like a leadoff man, and adopt as his main goal getting on base.
2. Every batter should also possess the power to hit home runs, in part because home run power forced opposing pitchers to pitch more cautiously, and led to walks, and high on-base percentages.
3. To anyone with the natural gifts to become a professional baseball player, hitting was less a physical than a mental skill. Or, at any rate, the aspects of hitting that could be taught were mental.

By 1995, Alderson had created a new baseball corporate culture around a single baseball statistic: on-base percentage. Scoring runs was, in the new view, less an art or a talent than a *process*. If you made the process a routine—if you got every player doing his part on the production line—you could pay a lot less for runs than the going rate. Alderson was building a system with Marine Corps intolerance for exceptions to the rules. "Sandy produced this long paper about the pros and cons of selective hitting," recalled Karl Kuehl, who was in charge of implementing Alderson's rules. "He wanted to really push the kids coming up through the minor leagues. No one had ever heard of on-base percentage, but when your being called to the major leagues depends on your on-base percentage, it gets your attention." The system's central tenet was, in Alderson's words, "the system was the star. The reason the system works is that everyone buys into it. If they don't, there is a weakness in the system." The unacceptable vice in a minor league player was a taste for bad pitches. The most praiseworthy virtue was the willingness to take a base on balls. No player was eligible for minor league awards, or was allowed to move up in the system, unless he had at least one walk in every ten bats.

The effect of Sandy Alderson's new rules was interesting to anyone who believed the pitcher, not the hitter, was chiefly responsible for the base on balls. More or less overnight, all of the A's minor league teams began to lead their respective leagues in walks. To ensure they never lost that lead, Alderson routinely reviewed the batting statistics of the teams, and leaned on managers whose teams were not walking. He noticed, for instance, that the Oakland Double-A affiliate was the exception in the organization: its players weren't drawing walks at the same frantic rate as the A's other minor league teams. "I got my reports," he said. "I can see they aren't taking any walks. I called the manager and said, 'They go up or you're fired.' And they went up. Quickly."

Even after the Marine Corps had come to the Oakland A's there remained a weakness in the system: the major league team. The mere presence of a free-swinging light hitter like Billy Beane on the big club in 1990 proved that Alderson's views were not the controlling ones. Around the big league clubhouse the GM trod more gingerly than around the minor league clubhouses. Alderson didn't march into Tony La Russa's office and tell him, "The walks go up or you're fired." No one did. There was no very good reason for this; it's just the way it was, because the guys who ran the front office typically had never played in the big leagues.

The need to treat the big league team as the sacrosanct province of people who *had* played in the big leagues struck Alderson, who liked the idea of order and discipline cascading unimpeded from the top, as a kind of madness. "In what other business," he asked, "do you leave the fate of the organization to a middle manager?" But that is what the Oakland A's, along with the rest of major league baseball, had always done. Tony La Russa was a middle manager and Tony La Russa had his own ideas about how to score runs, and those ideas guided the bats of his hitters. A player would come up through the A's farm system being told that he needed to be patient, that he needed to take his walks; and then the moment he got to the big club, he was told to unleash his natural aggression. Even players brainwashed by Alderson's minor league system in the new approach were susceptible to these arguments. Given the slightest opening, many of them regressed, and began hacking away. "It may have something to do with how dominant these players are as they come up," said Alderson. "Patience and discipline at the plate has never been reinforced. They say, 'They're not paying me to walk.' And so if you don't lean on them, they don't."

Before it had a chance to become a proper argument, the conflict between the old and the new baseball men was resolved by the budget crisis. Tony La Russa left when the new owners renounced the old habit of bankrolling millions of dollars in losses. Alderson set out to find a manager who would understand that he wasn't the boss, and landed upon the recently fired manager of the Houston Astros, Art Howe. "Art Howe was hired to implement the ideas of the front office, not his own," said Alderson. "And that was new."

Billy would say later that his wife left him because she was unnerved by his intensity—that she could even see it in his hands when he drove an automobile. At any rate, he soon found himself out of not only a baseball uniform but a wife as well. Baseball marriages were like that: their most vulnerable moment was immediately after a player retired, and it dawned on husband and wife that they'd actually be spending time together. "They end when the career ends," said Billy. "Until then you can put up with anything because you're always leaving the next day." His wife moved back to San Diego and took their infant daughter, christened Casey, with her. Billy spent his weeks scouting and his weekends speeding down, and then back up, the highway between Oakland and San Diego. He couldn't afford the plane tickets.

His motor was still fueled less by desire than anxieties—and he now had two of them. One was that he wouldn't know his own daughter. The other was that he wouldn't cut it in the front office. "If baseball's all you can do and you know that's all you can do," he said, "it breeds in you a certain creative desperation." When he wasn't speeding down some California highway he was jetting around the country watching games and listening to the other scouts talk about players. Whatever shred of doubt he'd had that most of them had no idea what they were talking about, he lost.

What he hadn't lost was his ferocious need to win. He had just transferred it to a different place, from playing to making decisions about players. But this time he had guidance—from a graduate of not one but *two* Ivy League colleges—and he was willing to follow it. "What Billy figured out at some point," said Sandy Alderson, "is that he wanted to be me more than he wanted to be Jose Canseco." In 1993 Alderson, impressed by the creative enthusiasm with which Billy seemed to attack every task he was given, brought him into the front office, made him his assistant, and told him his job was to go out and find undervalued minor league players. And then he handed Billy the pamphlet he'd commissioned from Eric Walker.

When Billy read Walker's pamphlet, he experienced—well, he couldn't quite describe the excitement of it. "It was the first thing I had ever read that tried to take an objective view of baseball," he said. "Something that was different than just a lot of people's subjective opinions. I was still very subjective in my own thinking but it made sense to me." It more than made sense to him: it explained him. The new, outsider's view of baseball was all about exposing the illusions created by the insiders on the field. Billy Beane had himself been one of those illusions.

Billy wasn't one to waste a lot of time worrying about whether he was motivated by a desire to succeed or the pursuit of truth. To his way of thinking the question was academic, since the pursuit of truth was, suddenly, the key to success. He was bright. He had a natural coruscating skepticism about baseball's traditional wisdom. He could see that Eric Walker's pamphlet was just the beginning of a radical, and rational, approach to the game—one that would concentrate unprecedented powers in the hands of the general manager. Where had Eric Walker come from, he wondered, and was there any more behind what he'd written? "Billy shed every one of his player-type prejudices and adapted," Alderson said. "Whereas most of the people like him would have said, 'That's not the way we did it when I played.'" In answer to Billy's question, Alderson pointed to a row of well-thumbed paperbacks by a writer named Bill James, who had opened Alderson's eyes to a new way of thinking about baseball. Alderson had collected pretty much everything Bill James had written, including four books self-published by James between 1977 and 1980 that still existed only as cheap mimeographs. Sandy Alderson had never met, or even spoken to, Bill James. He wasn't a typical baseball insider but he still recognized a distinction between people like himself, who actually *made* baseball decisions, and people like James, who just wrote about them. But he had found James's approach to the game completely persuasive, and had reshaped a professional baseball organization in James's spirit. That's why he had hired Eric Walker, in the hope of "getting some Bill James–like stuff that was proprietary to us."

For his part, Billy Beane had never heard of Bill James. "But that was the big moment," he said, "when I figured out that all the stuff Sandy was talking about was just derivative of Bill James." His mind had finally found an escape hatch. It led to a green field as far away from professional baseball as you could get and still be inside the park.

Chapter Four

FIELD OF IGNORANCE

I didn't care about the statistics in anything else. I didn't, and don't
pay attention to statistics on the stock market, the weather, the
crime rate, the gross national product, the circulation of magazines,
the ebb and flow of literacy among football fans and how many
people are going to starve to death before the year 2050 if I don't
start adopting them for $3.69 a month; just baseball. Now why is
that? It is because baseball statistics, unlike the statistics in
any other area, have acquired the powers of language.
—Bill James, *1985 Baseball Abstract*

THERE IS A CERTAIN KIND of writer whose motives are ulti-
mately mysterious. The writer born into a family of writers; the writer whose work is an attempt to make sense of
some private trauma; the writer who from the age of four is able
and willing to stay in his room and make up stories: each of these
creatures is a stereotype. What he writes may be good, but why he
writes isn't something you particularly want to hear more about.
The interesting case is a writer like Bill James. He grew up in a not
unhappy family in Mayetta, Kansas (population: 209), and the
closest he came to an uprooting experience was the move from
there down the Interstate Highway to Lawrence. There, at the
University of Kansas, James studied economics and literature. He
didn't know any literary types, had no apparent role models, and
was not encouraged in any way to commit his thoughts to paper.
After a shaggy dog story in the U.S. Army—he was the last man
from Kansas drafted to serve in Vietnam but never was sent—and

a fruitless layover in graduate school, he found a job as the night-watchman in a Stokely Van Camp pork and beans factory.

It was while guarding Stokely Van Camp's pork and beans that James stumbled seriously into putting his thoughts down on paper, in response to having things he absolutely needed to say that he was unable to convey any other way. "Every form of strength is also a form of weakness," he once wrote. "Pretty girls tend to become insufferable because, being pretty, their faults are too much tolerated. Possessions entrap men, and wealth paralyzes them. I learned to write because I am one of those people who somehow cannot manage the common communications of smiles and gestures, but must use words to get across things that other people would never need to say."

Even more oddly, everything James needed to say was either about baseball, or could be said only in the context of a discussion of baseball. "I'd probably be a writer if there was no such thing as baseball," he said, "but because there is such a thing as baseball I can't imagine writing about anything else." He was, from time to time, aware of the absurdity of devoting an entire adult life to the search for meaning in box scores. He never seems to have resisted his instinct to do it. "Now, look," he wrote to his readers, once he'd become an established, successful author, "both of my parents died of cancer, and I fully expect that it's going to get me, too, in time. It would be very easy for me to say that cancer research is more important to me than baseball—but I must admit that I don't do anything which would be consistent with such a belief. I think about cancer research a few times a month; I think about baseball virtually every waking hour of my life."

James's first book was self-published—photocopied and stapled together by himself—and ran just sixty-eight pages (production budget: $112.73). Its formal title was: *1977 Baseball Abstract: Featuring 18 Categories of Statistical Information That You Just Can't Find Anywhere Else.* To sell it, James took out a single one-

inch advertisement in *The Sporting News.* Seventy-five people
found it alluring enough to buy a copy. Opening its pale blue
cover, they found a short opening explanatory paragraph that
failed to explain anything much, followed by sixteen pages of
baseball statistics. Astonishingly short and abrupt paragraphs followed by pages and pages of numbers: that was James's quixotic
early approach to getting across what he had to say. Were it not for
the author's frequent assertion that it was one, there was no reason to think of the first *Baseball Abstract* as a book. ("In this next
section of this book . . .") And there was certainly no reason to
think that the writer had the capacity to lead the reader to a radical, entirely original understanding of his subject. What little
James actually wrote in his first book felt stage-frightened. The
questions he posed—Do some pitchers draw bigger crowds than
others? How much effect does an umpire crew have on the length
of a game?—could not possibly have interested anyone but the
nuttiest baseball nut and, in any case, couldn't be answered confidently with the data James had, from a single baseball season.

It wasn't until the end of the *1977 Baseball Abstract* that James
offered his cocktail party–sized readership a glimpse of his potential. The topic that finally gets him sufficiently worked up that he
devotes several entire pages to it of nothing but words is: fielding
statistics. The manner in which baseball people evaluate players'
fielding performance—adding up their errors, and applauding the
guy with the fewest—struck him as an outrage. "What is an
error?" he asked. "It is, without exception, the only major statistic in sports which is a record of what an observer thinks *should
have been accomplished.* It's a moral judgment, really, in the
peculiar quasi-morality of the locker room. . . . Basketball scorers
count mechanical errors, but those are a record of objective facts:
team A has the ball, then team B has the ball. . . . But the fact of a
baseball error is that *no* play has been made but that the scorer
thinks it should have. It is, uniquely, *a record of opinions.*"

James went on to explain that the concept of an error, like many baseball concepts, was tailored to an earlier, very different game. Errors had been invented in the late 1850s, when fielders didn't wear gloves, the outfield went unmowed and the infield ungroomed, and the ball was bashed around until it was lopsided. In 1860, a simple pop fly was an adventure. Any ball hit more than a few feet from a fielder on leave from the Civil War was unplayable. Under those circumstances, James conceded, it might have made some kind of sense to judge a fielder by his ability to cope with balls hit right at him. But a century later the statistic was still being used, unaided by any other, when anyone with eyes could see that balls hit at big league players were a trivial detail in a bigger picture. A talent for avoiding obvious failure was no great trait in a big league baseball player; the easiest way not to make an error was to be too slow to reach the ball in the first place. After all, wrote James, "you have to do something *right* to get an error; even if the ball is hit right at you, then you were standing in the right place to begin with."

The statistics were not merely inadequate; they lied. And the lies they told led the people who ran major league baseball teams to misjudge their players, and mismanage their games. James later reduced his complaint to a sentence: fielding statistics made sense only as numbers, not as language. Language, not numbers, is what interested him. Words, and the meaning they were designed to convey. "When the numbers acquire the significance of language," he later wrote, "they acquire the power to do all of the things which language can do: to become fiction and drama and poetry. . . . And it is not just baseball that these numbers, through a fractured mirror, describe. It is character. It is psychology, it is history, it is power, it is grace, glory, consistency, sacrifice, courage, it is success and failure, it is frustration and bad luck, it is ambition, it is overreaching, it is discipline. And it is victory and defeat, which is all that the idiot sub-conscious really understands." What to most people was a dull record of ephemeral events without deep meaning or lasting value was for James a safe deposit box containing life's secrets.

Baseball was theatre. But it could not be artful unless its performances could be properly understood. The meaning of these performances depended on the clarity of the statistics that measured them; bad fielding statistics were like a fog hanging over the stage. That raised an obvious question: why would the people in charge allow professional baseball to be distorted so obviously? The answer was equally obvious: they believed they could judge a player's performance simply by watching it. In this, James argued, they were deeply mistaken.

That was James's most general point, buried beneath his outrage about fielding statistics: the naked eye was an inadequate tool for learning what you needed to know to evaluate baseball players and baseball games:

Think about it. One absolutely cannot tell, by watching, the difference between a .300 hitter and a .275 hitter. The difference is one hit every two weeks. It might be that a reporter, seeing every game that the team plays, could sense that difference over the course of the year if no records were kept, but I doubt it. Certainly the average fan, seeing perhaps a tenth of the team's games, could never gauge two performances that accurately—in fact if you see both 15 games a year, there is a 40% chance that the .275 hitter will have more hits than the .300 hitter in the games that you see. The difference between a good hitter and an average hitter is simply not visible—it is a matter of record.

But the hitter is the center of attention. We notice what he does, bend over the scorecard with his name in mind. If he hits a smash down the third base line and the third baseman makes a diving stop and throws the runner out, then we notice and applaud the third baseman. But until the smash is hit, who is watching the third baseman? If he anticipates, if he adjusts for the hitter and moves over just two steps, then the same smash is a routine backhand stop—and nobody applauds. . . .

It was James's first sustained attack on baseball's conventional wisdom. He concluded it with a question:

So if we can't tell who the good fielders are accurately from the record books, and we can't tell accurately from watching, how can we tell?

"By counting things," he replied. Then he went on to propose a new statistic—the "range factor," he called it. A player's range factor was simply the number of *successful* plays he made in the field per game. There were obvious problems with range factors, too—an outfielder on a team staffed by fly ball pitchers, for instance, had more opportunities to make successful plays than an outfielder on a team staffed by sinker ball pitchers—but the details of the thing didn't matter. What mattered was James's ability to light a torch in a dark chamber and throw a new light on a dusty problem. He made you think. There was something bracing about the way he did it—his passion, his humor, his intolerance of stupidity, his preference for leaving an honest mess for others to clean up rather than a tidy lie for them to admire—that inspired others to join his cause. The cause was bigger than fielding statistics. The cause was the systematic search for new baseball knowledge.

The cause wasn't original. James was hardly the first person to notice that there was still stuff to be figured out about baseball, and that the game's underlying rationalities might be discerned through statistical analysis. Going right back to the invention of the box score in 1845, and its subsequent improvement in 1859 by a British-born journalist named Henry Chadwick, there had been numerate analysts who saw that baseball, more than other sports, gave you meaningful things to count, and that by counting them you could determine the value of the people who played the game.

But what got counted was often simply what was easiest to count, or what Henry Chadwick, whose reference point was cricket, had decided was important to count.

Chadwick was the critical figure in this history. To anyone who asked, "How could baseball statistics be so screwed up?," Henry Chadwick was usually the beginning, and occasionally the end, of the answer. Chadwick's stated goal in counting the events that occurred on a ball field was reform: he wanted players to be judged by their precise contributions to victory and defeat. He was as upset about the immorality he witnessed on the baseball diamond as he was about the drinking and gambling he found on the city streets—about which he also never tired of complaining. He longed to affix blame and credit for baseball plays, and to do it, he grossly oversimplified matters. Fielding errors were just one example of Chadwick's moralistic mind at work. Another was his interpretation of the base on balls. In cricket there was no such thing as a walk: Chadwick had to get his mind around a new idea. The tool was ill-designed for the task: Chadwick was better at popularizing baseball statistics than he was at thinking through their meaning. He decided that walks were caused entirely by the pitcher—that the hitter had nothing to do with them. In his initial box score Chadwick recorded a walk as an error; even in the later box scores, after he had listened to, or at least heard, the obvious objections from others, Chadwick never credited the hitter. He simply removed the walk altogether from the record books. "There is but one true criterion of skill at the bat," he wrote, "and that is the number of times bases are made on clean hits." Enter the batting average, ever since the chief measure of a player's offensive value.*

The more you examined these old measurement devices, the less apt they seemed. Chadwick, with help from others, had cre-

---

* For a fuller, more respectable account of the history of the box score, see Jules Tygiel's *Past Time: Baseball As History* (2000).

ated a system of perverse incentives for anyone who trotted out onto a baseball field. The fetish made of "runs batted in" was another good example of the general madness. RBI had come to be treated by baseball people as an individual achievement—free agents were *paid* for their reputation as RBI machines when clearly they were not. Big league players routinely swung at pitches they shouldn't to lard their RBI count. Why did they get so much credit for this? To knock runners in, runners needed to be on base when you came to bat. There was a huge element of luck in even having the opportunity, and what wasn't luck was, partly, the achievement of others. "The problem," wrote James, "is that baseball statistics are not pure accomplishments of men against other men, which is what we are in the habit of seeing them as. They are accomplishments of men in combination with their circumstances."

The failure of baseball people to acknowledge that fact in their statistics led to exactly the sort of moral corruption Henry Chadwick, in creating them, had sought to eliminate. The many little injustices and misunderstandings embedded in the game's records spawned exotic inefficiencies. Baseball strategies were often wrongheaded and baseball players were systematically misunderstood. Chadwick succeeded in creating a central role for statistics in baseball, but in doing it he created the greatest accounting scandal in professional sports.

Between Chadwick and James there had been fitful efforts to rethink old prejudices. The legendary GM Branch Rickey employed a professional statistician named Allan Roth who helped to compose an article under Rickey's byline in *Life* magazine in 1954 that argued for the importance of on-base and slugging percentages over batting average. A professor of mechanical engineering at Johns Hopkins, Earnshaw Cook, wrote two pompous books, in prose crafted to alienate converts, that argued for the relevance of statistical analysis in baseball. In the early 1960s, a pair of brothers employed by IBM used the company's computers to analyze baseball strategies and players. But the desire to use statistics to make baseball efficient—to measure and value precisely the events that occur on a baseball field, to give the numbers new powers of language—only became potent when it became practical.

When Bill James published his *1977 Baseball Abstract*, two changes were about to occur that would make his questions not only more answerable but also more valuable. First came radical advances in computer technology: this dramatically reduced the cost of compiling and analyzing vast amounts of baseball data. Then came the boom in baseball players' salaries: this dramatically raised the benefits of having such knowledge. "If we're going to pay these guys $150,000 a year to do this," James concluded in his essay on fielding, "we should at least know how good they are—which means knowing how much they allowed in the field just as much as it means knowing how much they created at bat." If this sounded compelling when baseball players were paid $150,000 a year, it sounded one hundred times more so when they were paid $15 million a year.

James's first proper essay was the preview to an astonishing literary career. There was but one question he left unasked, and it vibrated between his lines: if gross miscalculations of a person's value could occur on a baseball field, before a live audience of thirty thousand, and a television audience of millions more, what did that say about the measurement of performance in other lines of work? If professional baseball players could be over- or under-valued, who couldn't? Bad as they may have been, the statistics used to evaluate baseball players were probably far more accurate than anything used to measure the value of people who didn't play baseball for a living.

Still, had he left off writing in 1977, James would have been dismissed as just another crank who didn't know when to shut up about box scores. He didn't leave off in 1977. It didn't occur to him to be disappointed by a sale of seventy-five copies; he was encouraged! No author has ever been so energized by so little. As James's wife, Susan McCarthy, later put it, "instead of one page of a stolen base study lying on top of a couple of pages of pitcher data in the dungeon of a Stokely Van Camp's cardboard box for years and years, ideas and questions about issues he had been chewing on for a long time took up residence in a climate that allowed for growth and maturation."*

In 1978, James came out with a second book, and this time, before entering his discussion, he checked his modesty at the door. The book was titled *1978 Baseball Abstract: The 2nd Annual Edition of Baseball's Most Informative and Imaginative Review.* "I would like to produce here the most complete, detailed, and comprehensive picture of the game of baseball available anywhere," he wrote, "and I would like to avoid repeating anything that has ever been written before."

Word had spread this time: 250 people bought a copy. To an author who viewed a sale of 75 copies as encouragement, the sale of 250 was a bonanza. James's pen was now an unstoppable force. Every winter for the next nine years he wrote with greater confidence; every spring his growing audience found relatively less space devoted to numbers and more to James's words. The words might run on for many pages but they were typically presented as digressions from the numbers. Wishing to convey the history of his obsession with baseball, for instance, James buried it in a discussion of the year-end stats of the Kansas City Royals. Unable to supress his distaste for the rich men who bought baseball teams and spent huge sums of money on players, he left off writing about the Atlanta Braves and picked up the subject of their new owner.

---

* An invisible subplot of baseball fanaticism is its effect on the spouses of the fanatics. "Bill hid his interest in baseball when we first started dating," said his wife. "If I had known the extent of it, I'm not sure we'd have gotten very far."

"Ted Turner," he wrote, "seems never to have been tempted by moderation, by dignity or restraint. He is a man who plays hard at gentleman's games and whines when he loses that the victor was not a gentleman. No matter how hard he flees, he will always be pursued by an Awful Commonness, and that is what makes him a winner." (Yankees fans would soon learn that James was capable of greater contempt: "Turner is the man Steinbrenner dreams of being.")

The *Baseball Abstracts* were one long, elaborate aside, and the aside raised all sorts of strange new questions: If Mike Schmidt hit against the Cubs all the time, what would he hit? Did fleet young black players, as it seemed to James, actually lose their speed later in their careers than fleet young white players? Who were the best dead hitters? Even the most obscure questions about baseball, and its history, had practical implications. To calculate what Mike Schmidt would hit if he hit only against the Chicago Cubs, you needed to understand how hitting in Wrigley Field differed from hitting in other parks. To compare white and black speedsters, you needed to find a way to measure speed on the base paths and in the field; and once you'd done that, you might begin to ask questions about the importance of foot speed. To determine the best dead hitters, you needed to build tools to evaluate them, and those tools worked just as well on the living.

That last problem preoccupied James. From his second season on, he more or less set baseball defense to one side and concentrated on baseball offense. He explained to the readers of the second *Abstract* that his book contained roughly forty thousand baseball statistics. A few of them had been easy for him to obtain, but "the bulk of them were compiled one by one, picked out of the box scores and laboriously sorted into groups of about 30 or so, groups with titles like 'Double Plays turned in games started by Nino Espinosa,' and 'Triples hit by Larry Parrish in July.'" He freely admitted that collecting baseball statistics was, on the face of it, a bizarre way to spend one's time—unless one was obsessed by the baseball offense. "I am a mechanic with numbers," he wrote to readers of the third *Abstract*,

tinkering with the records of baseball games to see how the machinery of the baseball offense works. I do not start with the numbers any more than a mechanic starts with a monkey wrench. I start with the game, with the things that I see there and the things that people say there. And I ask: Is it true? Can you validate it? Can you measure it? How does it fit with the rest of the machinery? And for those answers I go to the record books. . . . What is remarkable to me is that I have so little company. Baseball keeps copious records, and people talk about them and argue about them and think about them a great deal. Why doesn't anybody use them? Why doesn't anybody say, in the face of this contention or that one, "Prove it"?

For what now seem like obvious reasons the baseball offense was more interesting to James than the other two potentially big fields of research, fielding and pitching. Hitting statistics were abundant and had, for James, the powers of language. They were, in his Teutonic coinage, "imagenumbers." Literary material. When you read them, they called to mind pictures. "Let us start with the number 191 in the hit column," he wrote,

and with the assertion that it is not possible for a flake (I would hope that no one reading this book doesn't know what a flake is) to get 191 hits in a season. It is possible for a bastard to do this. It is possible for a warthog to do this. It is possible for many people whom you would not want to marry your sister to do this. But to get 191 hits in a season demands (or seems to demand, which is as good for the drama) a consistency, a day-in, day-out devotion, a self-discipline, a willingness to play with pain and (to some degree) a predisposition to the team game which is wholly inconsistent with flakiness. It is entirely possible, on the other hand, for a flake to hit 48 homers. Hitting 48 homers is something done by large, slow men three-quarters thespian. . . .

James was an aesthete. But he was also a pragmatist: he had happened upon something broken and wanted to fix it. But he could only fix what he had the tools to fix. The power of statistical analysis depends on sample size: the larger the pile of data the analyst has to work with, the more confidently he can draw specific conclusions about it. A right-handed hitter who has gone two for ten against left-handed pitching cannot as reliably be predicted to hit .200 against lefties as a hitter who has gone 200 for 1,000. The offensive statistics available to James in 1978 were sufficiently comprehensive to reach specific, meaningful conclusions. Offense he could fix. He couldn't fix fielding because, as he had explained in his first *Abstract*, there wasn't the data available to make a meaningful appraisal of fielding. Pitching didn't need to be fixed. Or, at any rate, James didn't think it did.

In 1979, in the third, now annual, *Baseball Abstract*, James wrote, "a hitter should be measured by his success in that which he is trying to do, and that which he is trying to do is create runs. It is startling, when you think about it, how much confusion there is about this. I find it remarkable that, in listing offenses, the league will list first—meaning best—not the team which scored the most runs, but the team with the highest batting average. It should be obvious that the purpose of an offense is not to compile a high batting average." Because it was not obvious, at least to the people who ran baseball, James smelled a huge opportunity. How *did* runs score? "We can't directly see how many runs each player creates," he wrote, "but we can see how many runs each team creates."

He set out to build a model to predict how many runs a team would score, given its number of walks, hits, stolen bases, etc. He'd dig out the numbers for, say, the 1975 Red Sox. (Walks by individual players were still hard to find in 1975, thanks to Henry Chadwick, but team totals were available.) He could also find out how many runs the 1975 Red Sox scored. What he needed to determine was the relative importance to the team's scoring of the various things Red Sox players did at the plate and on the base paths—that is, assign weights to outs, walks, steals, singles, doubles, etc. There was nothing elegant or principled in the way he went about solving the problem. He simply tried out various equations on the right side of the equals sign until he found one that gave him the team run totals on the left side. The first version of what James called his "Runs Created" formula looked like this:

Runs Created = (Hits + Walks) × Total Bases/(At Bats + Walks)

Crude as it was, the equation could fairly be described as a scientific hypothesis: a model that would predict the number of runs a team would score given its walks, steals, singles, doubles, etc. You could plug actual numbers from past seasons into the right side and see if they gave you the runs the team scored that season. James was, in a sense, trying to predict the past. If the actual number of runs scored by the 1975 Boston Red Sox differed dramatically from the predicted number, his model was clearly false. If they were identical, James was probably onto something. As it turned out, James was onto something. His model came far closer, year in and year out, to describing the run totals of every big league baseball team than anything the teams themselves had come up with.

That, in turn, implied that professional baseball people had a false view of their offenses. It implied, specifically, that they didn't place enough value on walks and extra base hits, which featured prominently in the "Runs Created" model, and placed too much value on batting average and stolen bases, which James didn't even bother to include. It implied that sacrifices of any sort were aptly named, as they made no contribution whatsoever. That is: outs were more precious than baseball people believed, or seemed to believe. Not all baseball people, of course. The Jamesean analysis was consistent with an approach to the game championed most vocally by the former manager of the Baltimore Orioles, Earl Weaver. Weaver designed his offenses to maximize the chances of a three-run homer. He didn't bunt, and he had a special taste for guys who got on base and guys who hit home runs. Big ball, as opposed to small ball.

But once again, the details of James's equation didn't matter all that much. He was creating opportunities for scientists as much as doing science himself. Other, more technically adroit people would soon generate closer approximations of reality. What mattered was (a) it was a rational, testable hypothesis; and (b) James made it so clear and interesting that it provoked a lot of intelligent people to join the conversation. "The fact that the formulas work with the accuracy that they do is a way of saying there are essentially stable relationships between batting average, home runs, walks, other offensive elements—and runs," wrote James.

This kind of talk was catnip to people whose lives were devoted to discovering stable relationships in a seemingly unstable world: physicists, biologists, economists. There was a young statistician at the RAND Corporation, a future chair of the Harvard statistics department, named Carl Morris. "I'd been thinking about advanced ideas in baseball analysis," said Morris, "and was impressed that someone else was, too, who wrote about it in a very interesting way." Morris counted the days until the next *Baseball Abstract* appeared. James pointed the way to big questions that Morris could address more rigorously than even James could.

There was also a bright young government economist with the Office of Management and Budget named Eddie Epstein. He stumbled across the *Abstract* and decided he was in the wrong line of work. "I read the *Abstract*," he said, "and the light bulb went off:

I can do this! The way Bill laid out very clearly what could be gleaned from these mountains of baseball data. In the past an awful lot was thought to be unknowable." Epstein began to pester Edward Bennett Williams, the owner of the Baltimore Orioles, for a job.

Then there were the few hobbyists who had been active before James began writing his *Abstracts*. Dick Cramer was a research scientist for the pharmaceutical company then called SmithKline French (now GlaxoSmithKline), and so had access to a computer. By day he used the SmithKline computers to discover new drugs and by night he used them to test his own theories about baseball. For instance, Cramer had a hypothesis about clutch hitting: it didn't exist. No matter what the announcers said, and what the coaches believed, major league baseball players did not perform particularly well—or particularly badly—in critical situations. On the one hand, it made a funny kind of sense: no one who behaved differently under pressure would ever make it to the big leagues. On the other hand, it contradicted the sacred, received wisdom in baseball. The sheer counterintuitiveness of his notion delighted Cramer. "It violates everyone's personal experience of pressure, and how they cope with it," he said. And yet it was true, or impossible to disprove. Cramer had tested it and found no evidence that players hit differently in one situation than any other—with a pair of exceptions. Some left-handed hitters fared worse against lefties than righties, and some right-handed hitters fared worse against righties than lefties.

Cramer's work has subsequently withstood intense, repeated critical scrutiny, but until Bill James came along no one paid it any attention. "Until Bill came along," Cramer says, "it was just three or four of us writing letters to each other. Even my own family would say, 'This is a crazy way to spend your time.'"

Cramer, like James, understood that the search for baseball knowledge was constrained by the raw statistics, and began to think seriously about starting a company to collect better data about Major League Baseball games than did Major League Baseball. One of the men to whom Cramer wrote letters on the subject was Pete Palmer. Palmer worked as an engineer at Raytheon, on the software that supported the radar station in the Aleutian Islands that monitored Russian test missiles. At least that's what he did for money; for love he sat down with his charts and slide rule and analyzed baseball strategies. Both Palmer and Cramer had separately created their own models of the baseball offense that differed trivially from James's. (Together, they later dreamed up the stat now widely used to capture the primary importance to offense of slugging and on-base percentages: OPS, an acronym for on base plus slugging.) Palmer really was a gifted statistical mind, and he had done a lot of work, just for the hell of it, that demonstrated the foolishness of many conventional baseball strategies. Bunts, stolen bases, hit and runs—they all were mostly self-defeating and all had a common theme: fear of public humiliation.

"Managers tend to pick a strategy that is least likely to fail rather than pick a strategy that is most efficient," said Palmer. "The pain of looking bad is worse than the gain of making the best move." Palmer had written a book back in the 1960s revealing all this. The manuscript was still gathering dust on his desk when Bill James came along and created a market for it. In 1984, in the wake of Bill James's success, he was able to publish it: *The Hidden Game of Baseball*. "Bill proved there were buyers for this kind of thing," Palmer says. "I'm not sure the book would have seen the light of day otherwise."

James's literary powers combined with his willingness to answer his mail to create a movement. Research scientists at big companies, university professors of physics and economics and life sciences, professional statisticians, Wall Street analysts, bored lawyers, math wizards unable to hold down regular jobs—all these people were soon mailing James their ideas, criticisms, models, and questions. His readership must have been one of the strangest group of people ever assembled under one idea. Before he found a publisher, James had four readers he considered "celebrities." They were:

Norman Mailer

Baseball writer Dan Okrent

William Goldman, the screenwriter (*Butch Cassidy and the Sundance Kid*)

The guy who played "Squiggy" on the TV sitcom *Laverne & Shirley*

James's readers were hard to classify because he was hard to classify. The sheer quantity of brain power that hurled itself voluntarily and quixotically into the search for new baseball knowledge was either exhilarating or depressing, depending on how you felt about baseball. The same intellectual resources might have cured the common cold, or put a man on Pluto; instead, it was used to divine the logic hidden inside a baseball game, and create whole new ways of second-guessing the manager.

Four years into his experiment James was still self-publishing his *Baseball Abstract* but he was overwhelmed by reader mail. What began as an internal monologue became, first, a discussion among dozens of resourceful people, and then, finally, a series of arguments in which fools were not tolerated. (Most witheringly not by James: "Is baseball really 75% pitching? James J. Skipper attempted to answer this question in the 1980 *Baseball Research Journal*, by the ingenious method of asking everybody in sight what percentage of baseball was pitching, totaling up their answers, and dividing by the number of people in sight. . . .") By 1981, in response to a pile of letters asking him what he thought about a new baseball offense model created by the sports journalist Thomas Boswell, James was able and willing to write that "the world needs another offensive rating system like Custer needed more Indians (or, for that matter, like the Indians needed another Custer). . . . What we really need is for the amateurs to clear the floor." There was now such a thing as intellectually rigorous baseball analysts. James had given the field of study its name: sabermetrics.*

The swelling crowd of disciples and correspondents made James's movement more potent in a couple of ways. One was that it now had a form of peer review: by the early 1980s all the statistical work was being vetted by people, unlike James, who had a deep interest in, and understanding of, statistical theory. Baseball studies, previously an eccentric hobby, became formalized along the lines of an academic discipline. In one way it was an even more effective instrument of progress: all these exquisitely trained, brilliantly successful scientists and mathematicians were working for love, not money. And for a certain kind of hyperkinetic analytical, usually male mind there was no greater pleasure than searching for new truths about baseball. "Baseball is a soap opera that lends itself to probabilistic thinking," is how Dick Cramer described the pleasure.

The other advantage was that the growing army of baseball analysts was willing and able to generate new baseball data. James was forever moaning about the paucity of the information kept by major league baseball teams. Early in one of his *Baseball Abstracts* he had explained to his readers that "the answers that I arrive at—and thus the methods I have chosen—are never wholly satisfactory, almost never wholly disappointing. The most consistent problems that I have arise from the limitations on my information sources. All I have is the box scores." The reason he couldn't get more than the box scores is that the company that kept the score sheets for Major League Baseball, the Elias Sports Bureau, was perfectly unhelpful when James asked it for access to them. "The problem with the Elias Bureau," he wrote, "is that the Elias Bureau never turns loose of a statistic unless they get a dollar for it. Their overarching concern in life is to get every dollar

* The name derives from SABR, the acronym of the Society for American Baseball Research. In 2002, the society had about seven thousand members.

they can from you and give you as little as possible in return for it—like a lot of other businesses, I suppose, only with a more naked display of greed than is really usual."

James was shocked by the indifference of baseball insiders to the fans who took more than an ordinary interest. Major League Baseball had no sense of the fans as customers, and so hadn't the first clue of what the customer wanted. The customer wanted stats and Major League Baseball did its best not to give them to him. The people inside Major League Baseball were, if anything, hostile to the people outside Major League Baseball who wished to study the game. That struck James, who by now had perfected the art of sounding like a sane man in an insane world, as mad. "The entire basis of professional sports is the public's interest in what is going on," he wrote. "To deny the public access to information that it cares about is the logical equivalent of locking the stadiums and playing the games in private so that no one will find out what is happening."

In 1984, James wrote to what was now a rapidly expanding crowd of baseball nuts and proposed a radical idea: Take the accumulation of baseball statistics out of the hands of baseball insiders. Build an organization of hundreds of volunteer scorekeepers who would collect the stuff you needed to know to reduce baseball to a science. "What I propose here, so far as I know for the first time in a century, is to start over. . . . I am proposing to re-build the box score, not around the old one, but around the tool from which the box score is assembled: the score sheet." He then explained that much of the data collected by professional baseball teams—say, how right-handed hitters fared against left-handed pitching—wasn't available to the public. Worse, baseball teams didn't have the sense to know what to collect, and so an awful lot of critical data simply went unrecorded: how batters fared in different counts and different game situations, who was pitching when a base was stolen, how different outfielders affected the audacity of runners on the base paths, where hits landed and how hard they were hit, how many pitches a pitcher threw in a game. The lack of critical data meant that "we as analysts of the game are blocked off from the basic source of information which we need to undertake an incalculable variety of investigative studies."

The movement to take the understanding of professional baseball away from baseball professionals, dubbed by James "Project Scoresheet," soon combined with a small, failing business created by Dick Cramer, called STATS Inc., that was designed to do much the same thing. The goal of STATS Inc. had been, in Cramer's words, "to set down the primary events that occurred in a baseball game as completely as possible." Back in 1980, STATS Inc. had set out to sell this sort of information to baseball teams, but the teams wanted nothing to do with it. Cramer pressed on: to big league baseball games, beginning in the spring of 1981 with an exhibition game between the Chicago Cubs and the Oakland A's (future A's scout Matt Keough got the win), the company sent its own scorekeepers. Along with all the usual data, these poorly paid people recorded play-by-play information about the games that had never before been systematically collected: the pitch count at the end of at bats, pitch types and locations, the direction and distance of batted balls. They broke the field down into twenty-six wedges radiating out from home plate. A fly ball's distance was judged to be where it landed; a ground ball's, where it was picked up. If a player singled and advanced to second on an error by the right fielder, the play was recorded as two separate events. All of this was new and, to the movement analysts, essential if you wanted to get to the guts of the game.

The people who were paid to manage professional teams failed to see the point. They hadn't even bothered to compile the information they needed to analyze their actions intelligently. Presented with new information by STATS Inc., they showed little interest in it, even when it was offered to them gratis. The CEO of STATS Inc., John Dewan, said that "You had general managers and managers who had played the game. How could someone who all they knew is computers tell them *anything* that would make them more successful? I remember calling the White Sox, almost as a matter of courtesy, and telling them 'Hey, when Frank Thomas plays first base, he hits seventy points better than when he DH's.' Nobody cared to know it." Every eighteen months STATS Inc. would hire another bright, well-educated young man who simply could not believe that major league baseball teams did not want to know things that might help them win games. He would then proceed to hurl himself into the business of selling STATS Inc. to baseball teams. He always quit, disillusioned. "The people who run baseball are surrounded by people trying to give them advice," said James. "So they've built very effective walls to keep out anything."

It wasn't as simple as the unease of jocks in the presence of nerds. Professional baseball was happy to have intellectuals hanging around the clubhouse and the commissioner's office and the GM's suite. Well, perhaps not happy, but not disturbed either, so long as the intellectuals had no practical consequences for how baseball was played, and by whom. Baseball offered a comfortable seat to the polysyllabic wonders who quoted dead authors and blathered on about the poetry of motion. These people dignified the game, like a bow tie. They were harmless. What was threatening was cold, hard intelligence.

STATS Inc. founder Dick Cramer told a story with the flavor of the deeper problem. In the early days, through fluky circumstances, Cramer had sold his data collection and analysis service to the Houston Astros. The Astros' GM, Al Rosen, wanted to know how the team would be affected if the Astrodome's fences were moved in. Would the team, as currently composed, do better or worse in a smaller, more hitter-friendly park? Cramer ran the numbers—showing the relative propensity of the Astros versus their opponents to hit long pop flies—and told Rosen, "Sorry, if you do that, you lose more games." Instead of deciding not to move the fences in, Rosen decided that the information could never be made public. "All of a sudden it is classified information," said Cramer, "It was 'We can't tell anyone! My God, we can't let this information get out! Imagine the effect on our pitchers!'" They didn't want the information to inform the decision. They'd already made the decision. (They believed home runs sold tickets.) They wanted the information, in some sense, to avoid having to deal with its implications.

In 1985, STATS Inc. gave up trying to sell their superior data to teams and began to sell it to fans. Their timing could not have been better: the baseball fan was changing in a way that made him a natural customer of STATS Inc. A new kind of fan, with a quasi-practical interest in baseball statistics, had been invented. In 1980 a group of friends, led by *Sports Illustrated* writer Dan Okrent, met at La Rotisserie Française, a restaurant in Manhattan, and created what became known, to the confusion of a nation, as Rotisserie Baseball. Okrent can plausibly be said to have "discovered" Bill James. Okrent was one of those seventy-five people who, in 1977, ran across the one-inch ad in *The Sporting News* James took out and sent off his check to Lawrence, Kansas. Back came an unpromising mimeograph. Then he read it. "I was absolutely dumbstruck," he said. "I couldn't believe that (a) this guy existed and (b) he hadn't been discovered."

Okrent flew to Lawrence to make sure James indeed existed, then wrote a piece about him for *Sports Illustrated*. It was killed: James's arrival on the national sporting scene was delayed by a year, after the *Sports Illustrated* fact-checker spiked the piece. "She went through it line by line," recalled Okrent, "saying, 'Everyone knows this isn't true. Everyone knows that Nolan Ryan attracted a bigger crowd when he pitched, that Gene Tenace was a bad hitter, that . . .'" Conventional opinions about baseball players and baseball strategies had acquired the authority of fact, and the *Sports Illustrated* fact-checking department was not going to let evidence to the contrary see print. The following year, an editor who had been unable to shake Okrent's piece from his mind asked Okrent to try again. He did, and the piece was published, and Bill James was introduced to a wider audience. The year after that, 1982, a New York publisher, Ballantine Books, brought out the *Baseball Abstract*, and made it a national best-seller.

Many of James's new readers were Rotisserie Baseball fanatics. The game, which sought to simulate an actual baseball game, put the players in the role of general manager of a team of real life baseball players, which he picked himself from actual teams. Each morning he'd get up and go to the box scores in the newspaper to calculate how his "team" had done. Over the next decade some immeasurable but vast number of Americans—millions, certainly—took to the game, many of them obsessively. That they should have developed a special interest in Bill James was strange, in a way. The fantasy games were premised on the old-fashioned statistics, the pre-Jamesean understanding of baseball. The general manager of a Rotisserie team measured his success by toting up batting averages, RBIs, stolen bases, and so on. To win one's Rotisserie League you needed to behave pretty much like bone-headed general managers. You needed to overpay for RBIs and batting averages and stolen bases; you had no use for on-base and slugging percentages. You certainly didn't need access to the growing corpus of new baseball knowledge. Rotisserie Baseball was, if anything, a force for encouraging the conventional view of baseball.

Nevertheless! The fans were more keenly interested in the information they needed to make intelligent baseball decisions— even if they themselves did not directly benefit from making intelligent baseball decisions—than the people who ran the real teams. They needed it, or thought they needed it, to win their fantasy games. As James later admitted, the desire to win these games had been a chief motive for his original rethinking of the game. Before the sophisticated baseball fantasy leagues there had been sophisticated table-top baseball games. "I used to be in a table-game league," James confessed to his readers a decade later. "This was ten, twelve years ago. . . . It was during this period, in trying to win that league, that I became obsessed with how an offense works and why it doesn't work sometimes . . . with finding what information you would need to have to simulate baseball in a more accurate way. I had thought about these things before, of course, but to win that damn [table league] I had to know."

James knew better than just about anyone on the planet just how many people were taking to these fantasy games, and how widespread was the desire to play at being the general manager of a big league baseball team, and, therefore, how deep the interest in baseball statistics. He became an investor and creative director of the newly energized STATS Inc. The company grew rapidly—ESPN was a customer from the start and *USA Today* soon became one. It became the leading source of information to the baseball fan until it was sold in 1999 for $45 million to Fox News Corporation.

The company was a success, but of a curious kind: what should have happened didn't happen. What should have happened is this: real, as opposed to fantasy, general managers would engage with this new, growing body of knowledge. The Jamesean movement set the table for the geeks to rush in and take over the general management of the game. Everywhere one turned in competitive markets, technology was offering the people who understood it an edge. What was happening to capitalism should have happened to baseball: the technical man with his analytical magic should have risen to prominence in baseball management, just as he was rising to prominence on, say, Wall Street.

What the baseball professionals did do, on occasion, beginning in the early 1980s, was to hire some guy who knew how to switch on the computer. But they did this less with honest curiosity than in the spirit of a beleaguered visitor to Morocco hiring a tour guide: pay off one so that the seventy-five others will stop trying to trade you their camels for your wife. Which one you pay off is largely irrelevant. Some stat head would impress himself upon a general manager as the sort of guy who crunched numbers and the GM would find him a small office in the back.

The lack of discrimination of the few baseball GMs who went shopping for a James manqué led to what might be called *Elephant Man* moments. The *Elephant Man* moment came when the beat reporter for the local team pulled back the curtain on the front office and revealed the shriveled-up fellow with bizarre facial hair punching numbers into a Mac. The brains of the operation! The crowd invariably shrieked and recoiled. The most dramatic *Elephant Man* moment was probably when an oddity named Mike Gimbel hired by the Boston Red Sox didn't wait to be exposed but bodily hurled himself into the Boston sports pages, by claiming responsibility for the shrewd moves made by the Red Sox GM, Dan Duquette. The *Boston Globe* explained to Red Sox fans that this new intellectual force behind the team was "a Queens Community College dropout, a self-taught computer programmer and a Rotisserie League fanatic whose Brooklyn loft was raided three years ago by police because of his six pet caimans—South American alligators—that he kept in an indoor pond in his loft. The cops also confiscated his five turtles and an iguana." The New England Sports Service ran the same story with the headline: *Stats Freak Has Duquette's Ear.* "By day Gimbel lives in Brooklyn and works for the Bureau of Water Supply in New York," it began, groping for just the right combination of words and images to infuriate the Red Sox season ticket holder. "It's as if a computer savvy Ed Norton had become the Red Sox secret weapon. Gimbel is unorthodox in virtually every way. In 80 degree Florida weather yesterday, Gimbel appeared ready for a trip to Siberia, with long pants, a long sleeve shirt and a jacket. His approach to evaluating baseball is more out of the ordinary. He cautions against watching too many games. . . ."

Duquette waited until the end of the season, then let Gimbel know his contract wouldn't be renewed—thus proving to the world just how critical he was to the Boston Red Sox.

By the early 1990s it was clear that "sabermetrics," the search for new baseball knowledge, was an activity that would take place mainly outside of baseball. You could count on one hand the number of "sabermetricians" inside of baseball, and none of them appears to have had much effect. After a while they seemed more like fans who second-guessed the general manager than advisers who influenced decisions. They were forever waving printouts to show how foolish the GM had been not to have taken their advice. A man named Craig Wright spent many frustrating years as the sabermetrician with the Texas Rangers, and then many more consulting other big league teams. He eventually quit his profession altogether. "I needed to be a GM if I was going to see my stuff ever used," he said. "And I never even got asked to interview for a single GM job." Eddie Epstein—the young government economist whose interest in baseball analysis had been inflamed by James's writing—got himself hired by the Baltimore Orioles and the San Diego Padres but he, too, wound up quitting in a huff. The Padres executive responsible for hiring him, Larry Lucchino, freely acknowledged that the small group inside baseball searching for new baseball knowledge "was a cult. The cult status of it meant it was something that could be discarded easily. There was a profusion of new knowledge and it was ignored."

Well into the late 1990s you didn't have to look at big league baseball very closely to see its fierce unwillingness to rethink anything. It was as if it had been inoculated against outside ideas. For instance, a new kind of rich person named John Henry bought the Florida Marlins in January 1999. Most baseball owners were either heirs, or empire builders of one sort or another, or both. Henry had made his money in the intelligent end of the financial markets. He had an instinctive feel for the way statistical analysis could turn up inefficiencies in human affairs. Inefficiencies in the financial markets had made Henry a billionaire—and he saw some familiar idiocies in the market for baseball players. As Henry later wrote in a letter to ESPN's Rob Neyer:

People in both fields operate with beliefs and biases. To the extent you can eliminate both and replace them with data, you gain a clear advantage. Many people think they are smarter than others in the stock market and that the market itself has no intrinsic intelligence—as if it's inert. Many people think they are smarter than others in baseball and that the game on the field is simply what they think it is through their set of images/beliefs. Actual data from the market means more than individual perception/belief. The same is true in baseball.

Henry was, unsurprisingly, a longtime Bill James reader. Even after he became the owner of a real big league baseball team, Henry continued to play in a sophisticated fantasy league in which he deployed Jamesean tools and, as he put it, "cleaned up. I won every year." But the real baseball team he owned continued to be run as if Bill James had never existed, and it didn't clean up anything but its shattered pride after ninety-eight losses.

The problem Henry faced was social and political. For a man who had never played professional baseball to impose upon even a pathetic major league franchise an entirely new way of doing things meant alienating the baseball insiders he employed: the manager, the scouts, the players. In the end, he would have been ostracized by his own organization. And what was the point of being in baseball if you weren't *in* baseball?

Right from the start Bill James assumed he had been writing for, not a mass audience, but a tiny group of people intensely interested in baseball. He wound up with a mass audience and went largely unread by the people most intensely interested in baseball: the men who ran the teams. Right through the 1980s and 1990s, James experienced only two responses to his work from baseball professionals. The first was opportunism from player agents, who wanted him to help them to demonstrate, in salary arbitration meetings with the teams, that their clients were underpaid. The other was hostility from the subcontractors who kept the stats for Major League Baseball.

When the Jamesean movement first took shape, the attitude

toward baseball statistics inside the company whose job it was to keep the official statistics for Major League Baseball was an odd mixture of possessiveness and indifference. In the late 1970s, the baseball writer Dan Okrent, with two colleagues from book publishing, went to pitch an idea to the CEO of the Elias Sports Bureau, Seymour Siwoff. The idea, recalled Okrent, "was to try to persuade him to collaborate with us on a painstakingly detailed, under-the-fingernails things you never knew book about baseball stats. The image is indelible: We are sitting there with this guy who looks like a superannuated ferret, his pale skinny arms protruding from the billowing short sleeves of his white-on-white shirt, and he brushes us off with a dismissive wave of his hand. 'Boys,' he said, 'nobody gives a shit about this stuff.'"

In 1985 the Elias Bureau finally woke up and published a book, a virtual twin in outward appearance to the *1985 Baseball Abstract*, called the *1985 Elias Baseball Analyst*. (The superannuated ferret was a co-author.) Although the company finally divulged some of the statistics they had long withheld from James and other analysts, they failed to do anything much with them. The writers imitated James's prose style but, lacking anything interesting to say, they wound up sounding empty and arch. James was happy to confirm the casual reader's impression that the Elias Bureau had a whiff of Salieri about it. "When the *Baseball Abstract* hit the bestseller lists," James wrote in his final *Abstract*,

> the [Elias Bureau] launched their own competitor, the main purposes of which were to:
>   a) make money
>   b) steal all of my ideas
>   c) make as many disparaging comments as possible about me
> So that was a lot of fun.

The effect on James of being ignored by the people who stood to benefit the most from his work was to distance himself even further from those people. In his earlier writings James often tried to explain what he was up to, in such a way that it might invite baseball professionals to pay attention. His instinct, at first, was to assume that the people who actually managed baseball teams had some good reason for what they were doing, even when what they were doing struck him as foolish. A few years into his career, he clearly decided that baseball professionals would benefit from being smacked on the head by a two-by-four. In his commentary about the Cleveland Indians that year, for instance, he wrote that "during the winter I was told something about the Indians' front office that really shocked me. They're dumb. You know, not bright, slow." He went on to explain how he at first refused to accept stupidity as an explanation for the Indians' ineptitude because "there is so much hope invested in a ball club, there are so many people who care about the fortunes even of the Indians and who are honestly hurt, if only in passing (but we are all only passing) that it just seems inconceivable that these fortunes could be entrusted to someone who is incapable of taking care of them. Are children allowed to play catch with the family jewels? . . . I have a correspondent who is an avid Indians fan, a professor of math at a fine university. He understands what needs to be done. Why can't he be given the job?"

Seven years into his literary career, in the *1984 Baseball Abstract,* James formally gave up any hope that baseball insiders would be reasonable. "When I started writing I thought if I proved X was a stupid thing to do that people would stop doing X," he said. "I was wrong." He began his opening essay of 1984, ominously, by pointing out the boom in sports journalism that promised to take you "inside the game." The media had become hell-bent on giving the superficial impression of allowing the fan a glimpse of the heart of every matter. Just to glance at the titles on TV shows and magazine articles you might think that there was nothing left inside to uncover.

It was all a lie. "What has really happened," James wrote, "is that the walls between the public and the participants of sports are growing higher and higher and thicker and darker, and the media is developing a sense of desperation about the whole thing." What was true about baseball was true about other spheres of American public life and, to James, the only sensible approach was to drop the pretense and embrace one's status as an outsider. "This is *outside* baseball," he wrote. "This is a book about what baseball looks like if you step back from it and study it intensely and minutely, but from a distance." It wasn't that it was better to be an outsider; it was *necessary*. "Since we are outsiders," he wrote, "since the players are going to put up walls to keep us out here, let us use our position as outsiders to what advantage we can."

From here until James quit writing his *Abstract* four years later he might as well have declared open season on insiders. He became somewhat slower to concede baseball professionals might have a point. One sentence serves as a fair summary of James's attitude toward the inside: "I think, really, that this is one reason that so many intelligent people drift away from baseball (when they come of age), that if you care about it at all you have to realize, as soon as you acquire a taste for independent thought, that a great portion of the sport's traditional knowledge is ridiculous hokum."

As baseball's leading analyst, James slid between two stools. Baseball insiders thought of him as some weird kind of journalist who had no real business with them. Baseball outsiders thought of him as a statistician who knew technical things about baseball. A number cruncher. A propeller head. Even after he had become known for his books—even after he changed the way many readers thought not only about baseball but about other things too—James never got himself thought of as a "writer."* That was a pity.

---

* When the Library of America published its wonderful anthology of America's great baseball writing in 2001, it included pieces by Robert Frost and John Updike and other fancy literary types, none of whom ever said anything as interesting about baseball as Bill James, and yet, inexplicably, nothing at all by James.

A number cruncher is precisely what James was not. His work tested many hypotheses about baseball directly against hard data—and sometimes did violence to the laws of statistics. But it also tested, less intentionally, a hypothesis about literature: if you write well enough about a single subject, even a subject seemingly as trivial as baseball statistics, you needn't write about anything else.

The trouble was that baseball readers were not ready for what he had to say. The people who found him worth reading struck him, increasingly, as ridiculous. His skeptical detachment from the world around him helped him to become a writer but it left him ill-suited to be a best-selling one. "I hate to say it and I hope you're not one of them," he wrote in his final, 1988 Baseball Abstract, "but I am encountering more and more of my own readers that I don't even like, nitwits who glom onto something superficial in the book and misunderstand its underlying message. . . . Whereas I used to write one 'Dear Jackass' letter a year, I now write maybe thirty." The growing misunderstanding between himself and his readership was, he felt, not adding to the sum total of pleasure or interest in the universe. "I am no longer certain that the effects of my doing this kind of research are in the best interests of the average baseball fan," he explained. "I would like to pretend that the invasion of statistical gremlins crawling at random all over the telecast of damn near every baseball game is irrelevant to me, that I really had nothing to do with it. . . . I know better. I didn't create this mess, but I helped."

Intelligence about baseball had become equated in the public mind with the ability to recite arcane baseball stats. What James's wider audience had failed to understand was that the statistics were beside the point. The point was understanding; the point was to make life on earth just a bit more intelligible; and that point, somehow, had been lost. "I wonder," James wrote, "if we haven't become so numbed by all these numbers that we are no longer capable of truly assimilating any knowledge which might result from them."

His final essay in his final *Baseball Abstract* James entitled "Breakin' the Wand." "To most people it no doubt seemed that I was writing about statistics," he said, "but I wasn't, not ever; in the years I've been doing this book I have written no more than a couple of articles about baseball statistics. The secret of the success of this book is that I was dead in the center of the discussion. I was writing about exactly the same issues that everybody else was talking about, only in a different way."

With that, he quit. Claimed he was through being a sabermetrician. "It is a wonderful thing to know that you are right and the world is wrong," he concluded. "Would God that I might have that feeling again before I die." He never had a clue—not then, not later—that the world was not entirely wrong. No one ever called James to say that an actual big league baseball team had read him closely, understood everything he had said along with the spirit in which he had said it, and had set out to find even more new baseball knowledge with which to clobber the nitwits who never grasped what Bill James was all about.

Chapter Five

THE JEREMY BROWN
BLUE PLATE SPECIAL

What I have tried to do with my work is to
make baseball more fun.
—*The Bill James Newsletter*, 1985

WHEN YOU THINK of intellectuals influencing the course
of human affairs you think of physics, or political theory, or economics. You think of John Maynard Keynes's
condescending line about men of action—how they believe themselves guided by their own ideas even when they are unwittingly
in the thrall of some dead economist. You don't think of baseball,
because you don't think of baseball as having an intellectual
underpinning. But it does; it had just never been seriously observed
and closely questioned, in a writing style sufficiently compelling
to catch the attention of the people who actually played baseball.
Once it had been, it was only a matter of time—a long time—
before some man of action seized on newly revealed truths to gain
a competitive advantage.

By the time he became the general manager of the Oakland A's,
in 1997, Billy Beane had read all twelve of Bill James's *Abstracts*.
James had something to say specifically to Billy: you were on the
receiving end of a false idea of what makes a successful baseball

player. James also had something general to say to Billy, or any other general manager of a baseball team who had the guts, or the need, to listen: if you challenge the conventional wisdom, you will find ways to do things much better than they are currently done. A full decade after James stopped writing his *Abstracts*, there were still two fresh opportunities for a team willing to take them to heart. One was simply to take the knowledge developed by James and other analysts outside the game, and implement it inside the game. The other was to develop and extend that knowledge. The Oakland A's had done both, though it would be wrong to say that, in using James's ideas, they aped James. As the Elias Sports Bureau had proven when they tried to rip off the *Abstract*, it was impossible to ape James. The whole point of James was: don't be an ape! Think for yourself along rational lines. Hypothesize, test against the evidence, never accept that a question has been answered as well as it ever will be. Don't believe a thing is true just because some famous baseball player says that it is true. "Anyone who thinks he is aping me, isn't," said James.

As late as June 4, 2002, the day of that year's amateur player draft, there were still big questions about baseball crying out for answers; a baseball diamond was still a field of ignorance. No one had established the most efficient way to use relief pitchers. No one had established to the satisfaction of baseball intellectuals exactly which part of defense was pitching and which fielding, and so no one could say exactly how important fielding was. No one had solved the problem of fielding statistics. And no one had figured out how to make the amateur draft any more than the madness it had always been. James hadn't worried too much about the amateur draft—probably because the players' statistics, before the Internet came along, weren't available to him to analyze. But in a newsletter he wrote for eighteen months in the mid-1980s, to a tiny audience of subscribers, he had argued persuasively that the South was overscouted and the Great Lakes region was underscouted. He also looked into the history of the draft and discovered that "college players are a better investment than high school players by a huge, huge, laughably huge margin." The conventional wisdom of baseball insiders—that high school players were more likely to become superstars—was also demonstrably false. What James couldn't understand was why baseball teams refused to acknowledge that fact. "Anti-intellectual resentment is common in all of American life and it has many diverse expressions," he wrote, advancing one theory. "Refusing to draft college players might have been one of them."

Still, James had never tried to show how the statistics of a high school or a college player might be used to make judgments about his professional future. The question of whether college performance translated into a professional career simply hadn't been answered, at least not publicly. Privately, Paul DePodesta, the head of R&D for the Oakland A's, had made his own study of it.

As a result of that study, the Oakland A's front office, over the silent shrieks of their own older scouts, were about to implement a radical new idea about young men and baseball. Lives were about to change, of people who had no clue that they were on the receiving end of an idea. As the scouts poured into the draft room, and stuffed their lower lips with chaw, a catcher with a body deemed by all of baseball to be unsuited to the game sat waiting in Tuscaloosa, Alabama. Jeremy Brown had no idea why what was about to happen to him was about to happen to him.

The morning of the amateur draft, Billy Beane arrived at the Coliseum earlier than usual and took the place he had occupied for the previous seven days. At dawn the room seemed more glaringly impersonal than usual; its cinder-block walls were the bright white of an asylum cell. The only hint of a reality outside were the four cheaply framed posters of former A's stars: Rickey Henderson, Mark McGwire, Dennis Eckersley, Walt Weiss.

It was still early, a full hour before the draft, and the younger scouts trickled in to report their savings. It's actually against Major League Baseball rules for teams to negotiate with players before the draft, but every team does it anyway, though not, perhaps, with the A's enthusiasm. One of the first scouts to arrive is Rich Sparks ("Sparky"), who covers the Great Lakes region for the A's. Sparky has just finished a conversation with Steve Stanley, a center fielder from Notre Dame, and he's pleased. Steve Stanley was yet another example of the strange results you obtained when you ceased to prejudge a player by his appearance, and his less meaningful statistics, and simply looked at what he had accomplished according to his meaningful stats. The Major League Scouting Bureau lists Stanley at five foot seven and 155 pounds, but that's wildly generous. Despite his size—or perhaps because of it—Stanley has a gift for getting on base. To judge crudely, with the naked eye, he already plays a better center field than Terrence Long, the A's big league center fielder. And yet the scouts long ago decided Stanley wasn't big enough to play.

Stanley has told Sparky that he expected to go after the fifteenth round of the draft. In other words, he expects to be taken by a team simply to fill out its minor league roster, not because the team thinks he has a chance of making it to the big leagues. Sparky has just informed Stanley that the A's are willing to make him a second-round draft pick—and a genuine big league prospect—on the condition that he agree to sign for $200,000, or about half a million dollars less than every other second-round pick will sign for. Other teams will assume that Billy Beane is interested in all these oddballs because he can't afford normal players, and Billy encourages the view. And it's true he can't afford anyone else. On the long cafeteria table in front of Billy sat an invisible cash register, and inside it the $9.4 million his owner had given him to sign perhaps as many as thirty-five players. The A's seven first-round picks alone, paid what their equivalents had received the year before, would cost him more than $11 million. Billy uses his poverty to camouflage another fact, that he wants these oddballs more than the studs he cannot afford. He views Stanley as a legitimate second-round pick. Since no one else does, he might as well save money on him.

"Sparky, we all right?" asks Billy.

"Yeah, sure," says Sparky. "I thought he was going to jump through the phone when I told him."

Billy laughs. "Pumped, are we?"

"I think he'd play for free," says Sparky.

After Sparky comes Billy Owens ("Billy O"), the young scout who covers the Deep South and is thus responsible for all communication with the University of Alabama catcher, Jeremy Brown. "Billy O looks like a Jamaican drug lord, doesn't he?" shouts Billy Beane, as Billy O ambles into the draft room. Billy O doesn't bother to smile. Too much trouble. He somehow conveys the idea of a smile without moving a muscle.

"We're all right, huh?" says Billy.

"Yeah, we all right," says Billy O.

"Does he understand?"

"Oh he understands."

Billy O is what you'd get if you hammered Shaquille O'Neal on the head with a pile driver until he stood six foot two. He's big and wide and moves only when he is absolutely certain that movement is required for survival. He's shrewd, too, and can see what you mean even if you don't. Over the past few days Billy O has come to see that he has a novel task: giving Jeremy Brown a new opinion of himself. He took it in small steps; he didn't want to shock the kid. "That boy told me he'd be happy to go in the first nineteen rounds," says Billy O. "I told him, 'think top ten.' I'm telling you, that guy was so happy when I told him that. Next day I called him back and say, 'shrink that to five.' I'm not sure he believed me. Yesterday, I called him and said, 'You got a chance to make six figures and the first number is not going to be a one.' The boy had to sit down."

But it was what happened late the night before that really

struck Billy O. He'd called Jeremy Brown to tell him that the Oakland A's were thinking of drafting him with the fifth of their seven
first-round picks, the thirty-fifth overall pick. To that, Brown hadn't
said anything much at all. Just "Thank you very much but I need
to call you back." Seconds later he'd called back. It turned out he
thought the guy who had just called him wasn't Billy Owens, Oakland A's scout, but a college teammate of his masquerading as
Billy O. "He thought it was a crank call," says Billy O. "He said
he wanted to make sure it was me, and that I was serious."

Jeremy Brown, owner of the University of Alabama offensive
record books *as a catcher*, has been so perfectly conditioned by the
conventional scouting wisdom that he refused to believe that any
major league baseball team could think highly of him. As he eased
himself into the radically new evaluation of his talents, he heard
Billy O lay down the conditions. There were two. One was that he
would sign for the $350,000 the A's were offering, which was
nearly a million dollars less than the thirty-fifth pick of the draft
might expect to receive. The other was he needed to lose weight.
"I said this is the Oakland A's speaking to you, and the Oakland
A's do things differently," said Billy O, fresh from the strangest
pre-draft chat he'd ever had with an amateur player. "I told him
how this was the money and it was as much as he was ever gonna
get and it was non-negotiable. I said the Oakland A's are making a
commitment to you. You gotta make a commitment to us, with
your body."

It had to be the most energizing weight loss commercial in history, even if it was delivered by an unlikely pitchman. At the end
of it, Brown had sounded willing to agree to anything. At the same
time, he still didn't really believe any of it. And that worries Billy
Beane.

"You wanna go home tonight?" he now asks Billy O. What he's
really asking is: Do you think you need to be there in the flesh, to
keep Jeremy Brown sane? To remind him that the Oakland A's
have just radically increased his market value, and that he should

remain grateful long enough to sign their contract. Once Jeremy Brown becomes a first-round pick, the agents, heretofore oblivious of his existence, would be all over him, trying to persuade him to break the illicit verbal agreement he'd made with the A's.

"No," says Billy O, and takes his seat in the ring of scouts. "I told him those agents are going to be calling him and telling him all kinds of shit. The boy's all right."

"Hey," says Sparky, brightly, to Billy O, "your guy could eat my guy for dinner."

"And would," says Billy O, then shuts his mouth, to achieve perfect immobility.

Billy Beane's phone rings.

"Hey Kenny," he says. Kenny Williams, GM of the Chicago White Sox. Williams has been calling a lot lately. He wants to trade for the A's starting pitcher, Cory Lidle. But this morning it isn't Lidle he wants to talk about. He's calling because the White Sox hold the eighteenth pick in the draft, two behind the A's first selection, and he wants to find out who the A's plan to draft. He doesn't come right out and say it; instead, he probes Billy about players, thinking he might trick Billy into tipping his hand. "We're in front of you so don't try to play secret agent man," Billy finally says. "Don't worry, Blanton might get to you." Joe Blanton is a pitcher at the University of Kentucky. Billy likes him too.

Billy hangs up. "He's going to take Blanton," he says. A useful tidbit. It fills in the white space between the A's first pick and their second, the twenty-fourth of the entire draft.

No one is thinking about the twenty-fourth pick of the draft, however. The twenty-fourth pick of the draft feels years away, and irrelevant. With the twenty-fourth pick of the draft, and all the other picks they have after that, the A's will pursue players in whom no one else has seen the greatness. Jeremy Brown is the extreme example of the phenomenon, but there are many others.

Nick Swisher is a different story; Swisher many teams want. No one utters Swisher's name, but everyone knows that Billy's obsessed with the kid. Here in the asylum cell Swisher already feels *owned.* The scouts were already sharing their favorite Swisher stories. The Indians' GM, Mark Shapiro, goes to see Swisher play, and instead of sticking to his assigned role of intimidated young player under inspection by big league big shot, Swisher marches right up to Shapiro and says, "So what the hell's up with Finley's old lady?" (Chuck Finley is an Indians pitcher who had filed assault charges against his wife.) Great story! The kid has an attitude.

Billy has to work to hide how much he likes the sound of that descriptive noun. Attitude is "a subjective thing." Billy's stated goal is to remain "objective." All these terribly subjective statements about Swisher keep popping out of his mouth anyway. Swisher has an attitude. Swisher is fearless. Swisher "isn't going to let anything get between him and the big leagues." Swisher has "presence." The more you listen to Billy talk about Swisher, the more you realize that he isn't talking about Swisher. He's talking about Lenny Dykstra. Swisher is the same character as the one that had revealed Billy's shortcomings to himself—made it clear to him that he was never going to be the success everyone said he was born to be. That he'd need to figure out all by himself how to be something else. No wonder that on the subject of Nick Swisher Billy sounds somewhat less than "objective." He's talking about a ghost.

At first, there's no hint of trouble. The scouts have called around and have a fair idea of who will draft whom with the first fifteen picks. All is clear for the A's to draft Nick Swisher with the sixteenth pick of the draft. It's Billy's best friend in baseball, J. P. Ricciardi, the GM of the Blue Jays, who, twenty minutes before the draft, calls to tell Billy that all is no longer so clear. The sound of J.P.'s voice initially causes Billy to brighten but whatever he says causes Billy to say, "Fuck! I got to go." He punches his cell phone off and hurls it onto the table.

"Span fucked us," he says. "His agent just asked for $2.6 million and fucking Colorado can't get a contract done." Denard Span is a high school center fielder, who was meant to be drafted by the Colorado Rockies with the ninth pick of the draft. Now, it seems, he won't be.

When seventeen-year-old Denard Span announces that he won't stand for a penny less than $2.6 million, his stock plummets. No one wants to touch him out of fear they won't be able to persuade him to sign for a sensible sum of money. Span's name clatters down toward the bottom rungs of the first round, and triggers a mind-numbingly complex chain reaction at the top. The Mets, who hold the pick immediately before the A's, the fifteenth over-all, had been set to take one from a list of four pitchers: Jeff Francis, who was also on Billy's wish list, and three high schoolers, Clinton Everts, Chris Gruler, and Zack Greinke. Everts, Gruler, and Greinke were probably spoken for by the Expos, Reds, and Royals. That left Francis, free and clear to fall to the Mets with the fifteenth pick. Colorado's bungling of negotiations with their first choice had just screwed that up. Colorado was now taking Francis. That's what J.P. has just told Billy. He knows this because the Mets' next choice after their four pitchers was Russ Adams, whom the Blue Jays intended to take with the fourteenth pick. The Mets' next choice after Adams was Nick Swisher. Swisher—like Lenny!—was going to be a Met.

Billy calls Steve Phillips, the Mets' GM, out of some vague notion he might talk him out of taking Swisher. There is no more reason for him to think he can do this than there was for Kenny Williams to think he could trick Billy into tipping his hand. It is the nature of being the general manager of a baseball team that you have to remain on familiar terms with people you are continually trying to screw. In his six years on the job Billy has had such a gift for making grotesquely good deals—for finding what other people want, even if they shouldn't want it, and giving it to them in exchange for something a lot better—that he thinks he can do it here. But he can't; there's nothing to trade. It's against the rules to trade draft slots. The thirty or so people in the draft room hear one side of Billy's awkward conversation:

"What about Everts, you hear anything on that?" he asks, teasingly.

Pause. Phillips tells him that the Montreal Expos are taking Everts.

"What about Greinke or Gruler?"

Pause. Phillips tells him that they are being taken by the Royals and Reds.

"Yeah. I'm just as pissed as you are."

He hangs up, and, dropping the pretense that his pain is not unique in the universe, shouts, "Fuck!"

Anyone who walked in just then and tried to figure out what was happening would have been totally mystified. Thirty men sit in appalled silence watching one man fume. Finally Billy says, "They're taking Swisher." Just in case anyone in the draft room is feeling at ease with that fact, he rises and swats his chair across the room. We'd been here more than an hour, thinking about nothing but Swisher, and until that moment no one had mentioned Nick Swisher's name.

"We should be all right," says someone, recklessly.

"No. We're not all right," says Billy. He's in no mood to feel better. "Greinke, Gruler, and Everts aren't going to be there. Fucking Colorado's taking Francis. J.P. is going to take Adams, and once Adams is gone, we're fucked."

Nick Swisher is, at best, the Mets' sixth choice: the Mets don't even begin to appreciate what they are getting. The Mets are taking Swisher *reluctantly*. If Billy had the first pick in the entire draft he'd take Swisher with it. He appreciates Swisher more than any man on the planet and Swisher . . . should . . . have . . . been . . . his! And yet Swisher will be a Met, almost by default.

"Fuck!" he shouts again. He reaches for his snuff. He hasn't slept in two days. It's a tradition with him: he never sleeps the night before the draft. He's too excited. Draft day, he says, is the one day of the baseball year that gives him the purest pleasure.

Except when it goes wrong. He claws out a finger of snuff and jams it into his lip. His face reddens slightly. The draft room, at this moment, has an all-or-nothing feel to it. If the Oakland A's land Nick Swisher, nothing could mar the loveliness of the day. If they don't, nothing that happens afterward can make life worth living.

Any very large angry man can unsettle a room, even a room full of other large men, but Billy has a special talent for it. Five minutes after he's spoken to Phillips he is still so upset that no one in the room utters a peep, out of fear of setting off the bomb. The mood is exactly what it would be if every person in the room was handed his own personal vial of nitroglycerin. You could see why guys used to come down from the bullpen when Billy Beane hit, just to see what he would do if he struck out. To describe whatever he's feeling as anger doesn't do justice to it. It's an isolating rage: he believes, perhaps even wants to believe, that he is alone with his problem and no one can help him. That no one *should* help him.

The space around Billy's rage is perfectly still. Paul DePodesta stares quietly into his computer screen. Paul's seen Billy in this state often enough to know that it's not something you want to get in the middle of. Paul knows that Billy, to be Billy, needs to get worked up. "I think Swisher will get to us," Paul says quietly, "but I'm not going to say that right now."

Finally the miserable silence is punctuated by the ringing of scouting director Erik Kubota's cellphone—only instead of ringing it plays, absurdly, Pachelbel's Canon. Erik snatches it quickly off the table. "Oh, is that what it is?" he says into the phone, in a clipped tone, and hangs up. The draft room has become a symbolist play.

Billy's phone rings. It's Kenny Williams again. Williams is of no current interest to Billy. Nothing the White Sox do will alter Billy's chances of getting Swisher.

"What's up Kenny," Billy says rather than asks.

What's up is that Kenny has just heard that Billy isn't getting Swisher, and fears that Billy will take *his* first choice. Billy doesn't have time for other people's fears just now; if he's going to be miserable everyone else is going to be, too. "You were going to get Blanton," he says. "But you ain't getting him now."

He hangs up and calls Steve Phillips again. That's his style: if he doesn't get the answer he wants the first time, he calls again and again until he does. To come between him and what he was after at just that moment would have been as unwise as pitching a tent between a mother bear and her cub. Phillips answers on the first ring.

"Hear anything?" Billy asks.

Pause. Phillips says he hasn't.

"Yeah," says Billy, glumly. He begins to *sympathize* with Phillips for getting stuck with Swisher. Then Phillips says something new, that causes Billy's mood to shift. Frustration is shoved aside by curiosity.

"Oh really?"

Pause.

"Well, that's a fucking light at the end of the fucking tunnel."

He clicks off and turns to Paul. "He says if Kazmir gets to him he'll take him." Scott Kazmir is yet another high school pitcher in whom the A's haven't the slightest interest. Billy's so excited he doesn't even bother to say how foolish it is to take a high school pitcher with a first-round pick. Everyone looks up at the white board and tries to figure out if Kazmir, the Mets' new sixth choice, will get to the Mets. He might; no other team has said definitely that they will take him. But then no one has any idea what either the Detroit Tigers or the Milwaukee Brewers, who pick seventh and eighth, intend to do. Something not terribly bright, it was a fair bet, if they just continued doing what they had done in the past. And that was a problem: picking a high school pitcher like Kazmir is exactly the sort of not-so-bright decision both franchises had a knack for making.

"Fielder could help us here," says Chris Pittaro, finally.

Fielder is the semi-aptly named Prince Fielder, son of Cecil Fielder, who in 1990 hit fifty-one home runs for the Detroit Tigers, and who by the end of his career could hardly waddle around the bases after one of his mammoth shots into the upper deck, much less maneuver himself in front of a ground ball. "Cecil Fielder acknowledges a weight of 261," Bill James once wrote, "leaving unanswered the question of what he might weigh if he put his other foot on the scale." Cecil Fielder could have swallowed Jeremy Brown whole and had room left for dessert, and the son apparently has an even more troubling weight problem than his father. Here's an astonishing fact: Prince Fielder is too fat even for the Oakland A's. Of no other baseball player in the whole of North America can this be said. Pittaro seems to think that the Detroit Tigers might take Fielder anyway, for sentimental reasons. And if the Tigers take him, they trigger a chain reaction that ends with the Mets getting one of their first six choices.

Before anyone has a chance to figure out whether Kazmir will get to the Mets, the draft begins. As it does, the Oakland A's owner, Steve Schott, enters the room, followed shortly by the A's manager, Art Howe. Howe stands in the back of the room with his jaw jutting and a philosophical expression on his face, the way he does in the dugout during games. It is one of the mysteries of baseball that people outside it assume the manager is in charge of important personnel decisions. From the start to the end of this process Howe has been, as he is with all personnel decisions, left entirely in the dark.

The A's scouting director, Erik Kubota, takes up his position at the speakerphone and tells everyone else to shut up. Everyone in the draft room is about to learn just how new and different is the Oakland A's scientific selection of amateur baseball players. The A's front office has a list, never formally written out, of the twenty players they'd draft in a perfect world. That is, if money were no object and twenty-nine other teams were not also vying to draft the best amateur players in the country. The list is a pure expression of the new view of amateur players. On it are eight pitchers and twelve hitters—all, for the moment, just names.

Pitchers:	Position Players:
Jeremy Guthrie	Nick Swisher
Joe Blanton	Russ Adams
Jeff Francis	Khalil Greene
Luke Hagerty	John McCurdy
Ben Fritz	Mark Teahen
Robert Brownlie	Jeremy Brown
Stephen Obenchain	Steve Stanley
Bill Murphy	John Baker
	Mark Kiger
	Brian Stavisky
	Shaun Larkin
	Brant Colamarino

Two of the position players—Khalil Greene and Russ Adams—Billy already knew would be gone before the A's picked, and so he hadn't even bothered to discuss them during the meetings. His best friend J. P. Ricciardi would take Adams, and another close friend, Kevin Towers, the GM of the San Diego Padres, would take Greene. Two of the pitchers—Robert Brownlie and Jeremy Guthrie—were represented by the agent Scott Boras. Boras was famous for extracting more money than other agents for amateur players. If the team didn't pay whatever Boras asked, Boras would encourage his client to take a year off of baseball and reenter the draft the following year, when he might be selected by a team with real money. The effects of Boras's tactics on rich teams were astonishing. In 2001 the agent had squeezed a package worth $9.5 million out of Texas Rangers owner Tom Hicks for a college third baseman named Mark Teixeira. The guy who was picked ahead of Teixeira signed for $4.2 million, and the guy who was picked after him signed for $2.65 million, and yet somehow between these numbers Boras found $9.5 million. By finding the highest bidders for his players before the draft and scaring everyone else away from them, Boras was transforming the draft into a pure auction.

Billy couldn't afford auctions. He had $9.5 million to spend and Boras had let it be known that whichever team drafted Jeremy Guthrie was going to cough up a package worth $20 million—or Guthrie would return to Stanford for his senior year. The Cleveland Indians had agreed to pay the price, and so the Indians would take Guthrie with the twenty-second pick.

Of the sixteen players on his list he could afford, and stood any chance of getting, Billy thinks he might land as many as six. But the truth is he doesn't know. It was possible he'd only get one of the players on the wish list. By the time the A's made their second pick, the twenty-fourth of the draft, all of them might be gone. If they got six of the players on their wish list, Paul said, they'd be ecstatic. No team ever came away with six of their top twenty.

The room remains silent. The entire draft takes place over speakerphone, far away from the fans. In the draft Major League Baseball has brought to life Bill James's dystopic vision of closing the stadium to the fans and playing the game in private. Pro football and pro basketball make great public event of their drafts. They gather their famous coaches and players in a television studio and hand them paddles with big numbers on them to wave. Football and basketball fans are able to watch the future of their team unfold before their eyes. The Major League Baseball draft is a conference call—now broadcast on the Web.

The Pittsburgh Pirates, owners of the worst regular season record in the 2001 season, have the first overall pick. A voice from Pittsburgh crackles over the speakerphone:

"Redraft number 0090. Bullington, Bryan. Right-handed pitcher. Ball State University. Fishers, Indiana."

Just like that the first $4 million is spent, but at least it is spent on a college player. ("Redraft" means he has been drafted before.) The next five teams, among the most pathetic organizations in pro baseball, select high school players. Tampa Bay takes a high school shortstop named Melvin Upton; Cincinnati follows by taking the high school pitcher Chris Gruler; Baltimore follows suit with a high school pitcher named Adam Loewen; Montreal follows suit with yet another high school pitcher, Clinton Everts. The selections made are, from the A's point of view, delightfully mad. Eight of the first nine teams select high schoolers. The worst teams in baseball, the teams that can least afford for their draft to go wrong, have walked into the casino, ignored the odds, and made straight for the craps table.

Billy and Paul no longer think of the draft as a crapshoot. They are a pair of card counters at the blackjack tables; they think they've found a way to turn the odds inside the casino against the owner. They think they can take over the casino. Each time a team rolls the dice on a high school player, Billy punches his fist in the air: every player taken that he doesn't want boosts his chances of getting one he does want. When the Milwaukee Brewers take Prince Fielder with the eighth pick, the room explodes. It means that Scott Kazmir probably will be available to the Mets. And he is. And the Mets take him. (And spend $2.15 million to sign him.) Sixteen minutes into the draft Erik Kubota leans into the speakerphone, trying, and nearly succeeding, to sound cool and collected.

"Oakland selects Swisher, Nicholas. First baseman/center fielder. Ohio State University. Parkersburg, West Virginia. Son of ex-major leaguer Steve Swisher."

"Prince Fielder just saved our paint," says an old scout. Even the fat players who don't work for the A's do the A's work.

Billy is now on his feet. He's got Swisher in the bag: who else can he get? There's a new thrust about him, an unabridged expression on his face. He was a bond trader, who had made a killing in the morning and entered the afternoon free of fear. Feeling greedy. Certain that the fear in the market would present him with even more opportunities to exploit. Whatever happened now wasn't going to be bad. How good could it get? The anger is gone, lingering only as an afterthought in other people's minds. He was no longer in the batter's box. He was out in center field, poised to make a spectacular catch no one expected him to make. "Billy's a shark," J. P. Ricciardi had said, by way of explaining what distinguished Billy from every other GM in the game. "It's not just that he's smarter than the average bear. He's relentless—the most relentless person I have ever known."

Billy moves back and forth between his wish list and Paul and Erik. Paul to check his judgments, Erik to execute his wishes. Like any good bond trader, he loves making decisions. The quicker the better. He looks up at the names of the players on the white board and listens to the speakerphone crackle. Three pitchers from the wish list (Francis, Brownlie, and Guthrie) go quickly. Sixteen players that he badly wants to own remain at large. The A's second first-round pick is #24 (paid to them by the Yankees for the right to buy Jason Giambi), followed rapidly by #26, #30, #35, #37, #39. Billy has agreed with Erik and Paul to use #24 to get John McCurdy, a shortstop from the University of Maryland, the second hitter on the wish list. McCurdy was an ugly-looking fielder with the highest slugging percentage in the country. They'd turn him into a second baseman, where his fielding would matter less. Billy thought McCurdy might be the next Jeff Kent.

The White Sox come on the line. "Here goes Blanton," says Billy.

When Kenny Williams told Billy an hour before that the White

Sox were taking Blanton, Billy couldn't but agree that it showed disturbingly good judgment. Blanton was the second best pitcher in the draft, in Billy's view, behind Stanford pitcher Jeremy Guthrie.

A White Sox voice crackles on the speakerphone: "The White Sox selects redraft number 0103, Ring, Roger. Left-handed pitcher. San Diego State University. La Mesa, California."

"You fucking got to be kidding me!" hollers Billy, overjoyed. He doesn't pause to complain that Kenny Williams had told him he was taking Blanton. (Was he afraid Billy might take Ring?) "Ring over Blanton? A reliever over a starter?" Then it dawns on him: "Blanton's going to get to us." The second best right-handed pitcher in the draft. He says it but he can't quite believe it. He looks at the board and recalculates what the GMs with the next five picks will do. "You know what?" he says in a surer tone. "Blanton's going to be there at 24."

"Blanton *and* Swisher," says Erik. "That's a home run."

"The Giants won't take McCurdy, right?" says Billy. The San Francisco Giants had the twenty-fifth pick, the only pick between the A's next two. "Take Blanton with 24 and McCurdy with 26."

"Swisher and Blanton *and* McCurdy," says Erik "This is unfair." He clicks the button on the speakerphone, and his voice shaking like a man calling in to say he holds the winning Lotto ticket, takes Blanton with the twenty-fourth pick, pauses while the Giants make their pick, then takes McCurdy with the twenty-sixth.

Everyone in the room, even the people in the back who have no real idea what is going on, a group that includes both the manager and the owner of the Oakland A's, claps and cheers. The entire room assumes that if Billy gets what he wants it can only be good for the future of the franchise. This is now the Billy Beane Show, and it's not over yet.

Billy stares at the board. "Fritz," he says. "It'd be unbelievable if we could get Fritz too." Benjamin Fritz, right-handed pitcher from Fresno State. Third best right-handed pitcher in the draft, in the opinion of Paul DePodesta's computer.

"There's no chance Teahen's gone before 39, right?" says Paul quickly. He can see what Billy is doing. Having realized that he can get most of the best hitters, Billy is now seeing if he can get the best pitchers, too. Paul's view—the "objective" one—is that the hitters are a much better bet than the pitchers. He thinks the best thing to do with pitchers is draft them in bulk, lower down. He doesn't want to risk losing his hitters.

"Teahen will be there at 39," says Billy.

No one else in the room is willing to confirm it.

"Take Fritz with 30, Brown with 35, and Teahen with 37," Billy says. Erik leans into the speakerphone, and listens. The Arizona Diamondbacks take yet another high school player with the twenty-seventh pick and the Seattle Mariners take another with the twenty-eighth. The Astros take a college player, not Fritz, with the twenty-ninth. Erik takes Fritz with the thirtieth.

"We just got two of the three best right-handed pitchers in the country, and two of the four best position players," says Paul.

"This doesn't happen," says Billy. "Don't think this is normal."

As the thirty-fifth pick approaches, Erik once again leans into the speaker phone. If he leaned in just a bit more closely he might hear phones around the league clicking off, so that people could laugh without being heard. For they do laugh. They will make fun of what the A's are about to do; and there will be a lesson in that. The inability to envision a certain kind of person doing a certain kind of thing because you've never seen someone who looks like him do it before is not just a vice. It's a luxury. What begins as a failure of the imagination ends as a market inefficiency: when you rule out an entire class of people from doing a job simply by their appearance, you are less likely to find the best person for the job.

When asked which current or former major league player Jeremy Brown reminded him of, Paul stewed for two days, and finally said, "He has no equivalent." The kid himself is down in

Tuscaloosa, listening to the Webcast of the conference call, biting his nails because he *still* doesn't quite believe that the A's will take him in the first round. He's told no one except his parents and his girlfriend and them he's made swear they won't tell anyone else, in case it doesn't happen. Some part of him still thinks he's being set up to be a laughingstock. That part of him dies the moment he hears his name called.

"Oakland selects redraft number 1172. Brown, Jeremy. Catcher. University of Alabama. Hueytown, Alabama."

Minutes after Erik speaks his name, Jeremy Brown's phone begins to ring. First it's family and friends, then agents. All these agents he's never heard of want to be in his life. *Scott Boras* suddenly wants to represent Jeremy Brown. The agents will tell him that they can get him at least half a million dollars more than the A's have promised. He'll have to tell them that he's made a deal with the A's on his own, and that he intends to keep his end of it. And he does.

The next two hours are, to Billy Beane, a revelation. When the dust settles on the first seven rounds, the A's have acquired five more of the hitters from Billy and Paul's wish list—Teahen, Baker, Kiger, Stavisky, and Colamarino. When in the seventh round Erik leans in and takes the last of these, an ambidextrous first baseman from the University of Pittsburgh named Brant Colamarino, Paul wears an expression of pure bliss. "No one else in baseball will agree," he says, "but Colamarino might be the best hitter in the country." That told you how contrary the A's measuring devices were: they were able to draft possibly the best hitter in the country with the 218th pick of the draft. Then Paul says, "You know what gets me excited about a guy? I get excited about a guy when he has something about him that causes everyone else to overlook him and I know that it is something that just doesn't matter." When Brant Colamarino removes his shirt for the first time in an A's minor league locker room he inspires his coaches to inform Billy that "Colarmarino has titties." Colamarino, like Jeremy

Brown, does not look the way a young baseball player is meant to look. Titties are one of those things that just don't matter in a ballplayer. Billy's only question for the coaches was whether a male brassiere should be called a "manzier" or a "bro."

Most every other team looks at the market pretty much the same way, or at any rate acts as if they do. Most teams, if they kept a wish list of twenty players, would feel blessed to have snagged three of them. The combination of having seven first-round draft picks, a deeply quirky view of baseball players, and a general manager newly willing to impose that view on his scouting department has created something like a separate market in Oakland. From their wish list of twenty they had nabbed, incredibly, thirteen players: four pitchers and nine hitters. They had drafted players dismissed by their own scouts as too short or too skinny or too fat or too slow. They had drafted pitchers who didn't throw hard enough for the scouts and hitters who hadn't enough power. They'd drafted kids in the first round who didn't think they'd get drafted before the fifteenth round, and kids in lower rounds who didn't think they'd get drafted at all. They had drafted *ballplayers*.

It was as if a big new market-moving Wall Street money manager had sprung into being, and bought shares only in vegetarian restaurants, or electric car manufacturers. With a difference. A revaluation in the stock market has consequences for companies and for money managers. The pieces of paper don't particularly care what you think of their intrinsic value. A revaluation in the market for baseball players resonates in the lives of young men. It was as if a signal had radiated out from the Oakland A's draft room and sought, laserlike, those guys who for their whole career had seen their accomplishments understood with an asterisk. The footnote at the bottom of the page said, "He'll never go anywhere because he doesn't *look* like a big league ballplayer."

Billy Beane was a human arsenal built, inadvertently, by professional baseball to attack its customs and rituals. He thought himself to be fighting a war against subjective judgments, but he

was doing something else, too. At one point Chris Pittaro said that
the thing that struck him about Billy—what set him apart from
most baseball insiders—was his desire to find players unlike himself. Billy Beane had gone looking for, and found, his antitheses.
Young men who failed the first test of looking good in a uniform.
Young men who couldn't play anything but baseball. Young men
who had gone to college.

The fat scout ambles in. He's one of the older scouts, and like
most of the others, he'll leave the Oakland A's at the end of the
season, and find a team that cares about what he knows. All these
misshapen players coming in will drive all of these old scouts out.
But for now the older scouts are, mainly, amused. "Just talked to
Kiger," the fat scout says laconically. Mark Kiger plays shortstop
for the University of Florida. A machine for wearing down opposing pitchers, and getting himself on base. Too small to play pro
ball—or so they said. Now a fifth-round draft choice of the Oakland A's.

"What did he say?" asks Billy

"'Thank you. Thank you. Thank you,'" says the fat scout, and
then laughs. "He just wanted to get drafted."

It counted as one of the happiest days of Billy Beane's career. He
can't have known whether he had simply found a new way of fix-
ing irrational hopes upon a young man, or if he had, as he hoped,
eliminated hope from the equation. But he thought he knew. At
the end of the day he actually looked up with a big smile and said,
"This is maybe the funnest day I have ever had in baseball." Then
he walked out the back door of the draft room and into the Coliseum. He had another, bigger missile to fire at the conventional
wisdom of major league baseball. It was called the Oakland A's.

Chapter Six

THE SCIENCE OF WINNING AN UNFAIR GAME

HERE WAS NO simple way to approach the problem that Billy Beane was trying to solve. It read like an extra credit question on an algebra quiz: You have $40 million to spend on twenty-five baseball players. Your opponent has already spent $126 million on its own twenty-five players, and holds perhaps another $100 million in reserve. What do you do with your forty million to avoid humiliating defeat? "What you don't do," said Billy, "is what the Yankees do. If we do what the Yankees do, we lose every time, because they're doing it with three times more money than we are." A poor team couldn't afford to go out shopping for big league stars in the prime of their careers. It couldn't even afford to go out and buy averagely priced players. The average big league salary was $2.3 million. The average A's opening day salary was a bit less than $1.5 million. The poor team was forced to find bargains: young players and whatever older guys the market had undervalued. It would seem highly unlikely, given the wage inflation in pro baseball over the past twenty-five years, that any established big league player was underpriced. If the market was even close to rational, all the real talent would have been bought up by the rich teams, and the Oakland A's wouldn't have stood a chance. Yet they stood a chance. Why?

Oddly enough, Major League Baseball had asked that very question, in its own half-assed, incurious way. After the 1999 season, Major League Baseball had created something it called the Commissioner's Blue Ribbon Panel on Baseball Economics, whose job it was to produce a document called *The Blue Ribbon Panel Report*. Its stated purpose was to examine "the question of whether baseball's current economic system has created a problem of competitive imbalance in the game." The baseball commissioner, Bud Selig, had invited four men of sound reputation—former U.S. senator George Mitchell, Yale president Richard Levin, the columnist George Will, and former chairman of the U.S. Federal Reserve Paul Volcker—to write a report on the economic inequalities in baseball. Selig owned maybe the most pathetic poor team in all of baseball, the Milwaukee Brewers. He no doubt wanted to believe that the Brewers' trouble was poverty, not stupidity. He had an obvious financial interest in the commission reaching the conclusion that players' salaries needed to be constrained and that rich teams should subsidize poor ones. He expressed this interest by trying to pad the Blue Ribbon Panel Commission with other owners of poor, pathetic baseball teams. But the four eminences objected to this transparent attempt to undermine their authority, and Selig agreed that the owners would merely sit in the room, observing the eminences deliberate.

It didn't matter. In July 2000, the panel did pretty much exactly what Bud Selig hoped it would do: conclude that poor teams didn't stand a chance, that their hopelessness was Bad for Baseball, and that a way must be found to minimize the distinction between rich and poor teams. George Will, the conservative columnist, was, oddly enough, the most outspoken proponent of baseball socialism. One dramatic fact Will often used to incite alarm was that the ratio of the payrolls of the seven richest and seven poor-est teams in baseball was 4:1, while in pro basketball it was 1.75:1 and in pro football 1.5:1. Baseball was the major American sport in which money bought success, he said, and that was a crime against the game. When fans of the Brewers and the Royals and the Devil Rays figured out that their teams existed only so that the New York Yankees might routinely pummel them, they would abandon the sport altogether. At stake was nothing less than the future of professional baseball.

There was something to be said for these arguments but there was also something to be said against them, and, according to two people who watched the proceedings, only one commissioner was willing to say it: Paul Volcker. Volcker was also the only commis-sioner with a financial background. To the growing annoyance of the others, he kept asking two provocative questions:

1. If poor teams were in such dire financial condition, why did rich guys keep paying higher prices to buy them?
2. If poor teams had no hope, how did the Oakland A's, with the second lowest payroll in all of baseball, win so many games?

The owners didn't have a good answer to the first question, but to answer the second they dragged in Billy Beane to explain him-self. The odd thing was that the previous season, 1999, the A's had finished 87–75 and missed the play-offs. Still, they had improved dramatically from 1998, Billy's first year on the job, when they'd gone 74–88. And they were looking even stronger in 2000. Volcker smelled a rat. If results in pro baseball were so clearly determined by financial resources, how could there be even a single excep-tion? How could a poor team improve so dramatically? Paul DePodesta wrote Billy Beane's presentation and Billy flew off to New York to explain to Volcker why he was a fluke. He was happy to do it. He hadn't the slightest interest in stopping the Blue Rib-bon Panel from concluding that his life was unfair. He'd be

delighted to see the cost of players constrained, or, even better, the
Yankees made to give him some of their money. When he got up
before the panel, Billy flashed a slide up on the overhead projector.
It read:

"MAJOR LEAGUE"
*Movie about the hapless Cleveland Indians

In order to assemble a losing team, the owner distributes a
list of players to be invited to spring training. The baseball
executives say that most of these players are way past their
prime. Fans see the list in the paper and remark, "I've never
even heard of half these guys."

Our situation closely resembles the movie.

When it suited his purposes Billy could throw the best pity party
this side of the Last Supper. He told the Blue Ribbon Panel that the
Oakland A's inability to afford famous stars meant that no matter
how well the team performed, the fans stayed away—which was
the opposite of the truth. All the A's marketing studies showed
that the main thing fans cared about was winning. Win with
nobodies and the fans showed up, and the nobodies *became* stars;
lose with stars and the fans stayed home, and the stars became
nobodies. Assembling nobodies into a ruthlessly efficient machine
for winning baseball games, and watching them become stars, was
one of the pleasures of running a poor baseball team.

Billy also told the Blue Ribbon Panel that his inability to pay
the going rate for baseball players meant that his success was
likely to be ephemeral. It might have been what they wanted to
hear but it wasn't what he believed. What he believed was what
Paul Volcker seemed to suspect, that the market for baseball players was so inefficient, and the general grasp of sound baseball
strategy so weak, that superior management could still run circles
around taller piles of cash. He then went out and created more evi-

dence in support of his belief. Having won 87 games in 1999, the Oakland A's went on to win 91 games in 2000, and an astonishing 102 games in 2001, and made the play-offs both years.

They weren't getting worse, they were getting better. The rapidly expanding difference between the size of everyone else's money pile and Oakland's had no apparent effect. Each year the Oakland A's seemed more the financial underdog and each year they won more games. Maybe they were just lucky. Or maybe they knew something other people didn't. Maybe they were, as they privately thought, becoming more *efficient*. When, in 2001, for the second year in a row, they lost to the Yankees in the fifth and deciding game of the play-offs, the Oakland front office was certain that theirs had been the better team and that it was the Yankees who had gotten lucky—and that the Yankees front office knew it. And that some fraction of the $120 million the Yankees had paid Jason Giambi after the 2001 play-offs to lure him away from the Oakland A's was to prevent him from ever again playing for the Oakland A's.

At any rate, by the beginning of the 2002 season, the Oakland A's, by winning so much with so little, had become something of an embarrassment to Bud Selig and, by extension, Major League Baseball. "An aberration" is what the baseball commissioner, and the people who worked for him, called the team, and when you asked them what they meant by that nebulous word, they said, though not for attribution, "They've been lucky." This was the year the luck of the A's was meant to run out. The relative size of the team's payroll had shrunk yet again. The *difference* between the Yankees' and A's opening day payrolls had ballooned from $62 million in 1999 to $90 million in 2002. The Blue Ribbon Panel's nightmare scenario for poor teams had become a reality for the 2002 Oakland A's. They had lost to free agency—and thus, to richer teams—three of their proven stars: Jason Isringhausen, Johnny Damon, and Giambi.

To a financial determinist like Bud Selig, the wonder must have been that they hadn't simply given up. Of course, no one in pro sports ever admits to quitting. But it was perfectly possible to abandon all hope of winning and at the same time show up every day for work to collect a paycheck. Professional sports had a word for this: "rebuilding." That's what half a dozen big league teams did more or less all the time. The Kansas City Royals had been rebuilding for the past four or five years. Bud Selig's Brewers had been taking a dive for at least a decade. The A's didn't do this, for the simple reason that they actually believed they were going to keep on winning—perhaps not so many games as they had in 2001, but enough to get themselves back to the play-offs.

Before the 2002 season, Paul DePodesta had reduced the coming six months to a math problem. He judged how many wins it would take to make the play-offs: 95. He then calculated how many more runs the Oakland A's would need to score than they allowed to win 95 games: 135. (The idea that there was a stable relationship between season run totals and season wins was another Jamesean discovery.) Then, using the A's players' past performance as a guide, he made reasoned arguments about how many runs they would actually score and allow. If they didn't suffer an abnormally large number of injuries, he said, the team would score between 800 and 820 runs and give up between 650 and 670 runs.* From that he predicted the team would win between 93 and 97 games and probably wind up in the play-offs. "There aren't a lot of teams that win ninety-five games and don't make it to the play-offs," he said. "If we win ninety-five games and don't make the play-offs, we're fine with that."

The 2001 Oakland A's had won 102 regular season games. The 2002 Oakland A's entered the season without the three players widely regarded by the market to be among their best and the expected result was a net loss of seven wins. How could that be? The only way to understand the math was to look a bit more

---

* They wound up scoring 800 and allowing 653.

closely at what, exactly, the team lost, or believed they lost, when other, richer teams hired away each of the three stars.

The first, and easiest, player to understand was their old flame-throwing closer, Jason Isringhausen. When Billy Beane had traded for him in the middle of the 1999 season, Isringhausen was pitching in the minor leagues with the New York Mets. To get him and a more expensive pitcher named Greg McMichael *and* the money to pay McMichael's salary, all Billy Beane had given up was his own established closer, Billy Taylor. Taylor, who ceased to be an effective pitcher more or less immediately upon joining the Mets, Billy Beane had himself plucked from the minor leagues for a few thousand dollars a few years earlier.

The central insight that led him both to turn minor league nobodies into successful big league closers and to refuse to pay them the many millions a year they demanded once they became free agents was that it was more efficient to create a closer than to buy one. Established closers were systematically overpriced, in large part because of the statistic by which closers were judged in the marketplace: "saves." The very word made the guy who achieved them sound vitally important. But the situation typically described by the save—the bases empty in the ninth inning with the team leading—was clearly far less critical than a lot of other situations pitchers faced. The closer's statistic did not have the power of language; it was just a number. You could take a slightly above average pitcher and drop him into the closer's role, let him accumulate some gaudy number of saves, and then sell him off. You could, in essence, buy a stock, pump it up with false publicity, and sell it off for much more than you'd paid for it. Billy Beane had already done it twice, and assumed he could do so over and over again.

Jason Isringhausen's departure wasn't a loss to the Oakland A's but a happy consequence of a money machine known as "Selling the Closer." In return for losing Isringhausen to the St. Louis Cardinals, the A's had received two new assets: the Cardinals' first-round draft pick, along with a first-round compensation pick. The former they'd used to draft Benjamin Fritz, a pitcher they judged to have a brighter and cheaper future than Isringhausen; the latter, to acquire Jeremy Brown.

The Blue Ribbon Commission had asked the wrong question. The question wasn't whether a baseball team could keep its stars even after they had finished with their six years of indentured servitude and became free agents. The question was: how did a baseball team find stars in the first place, and could it find new ones to replace the old ones it lost? How fungible were baseball players? The short answer was: a lot more fungible than the people who ran baseball teams believed.

Finding pitchers who could become successful closers wasn't all that difficult. To fill the hole at the back of his bullpen Billy had traded to the Toronto Blue Jays a minor league third baseman, Eric Hinske, for Billy Koch, another crude fireballer. He knew that Hinske was very good—he'd wind up being voted 2002 Rookie of the Year in the American League—but the Oakland A's already had an even better third baseman, Eric Chavez. Plus, Billy knew that, barring some disaster, Koch, too, would gain a lot of value as an asset. Koch would get his saves and be perceived by other teams to be a much more critical piece of a successful team than he actually was, whereupon the A's would trade him for something cheaper, younger, and possibly even better.

The loss of Johnny Damon, the A's former center fielder, presented a different sort of problem. When Damon signed with Boston, the A's took the Red Sox's first-round pick (to select Nick Swisher) plus a compensation pick. But Damon left two glaring holes: on defense in center field, on offense in the leadoff spot. Of the two the offense was the easiest to understand, and dismiss. When fans watched Damon, they saw the sort of thrilling leadoff hitter that a team simply had to have if it wanted to be competitive. When the A's front office watched Damon, they saw something else: an imperfect understanding of where runs come from.

Paul DePodesta had been hired by Billy Beane before the 1999 season, but well before that he had studied the question of why teams win. Not long after he'd graduated from Harvard, in the mid-nineties, he'd plugged the statistics of every baseball team from the twentieth century into an equation and tested which of them correlated most closely with winning percentage. He'd found only two, both offensive statistics, inextricably linked to baseball success: on-base percentage and slugging percentage. Everything else was far less important.

Not long after he arrived in Oakland, Paul asked himself a question: what was the relative importance of on-base and slugging percentage? His answer began with a thought experiment: if a team had an on-base percentage of 1.000 (referred to as "a thousand")—that is, every hitter got on base—how many runs would it score?* An infinite number of runs, since the team would never make an out. If a team had a slugging percentage of 1.000—meaning, it gained a base for each hitter that came to the plate—how many runs would it score? That depended on how it was achieved, but it would typically be a lot less than an infinite number. A team might send four hitters to the plate in an inning, for instance. The first man hits a home run, the next three make outs. Four plate appearances have produced four total bases and thus a slugging percentage of 1.000 and yet have scored only one run in the inning.

---

* These "percentages" are designed to drive anyone who thinks twice about them mad. It's one thing to give 110 percent for the team, but it is another to get on base 1,000 percent of the time. On-base "percentage" is actually on-base "per thousand." A batter who gets on base four out of ten times has an on-base "percentage" of four hundred (.400). Slugging "percentage" is even more mind-bending, as it is actually "per four thousand." A perfect slugging "percentage"—achieved by hitting a home run every time—is four thousand: four bases for every plate appearance. But for practical purposes, on-base and slugging are assumed to be measured on identical scales. At any rate, the majority of big league players have on-base percentages between three hundred (.300) and four hundred (.400) and slugging percentages between three hundred and fifty (.350) and five hundred and fifty (.550).

Baseball fans and announcers were just then getting around to the Jamesean obsession with on-base and slugging percentages. The game, slowly, was turning its attention to the new statistic, OPS (on base plus slugging). OPS was the simple addition of on-base and slugging percentages. Crude as it was, it was a much better indicator than any other offensive statistic of the number of runs a team would score. Simply adding the two statistics together, however, implied they were of equal importance. If the goal was to raise a team's OPS, an extra percentage point of on-base was as good as an extra percentage point of slugging.

Before his thought experiment Paul had felt uneasy with this crude assumption; now he saw that the assumption was absurd. An extra point of on-base percentage was clearly more valuable than an extra point of slugging percentage—but by how much? He proceeded to tinker with his own version of Bill James's "Runs Created" formula. When he was finished, he had a model for predicting run production that was more accurate than any he knew of. In his model an extra point of on-base percentage was worth three times an extra point of slugging percentage.

Paul's argument was radical even by sabermetric standards. Bill James and others had stressed the importance of on-base percentage, but even they didn't think it was worth three times as much as slugging. Most offensive models assumed that an extra point of on-base percentage was worth, at most, one and a half times an extra point of slugging percentage. In major league baseball itself, where on-base percentage was not nearly so highly valued as it was by sabermetricians, Paul's argument was practically heresy.

Paul walked across the hall from his office and laid out his argument to Billy Beane, who thought it was the best argument he had heard in a long time. Heresy was good: heresy meant opportunity. A player's ability to get on base—especially when he got on base in unspectacular ways—tended to be dramatically underpriced in relation to other abilities. Never mind fielding skills and foot speed. The ability to get on base—to avoid making outs—was underpriced compared to the ability to hit with power. The one attribute most critical to the success of a baseball team was an attribute they could afford to buy. At that moment, what had been a far more than ordinary interest in a player's ability to get on base became, for the Oakland A's front office, an obsession.

To most of baseball Johnny Damon, on offense, was an extraordinarily valuable leadoff hitter with a gift for stealing bases. To Billy Beane and Paul DePodesta, Damon was a delightful human being, a pleasure to have around, but an easily replaceable offensive player. His on-base percentage in 2001 had been .324, or roughly 10 points below the league average. True, he stole some bases, but stealing bases involved taking a risk the Oakland front office did not trust even Johnny Damon to take. The math of the matter changed with the situation, but, broadly speaking, an attempted steal had to succeed about 70 percent of the time before it contributed positively to run totals.

The offense Damon had provided the 2001 Oakland A's was fairly easy to replace; Damon's defense was not. The question was how to measure what the Oakland A's lost when Terrence Long, and not Johnny Damon, played center field. The short answer was that they couldn't, not precisely. But they could get closer than most to an accurate answer—or thought that they could. Something had happened since Bill James first complained about the meaninglessness of fielding statistics. That something was new information, and a new way of thinking about an old problem. Oddly, the impulse to do this thinking had arisen on Wall Street.

IN THE EARLY 1980S, the U.S. financial markets underwent an astonishing transformation. A combination of computing power and intellectual progress led to the creation of whole new markets in financial futures and options. Options and futures were really just fragments of stocks and bonds, but the fragments soon became so arcane and inexplicable that Wall Street created a single word to describe them all: "derivatives." In one big way these new securities differed from traditional stocks and bonds: they had a certain, precisely quantifiable, value. It was impossible for anyone to say what a simple stock or bond should be worth. Their value was a matter of financial opinion; they were worth whatever the market said they were worth. But *fragments* of a stock or bond, when you glued them back together, must be worth exactly what the stock or bond was worth. If they were worth more or less than the original article, the market was said to be "inefficient," and a trader could make a fortune trading the fragments against the original.

For the better part of a decade there were huge, virtually riskless profits to be made by people who figured this out. The sort of people who quickly grasped the math of the matter were not typical traders. They were highly trained mathematicians and statisticians and scientists who had abandoned whatever they were doing at Harvard or Stanford or MIT to make a killing on Wall Street. The fantastic sums of money hauled in by the sophisticated traders transformed the culture on Wall Street, and made quantitative analysis, as opposed to gut feel, the respectable way to go about making bets in the market. The chief economic consequence of the creation of derivative securities was to price risk more accurately, and distribute it more efficiently, than ever before in the long, risk-obsessed history of financial man. The chief social consequence was to hammer into the minds of a generation of extremely ambitious people a new connection between "inefficiency" and "opportunity," and to reinforce an older one, between "brains" and "money."

Ken Mauriello and Jack Armbruster had been part of that generation. Ken analyzed the value of derivative securities, and Jack traded them, for one of the more profitable Chicago trading firms. Their firm priced financial risk as finely as it had ever been priced. "In the late 1980s Kenny started looking at taking the same approach to Major League baseball players," said Armbruster.

"Looking at the places where the stats don't tell the whole truth—or even lie about the situation." Mauriello and Armbruster's goal was to value the events that occurred on a baseball field more accurately than they ever had been valued. In 1994, they stopped analyzing derivatives and formed a company to analyze baseball players, called AVM Systems.

Ken Mauriello had seen a connection between the new complex financial markets and baseball: "the inefficiency caused by sloppy data." As Bill James had shown, baseball data conflated luck and skill, and simply ignored a lot of what happened during a baseball game. With two outs and a runner on second base a pitcher makes a great pitch: the batter hits a bloop into left field that would have been caught had the left fielder not been Albert Belle. The shrewd runner at second base, knowing that Albert Belle is slow not just to the ball but also to the plate, beats the throw home. In the record books the batter was credited with having succeeded, the pitcher with having failed, and the left fielder and the runner with having been present on the scene. This was a grotesque failure of justice. The pitcher and runner deserved to have their accounts credited, the batter and left fielder to have theirs debited (the former should have popped out; the latter somehow had avoided committing an "error" and at the same time put runs on the board for the other team).

There was hardly a play in baseball that, to be precisely valued, didn't need to be adjusted for the players involved, or the ballpark in which it occurred. What AVM's system really wanted to know was: in every event that occurs on a baseball field, how—and how much—should the players involved be held responsible, and therefore debited and credited? Answer the question and you could answer many others. For example: How many doubles does Albert Belle need to hit to make up for the fly balls he doesn't catch?

How to account for a player's performances was obvious: runs. Runs were the money of baseball, the common denominator of everything that occurred on a field. *How much* each tiny event on a baseball field was worth was a more complicated issue. AVM dealt with it by collecting ten years of data from major league baseball games, of every ball that was put into play. Every event that followed a ball being put into play was compared by the system to what had typically happened during the previous ten years. "No matter what happens in a baseball game," said Armbruster, "it has happened thousands of times before." The performance of the players involved was always judged against the average.

A lot of this was no different from what Bill James and Dick Cramer had set out to do ten years earlier, when they created STATS Inc. The original contribution to new baseball knowledge of AVM Systems was how much more precisely it analyzed data, and how much more exactly it valued the performances of the players. Mauriello and Armbruster began by turning every major league diamond into a mathematical matrix of location points. Every point they marked with a number. They then reclassified every ball that was hit. There was no such thing in their record as a double; that was too sloppy. There were no such thing as pop flies, line drives, and grounders: finer distinctions needed to be made. A ball was hit with a certain velocity and trajectory to a certain grid on the field. In the AVM recording of a baseball game, a line drive double in the left-center gap became a ball hit with a certain force that landed on point #643.

The system then carved up what happened in every baseball play into countless tiny, meaningful fragments. Derivatives. "There are all sorts of things that happen in the context of a baseball play," said Armbruster, "that just never got recorded." A tiny example: after a single to right field a runner who had been on first base, seeing that Raul Mondesi is the right fielder, stops at second base instead of dashing to third. Runners seldom tried to go from first to third on balls hit to right field when Raul Mondesi was playing there. That was obviously worth something: what? Just as it never occurred to anyone on Wall Street to think about the value of pieces of a stock or a bond until there was a pile of money to be made from the exercise, it never occurred to anyone in the market for baseball players to assign values to the minute components of a baseball player's performance—until baseball players became breathtakingly expensive.

Bill James's work had been all about challenging the traditional understanding of the game, by questioning the meaning of its statistics. The financial experts at AVM took this idea even further, by recording the events that occurred on a baseball field without any reference whatsoever to the traditional statistics. It wasn't just circumstantial statistics such as "RBIs" and "saves" that the AVM model ignored. It ignored all conventional baseball statistics. The system replaced the game seen by the ordinary fan with an abstraction. In AVM's computers the game became a collection of derivatives, a parallel world in which baseball players could be evaluated more accurately than they were evaluated in the real world.

Paul DePodesta was an intern for the Cleveland Indians when he met the former Wall Street traders turned baseball analysts, making their first sales trip around Major League Baseball. He remembers his reaction to their presentation: *Oh my God.* "It opened my eyes for me," said Paul. "The biggest thing that AVM does is extract the element of luck. Everyone in baseball knows how much luck is involved in the game but they all say, 'The luck evens out.' What AVM was saying is that it doesn't. It's not good enough to say, 'Aw, it just evens out.'"

An insight born in the financial markets took root in the minds of a young man who would soon have the power to put it to use inside Major League Baseball. Not long after Billy Beane had hired Paul DePodesta, in 1998, Paul persuaded Billy to hire AVM Systems. "They were still interesting to me," Paul said, "because they weren't churning conventional statistics in unconventional ways, which is what everyone else does." AVM Systems was a luxury only a rich team could afford but that only a poor team, desperate for any edge, would think to use. Billy and Paul used the

AVM system for a couple of years and then, to save money, copied what AVM did. Once Paul finished replicating the parallel world of derivatives, he and Billy could begin to answer more accurately the question about Johnny Damon's defense.

Every event on a baseball field Paul understood as having an "expected run value." You don't need to be able to calculate expected run values to understand them. Everything that happens on a baseball field alters, often very subtly, a team's chances of scoring runs. Every event on a baseball field changes, often imperceptibly, the state of the game. For example, the value of having no runners on base with nobody out and no count on the batter is roughly .55 runs, because that is what a baseball team, on average, will score in that situation. If the batter smacks a double, he changes the "state" of the game: it's now nobody out with a runner on second base. The expected run value of that new "state" is 1.1 runs. It follows that the contribution of a leadoff double to a team's expected runs is .55 runs (1.1 minus .55). If the batter, instead of hitting a double, strikes out, he lowers the team's expected run value to roughly .30 runs. The cost of making that out was therefore .25 runs—the difference between the value of the original state of the game and the state the batter left it in.

But those calculations really only scratch the surface of the problem. If you want to strip out the luck and get to a deeper understanding of the value of a player's performance you have to pose the baseball equivalent of existential questions. For instance: what is a double? It really isn't enough to say that a double is when a runner hits a ball and gets to second base without a fielder's error. Anyone who has seen a baseball game knows that all doubles are not alike. There are doubles that should have been caught—just as there are balls that are hit that should have been doubles but were plucked from the air by preternaturally gifted fielders. There are lucky doubles and unlucky outs. To strip out the luck what you need, really, is something like a Platonic idea of a double.

A set of Platonic ideas is one of the gifts the Wall Street traders gave to Paul DePodesta. The precision of the AVM system, copied by Paul, enabled him to think about every event that occurred on a baseball field in a new and more satisfying way. Any ball hit any-place on a baseball field had been hit just that way thousands of times before: the average of all those hits was the Platonic idea. Call it a line drive hit at x trajectory and y speed to point #968. From the ten years worth of data, you can see that there have been 8,642 practically identical hits. You can see that 92 percent of the time the hit went for a double, 4 percent for a single, and 4 percent it was caught. Suppose the average value of that event is .50 of a run. *No matter what actually happened*, the system credits the hitter with having generated .50 of a run, and the pitcher with having given up .50 of a run. If Johnny Damon happens to get one of his trademark jumps and makes a sprawling catch, he is cred-ited with saving his team .50 of a run.

The beauty of the value of that hit (or catch) was that the game gave it to you; the game *told* you how valuable every event was, by telling you how valuable it had been, on average, over the past ten years. By listening to what the game told him about the value of events, Paul could take every ball hit between in the area broadly defined as center field and determine its "expected run value."

Which brings us back to Johnny Damon. Over the 2001 season many hundreds of balls had been hit by opponents of the Oakland A's in the vicinity typically covered by the center fielder. By total-ing up the outcomes when Johnny Damon was in the field, and comparing them to the average, Paul was able to see how many runs Damon had saved the team. He was also able to estimate how many runs Damon's likely replacement, Terrence Long, would cost the team. Some of this you could see with the naked eye, of course. You could see Johnny Damon break the instant the ball left the bat. You could see Terrence Long freeze, or even take off in the wrong direction, when the ball was in midflight. You didn't

really need Wall Street traders to tell you which one was the better center fielder. The system born on Wall Street simply helped
Paul to put a price on the difference. There was no longer any need
to guess. There was no need for gut instinct, or conventional fielding statistics. The total cost of having Terrence Long, rather than
Johnny Damon, in center field was fifteen runs, or about a run
every ten games.

Fifteen runs was not a trivial number. In the end, Paul concluded that Johnny Damon's fielding was more important than
Billy Beane believed—the first pamphlet Billy had read on the subject had said that fielding was "no more than 5%" of baseball—but
not so much more that you wanted to pay Johnny Damon the $8
million a year his agent was asking for. And the truth was that you
still couldn't make perfectly definitive statements about fielding.
"There was still no exact number," Paul said, "because the system
doesn't measure where a defensive player started from. It doesn't
tell you how far a guy had to go to catch a ball." What looked like
superior defense might have been brilliant defensive positioning
by the bench coach.

There was one other big glitch: these sorts of calculations could
value only past performance. No matter how accurately you valued past performance, it was still an uncertain guide to future performance. Johnny Damon (or Terrence Long) might lose a step.
Johnny Damon (or Terrence Long) might take to drink, or get
divorced. Johnny Damon (or Terrence Long) might decide that
he'd made enough money already and lose his middle-class enthusiasm for running down fly balls. In human behavior there was
always uncertainty and risk. The goal of the Oakland front office
was simply to minimize the risk. Their solution wasn't perfect, it
was just better than the hoary alternative, rendering decisions by
gut feeling.

Of one thing they were certain: their system brought you a lot
closer to the true value of a player's performances than anything
else like it. And it reinforced the Oakland A's working theory that

a guy's hitting ability had a far greater effect than his fielding ability on a team's performance. Albert Belle missed more fly balls than any other left fielder in baseball, but the system proved that he more than made up for it by swatting more doubles. Or as Paul put it, "The variance between the best and worst fielders on the outcome of a game is a lot smaller than the variance between the best hitters and the worst hitters." The market as a whole failed to grasp this fact, and so placed higher prices than it should on defensive skills. Thus the practical answer to the question about Johnny Damon's defense: it would probably cost more to replace than it was worth. Anyone who could play center field so well as Damon was either a lot worse offensively than Damon, or overpriced. The most efficient way to offset the loss of Johnny Damon's defense was to add more offense.

The Blue Ribbon Panel Report believed that a poor team could never survive the loss to free agency of its proven stars. But the business was more complicated than that. The departures of Johnny Damon and Jason Isringhausen, both proven stars, were not great blows to the Oakland A's. The loss of Isringhausen was not really a loss at all but a piece of ruthless profiteering. Damon's was a loss but nothing like the $32 million for four years the Red Sox had guaranteed him. If the Oakland A's had lost just those two players Paul's computer might have predicted that the team in 2002 would win as many games as they had in 2001. But they'd also lost Jason Giambi, and Jason Giambi was another matter. Giambi was maybe the worst defensive first baseman in the big leagues but he was a machine for creating runs, one of the most *efficient* offensive players in the game. Worse, Giambi was back in Oakland, playing for the other team.

Chapter Seven

GIAMBI'S HOLE

We're going to run the organization from the top down.
We're controlling player personnel. That's our job. I don't
apologize for that. There's this belief that a baseball team
starts with the manager first. It doesn't.
—Billy Beane, quoted in the *Boston Herald*, January 16, 2003

T HE OAKLAND A'S clubhouse was famously the cheapest
and least charming real estate in professional baseball and
the video room was the meanest corner of it. Off-limits to
reporters, just a few yards down the hall from the showers, the
video room was where the players came to hide from newspaper
reporters, and to study themselves. One wall was stacked with old
tapes of A's games, the other with decrepit video equipment.
Stained Formica desks, a pair of old video screens on each one,
squatted on either end of the room. The only decoration was a
plastic map of the United States—because occasionally the players wanted to see which states they'd fly over on the next road
trip—and two pieces of a bat split against one of the Formica desks
by former A's outfielder Matt Stairs. About six baseball players
could fit inside the room at once, and often did.

Between Matt Stairs's broken bat and the U.S. map usually sat
a young man named Dan Feinstein—Feiny, everyone called him.
Twenty minutes before game time all that was left of the players

in the video room was Miguel Tejada's Fig Newton wrappers. Feiny spotted them and shook his head. The A's shortstop was one of those people who had to be told to clean up his own mess, and Feiny was one of those people who wouldn't hesitate to do it.

Feiny was putting his college degree in medieval European history to work preparing videotapes for the Oakland A's. He took pride in his decrepit little space. Feiny argued that while rich teams had far more expansive and tasteful facilities, they paid a price for their luxury: their players never had to share close quarters. They weren't forced to get to know one another by smell. Feiny came to know all of the Oakland players, by smell and swing, and he was determined that they should also know themselves. The night I arrived, the A's were playing the New York Yankees, for whom David Wells was scheduled to pitch. Next to Feiny there was a long row of tapes: Tejada vs. Wells. Menechino vs. Wells. Chavez vs. Wells. I looked at the tapes, and then at Feiny, who said, "I don't have a good feeling about tonight." "Why not?" I asked. "They're better than us," he said.

Next to Feiny, at one end of the video room, sat David Forst, twenty-five-year-old former Harvard shortstop. Two years earlier, after he'd graduated with an honors degree in sociology, Forst had been invited to the Red Sox spring training camp. Dismissed in the final cut, he sent his résumé around big league front offices and it caught Paul DePodesta's eye. And so, surely for the first time since the dead ball era, the Harvard Old Boys' network came to baseball. Paul himself sat at the desk on the other end of the room. I ask them if it ever troubled them to devote their lives, and expensive educations, to a trivial game. They look at me as if I've lost my mind, and Paul actually laughed. "Oh, you mean as opposed to working in some deeply meaningful job on Wall Street?" he said.

It wasn't hard to see what Billy had seen in Paul when he'd hired him: an antidote to himself. Billy was an undisciplined omnivore. He let everything in and then worried about the consequences later. He ate about ten thousand calories of junk food each day on the assumption that he could always run them off. Ideas he consumed as rapidly and indiscriminately as cheese puffs. He had been put on this earth to devour all of it; Paul, on the other hand, seemed to be trying to establish some kind of record for fuel efficiency. Food he treated with suspicion, as if the world's chefs were conspiring to poison him. He'd somehow gotten through a private prep school and college without ever allowing a sip of alcohol to pass his lips, not because he had any conventional moral objection to drinking but because research had established that alcohol killed brain cells. About his career he was fantastically deliberate. He'd already turned down one lucrative offer, from the Toronto Blue Jays, to become, at twenty-eight, the youngest general manager in the history of baseball, and he was prepared to turn down more until exactly the right one came along. Paul was finicky about ideas, too, but he had let in one big one: that there was still such a thing as new baseball knowledge.

Paul was obviously a creature of reason but, beneath his reason, other qualities percolated. He'd played sports in high school, and then proved that a young man with the build of St. Francis of Assisi could play wide receiver for the Harvard varsity football team. ("He had the big heart," said his former coach, Mac Singleton.) Paul wasn't the sort of person who typically rises to power inside a big league organization, and yet he had. He was an outsider who had found a way to enter a place designed to keep outsiders out. Billy Beane had turned himself into a human bridge between two warring countries—the fiefdom of Playing Pro Ball and the Republic of Thinking About How to Play Pro Ball—and Paul was dashing across it. Under his arm he carried both the toolkit and the spirit of Bill James. "The thing that Bill James did that we try to do," Paul said, "is that he asked the question *why*."

The question Paul might have been asking on this night early in the 2002 season was: why the hell did we let Jason Giambi leave? The question that he had, in fact, asked was: why does it matter that we let Jason Giambi leave?

The A's front office realized right away, of course, that they couldn't replace Jason Giambi with another first baseman just like him. There wasn't another first baseman just like him and if there were they couldn't have afforded him and in any case that's not how they thought about the holes they had to fill. "The important thing is not to recreate the individual," Billy Beane would later say. "The important thing is to recreate the *aggregate*." He couldn't and wouldn't find another Jason Giambi; but he could find the pieces of Giambi he could least afford to be without, and buy them for a tiny fraction of the cost of Giambi himself.

The A's front office had broken down Giambi into his obvious offensive statistics—walks, singles, doubles, home runs—along with his less obvious ones—pitches seen per plate appearance, walk to strikeout ratio—and asked: which can we afford to replace? And they realized that they could afford, in a roundabout way, to replace his most critical offensive trait, his on-base percentage, along with several less obvious ones.

The previous season Giambi's on-base percentage had been .477, the highest in the American League by 50 points. (Seattle's Edgar Martinez had been second at .423; the average American League on-base percentage was .334.) There was no one player who got on base half the time he came to bat that the A's could afford; on the other hand, Jason Giambi wasn't the only player in the Oakland A's lineup who needed replacing. Johnny Damon (on-base percentage .324) was gone from center field, and the designated hitter Olmedo Saenz (.291) was headed for the bench. The average on-base percentage of those three players (.364) was what Billy and Paul had set out to replace. They went looking for three players who could play, between them, first base, outfield, and DH, and who shared an ability to get on base at a rate thirty points higher than the average big league player. The astonishing thing, given how important on-base percentage was, or the Oakland A's front office believed it was, was how little it cost. To buy it they simply had to be willing to sacrifice other qualities in a player— such as the ability to outrun the hot dog vendor in a sixty-yard dash. "We don't get the guys who are perfect," said Paul. "There has to be something wrong with them for them to get to us." To fill the hole left by Giambi, the A's had gone out and acquired, or promoted from within the organization, three players most teams didn't want to have anything to do with: former Yankee outfielder David Justice; former Red Sox catcher Scott Hatteberg; and Jason Giambi's little brother, Jeremy. They could only afford them, Paul explained, because all were widely viewed by Major League Baseball executives as defective.

As the Oakland A's trot out to their positions in the field, Paul takes his usual seat in front of one of the video screens. The camera pans to left field. There stands Jeremy Giambi, shifting back and forth unhappily, like a man waiting for an unpleasant phone call. He must know that he is standing in a place where he faces almost certain public humiliation. Paul can guess what Jeremy is thinking: *Please don't hit it to me.* Perhaps also: *If you do hit it to me, please be so kind as to hit it* at *me.*

On the second pitch of the game, Alfonso Soriano doesn't. The Yankees' second baseman takes a fastball in the middle of the plate from A's pitcher Eric Hiljus and smacks it deep into left field. Jeremy Giambi makes his way frantically back toward the left field wall, like a postman trying to escape a mad dog. He is the slowest man on the slowest team in professional baseball. When he runs, he manages somehow at the same time to convey personal embarrassment. He is too busy right now to wonder why he is playing left field at all, but he well might. He is playing left field not because he has any particular gift for plucking balls from the air but because he is even more gloriously inept when faced with the task of picking them up off the ground. Jeremy Giambi is in

left field, to be exact, because the most efficient distribution of the
A's resources was to stick him there.

Jeremy Giambi believes he has reached the wall before he does.
He gropes the air behind him with his free hand, then he looks up.
Somewhere in the night sky is a ball; where, apparently, he is
unsure. He jumps, or, at any rate, simulates the act of jumping.
The ball somehow flies under his glove and bangs off the wall for
a double. As Soriano zips around first base, I yell at the television—I hadn't come here to watch the underdog lose—and only
just stop myself from saying that the fans should sue for malprac-
tice. There was something indecent about hurling abuse at Oakland A's fielders, like hollering at cripples. It wasn't their fault
they'd landed in the middle of a lab experiment. Jeremy Giambi
never *asked* to play left field.

Paul DePodesta hardly blinks. Life with no money was filled
with embarrassing little trade-offs. The trick is to know precisely
what trade-offs you were making. A farce in left field is merely the
price of doing business with Jeremy Giambi's bat. But it's a complex transaction. The game is only two pitches old and already the
cost is felt.

Soriano is standing on third base and Derek Jeter on first (infield
single) when Jason Giambi first comes to the plate. The three Yankees on the field will be paid nearly as much this year as the A's
entire twenty-five-man roster. Giambi—Giambi's money—transforms the arena. If you drilled a hole in either the roof or the front
wall of the video room you would quickly reach the largest crowd
in Oakland A's history: 54,513 people had come tonight, and not
merely because the New York Yankees were in town. They'd
come because the past two years the A's had been within a few
outs of knocking the Yankees from the play-offs. They'd come to
watch the latest plot twist in one of the great David and Goliath
stories in professional sports: Goliath, dissatisfied with his size
advantage, has bought David's sling. The Oakland fans wave signs

at Giambi: TRAITOR. SELLOUT. GREED. They scream worse things. Yet in here, in the video room, their voices still cannot be heard. Six television screens display a soundless frenzy. No one in the video room so much as sighs. They have no interest in morality tales. Morality is for fans.

As Jason Giambi steps into the batter's box, the TV cameras flash back and forth between him and his younger brother in left field. The announcers wish to draw out a few comparisons. Poor Jeremy. He still needed a baseball genius to divine his true worth but any moron could see the value of his older brother, at the plate. In all of baseball for the past few years there has been only one batter more useful to an offense: Barry Bonds. Giambi has all the crude offensive attributes—home runs, high batting average, a perennially high number of RBIs. He also has the subtler attributes. When he's in the lineup, for instance, the opposing pitcher is forced to throw a lot more pitches than when he isn't. The more pitches the opposing starting pitcher throws, the earlier he'll be relieved. Relief pitchers aren't starting pitchers for a reason: they aren't as good. When a team wades into the opponent's bullpen in the first game of a series, it feasts, in games two and three, on pitching that is not merely inferior but exhausted. "Baseball is a war of attrition," Billy Beane was fond of saying, "and what's being attrited is pitchers' arms."

A hitter like Giambi performed many imperceptible services for his team. His ability to wear down first string pitchers gave everyone else more chances to hit against the second string. This ability, like every other, grew directly from his perfect understanding of the strike zone. He had the hitter's equivalent of perfect pitch, and the young men in the video room are attuned to its value.

"Watch," says Paul, as $17 million a year of hitter steps up to the plate and stares blankly at $237,500 of pitcher. "Giambi's cut the strike zone completely in half." It isn't Giambi's obvious powers that have him excited. It's his self-control, and the effect it has on pitchers. Giambi makes it nearly impossible for even a very good pitcher to do what he routinely does with lesser hitters: control the encounter. And Eric Hiljus isn't, tonight, a very good pitcher.

David points to the screen and shows me the sliver of the plate over which a pitch must pass for Giambi to swing at it. The line he traces omits a chunk of the inner half of the plate. "He has a hole on the inside where he can't do much with a pitch and so he lays off it," says David.

Every hitter has a hole. "The strike zone is too big to cover it all," as Paul says. Ted Williams wrote a book, called *The Science of Hitting*, in which he imagined the strike zone as a grid of seventy-seven baseballs and further imagined what he could, and couldn't, do with a baseball thrown to each of the seventy-seven spots. There were eleven spots, all low and most away, where, if the pitch was thrown to them and Ted Williams swung, he hit under .270. Barry Bonds, during spring training, had given an interview with ESPN in which he as much as said, "if you make your pitch, you can get me out." The issue wasn't whether a hitter had a weakness, but where it was. Every pitcher in the big leagues knew that Giambi's hole was waist-high, on the inside corner of the plate. It was about the size of a pint of milk, two baseballs in height and one baseball in width.

Which raised an obvious question: why don't the pitchers just aim for the milk pint? When I ask it, Feiny smiles and shakes his head. "They do," David says. "But he's so good he'll step back and rip one foul into the upper deck. After that, the pitcher won't ever go inside again."

"And his weakness is right next to his greatest strength," says Paul. "If they miss by two inches over the plate, the ball is gone. The pitcher is out there thinking: 'I can get him out there. But if I miss by even a fraction, he'll destroy me.'"

It's not clear what Eric Hiljus is thinking—other than he has no interest in flirting with the inside part of the plate. His first pitch is a ball just off the outside corner; his second pitch, a fastball, closer to the middle. Giambi yanks it into right field for a single that drives Soriano home.

The A's hitters go quietly in the first. In the top of the second, Eric Hiljus continues to indulge Yankee hitters with fastballs down the middle of the plate and they strike for four more runs, three on a home run by Derek Jeter. About the third time that I shout while the rest of the video room remains silent, I realize I am not only watching the game differently but am watching a different game. My eyes keep drifting to the one TV screen that, almost apologetically, displays the commercial broadcast. They focus on a different screen—an internal feed directly from the center field camera—that offers them the clearest view of the strike zone. I'm watching the whole game, and responding the way an ordinary fan responds. I'm looking for story lines and dramatic events and other fuel for my emotions. They're watching fragments—not the game itself but derivatives of the game—and responding, so far as I can tell, not at all. Finally, I say something about it.

"It's looking at process rather than outcomes," Paul says. "Too many people make decisions based on outcomes rather than process."

The route a pitch takes to the catcher's mitt *is* an outcome, I say. It's just a more subtle outcome.

"It's not what happened," says Paul, "it's how our guy approached it."

It's impossible to determine, from the stands or the dugout or the luxury suites or even the commercial broadcast, whether a ball traveling 90 miles an hour was half an inch off or half an inch over home plate. Only here, in the video room, can they see the biggest thing they feel they need to know to evaluate their players: whether a pitch is a ball or a strike. "The strike zone is the heart of the game," Bill James had written, and their behavior underscored the fact.

When the Yankees finish pummeling Eric Hiljus, and the A's

come to bat, David pulls out a neatly typed piece of paper that hints at Paul's meaning. It reads:

Tejada: 38%
Chavez: 34%
Long: 31%
Hernandez: 29%
Pena: 27%
Menechino: 19%
Justice: 18%
Giambi: 17%
Hatteberg: 14%

The A's front office record every pitch thrown to Oakland A's hitters, both by type and location. They've mined these to determine the percentage of pitches outside the strike zone each player has swung at. Each plate appearance they think of as a miniature game in itself, in which the odds shift constantly. The odds depend on who is pitching and who is hitting, of course, but they also depend on the minute events within the event. Every plate appearance was like a hand of blackjack; the tone of it changed with each dealt card. A first-pitch strike, for instance, lowered a hitter's batting average by about seventy-five points, and a first-pitch ball raised them about as much. But it wasn't the first pitch that held the most drama for the cognoscenti; it was the third. "The difference between 1–2 and 2–1 in terms of expected outcomes is just enormous," says Paul. "It's the largest variance of expected outcomes of any one pitch. On 2–1 most average major league hitters become all-stars, yet on 1–2 they become anemic nine-hole hitters. People talk about first-pitch strikes. But it's really the first two out of three."

Any ball out of the strike zone was an opportunity for a batter to shift the odds in his favor. All you had to do was: not swing! The bottom half of the A's lineup was systematically, willfully, shifting the odds in the pitchers' favor. "I envy casino managers," says Paul. "At least they can be sure that their blackjack dealers won't hit on 19."

The entire bottom half of the A's lineup—Miguel Tejada, Eric Chavez, Ramon Hernandez, Carlos Pena, and Terrence Long—is playing a different, more reckless game than the top half—Jeremy Giambi, Scott Hatteberg, David Justice, Frank Menechino. The top half is hitting with discipline, and avoiding swinging at bad pitches. The bottom half is hacking away. The odd thing about this is that the top half was acquired through trades from other clubs, and the bottom half, with the exception of Terrence Long and Carlos Pena, is homegrown.

The guys who aren't behaving properly at the plate are precisely those who have had the approach drilled into them by A's hitting coaches from the moment they became pro players. The seemingly inverse correlation between the amount of discipline exhibited by a big league hitter and the amount of time his team has spent trying to *teach* him discipline has led Billy Beane to conclude that discipline can't be taught. (Actually what he says is, "It can be taught, but we'd have to take guys in diapers to do it.") You could see just by looking at David's list why Billy felt he had to seize control of the amateur draft from his scouts. What most scouts thought of as a learned skill of secondary importance the A's management had come, through hard experience, to view virtually as a genetic trait, and the one most likely to lead to baseball success.

Which raises another obvious question: if Miguel Tejada and Ramon Hernandez and Eric Chavez are still swinging at bad pitches after years of being told not to, how can any list make a difference? This time when I ask it, Feiny doesn't smile at my stupidity. "They've spent five years with Miggy [they all call Tejada "Miggy"] in here trying to teach him what not to swing at," he says, "and he still swings at it."

"When you have it on paper, it's evidence," says David. "They say they don't believe you, but when you show them they're hitting .140 when they swing at the first pitch, it gets their attention. Sometimes."

David Justice interrupts the conversation. Seconds after the A's come into the dugout, Justice, who has been playing right field, appears in the video room. "Feiny, can I see my at bat?" he asks. He's not even breathing hard. The great thing about baseball players, from the point of view of personal hygiene, is how seldom they break a sweat.

Justice sits and watches a replay of himself being called out on strikes. The third strike was clearly off the plate by about three inches. He races through the first few pitches to get to the bad call. "The ump set up on the inside," Justice says, when he gets to the final pitch. "He can't even see that outside pitch."

He has a point: an umpire has to choose which of the catcher's shoulders to look out over and he's chosen to look out over the inside part of the plate. Justice wants to rewind the tape and prove his case all over again, but the A's least disciplined hitters are up and out with amazing speed. The war of attrition is turning into a rout. Eric Hiljus has thrown fifty-four pitches in the first two innings. David Wells throws twelve pitches in the first and just six more—two each to Tejada, Chavez, and Long—in the second before he strolls back to the dugout. Justice can't even finish complaining before he has to run out and play right field.

Justice was the second of three defective parts the A's front office had hired to replace Jason Giambi's bat. "Defective" wasn't actually the word Paul had used. "Warts" was. As in, "What gets me really excited about a guy is when he has warts, and everyone knows he has warts, and the warts just don't matter." All you had to do to see what Paul might mean by warts was to stroll through the Oakland A's clubhouse as the players emerged from the showers: not a pretty sight. Justice was an exception, however. Justice was still a physical specimen. He looked as handsome and cocky and fit as ever. Warts? For chrissake, I thought, he's *David Justice.*

He has more postseason hits than any player in history. He's Halle
Berry's ex. Whatever had happened between him and Halle Berry,
it was hard to find any obvious fault with David Justice.

"What's wrong with him?" I ask, once he's gone.

"He's thirty-six," says Paul.

The previous year Justice had started to show his age. He'd
taken swings in the World Series that looked positively amateur-
ish. But he'd also played most of the year injured and it was hard
to say how much of his drastic decline was a result of the injury
and how much of it was caused by old age. A baseball player typically ripens in his late twenties; as he enters his mid-thirties, he's
treated as guilty until he proves his innocence. Last year Justice
had as much as confessed to the baseball crime of aging. And this
is what had made him an Oakland A. In his prime, Justice had
been the sort of sensational hitter the Oakland A's could never
have afforded to buy on the open market. They could afford him
now only because no one else wanted him: the rest of baseball
looked at Justice and saw a has-been. Billy Beane had cut a deal
with the Yankees that left the A's with Justice for one year at a
salary of $3.5 million, half what the Yankees had paid him the
year before. The Yankees picked up the other half. The Yankees
were, in effect, paying David Justice to play against them. I tell
Paul that doesn't sound like a good way to beat the Yankees.

"He's an experiment for us," says Paul. "We see this as a game
of skill, not an athletic event. What we want to see is: at an age of
physical decline does the skill maintain its level, even when a
player no longer has the physical ability to exploit it?"

It was a funny way to put it: an experiment. What general truth
could be found out from the study of one man?

Justice isn't one man, Paul says. He's a type: an aging slugger of
a particular sort. Paul has made another study. He'd found that an
extraordinary ability to get on base was more likely to stay with a
player to the end of his career than, say, an extraordinary ability to
hit home runs. Players who walked a lot tended actually to walk

even more as they got older, and Justice walked a lot. Just a few years ago Justice's ability to wait for pitches he could drive—to not get himself out by swinging at a pitcher's pitch—had enabled him to hit lots of home runs, too. Much of his power was now gone. His new Oakland teammates witnessed his dissipation up close. After he'd hit a long fly ball, Justice would return to the A's dugout and say, matter of factly, "That used to be out." There was something morbid about it, like watching a death, play-by-play.

The A's front office didn't care. They sought only to milk the last few ounces of superior on-base percentage out of David Justice before he expired.

"Does Justice have any idea that you think of him this way?" I asked.

"No."

He didn't. None of them did. At no point were the lab rats informed of the details of the experiment. They were praised for their walks, and criticized for swinging at pitches out of the strike zone. But they weren't ever told that the front office had reduced offense to a science, or thought they had. They had no idea that their management had reduced them to their essential baseball ingredients and these did not include guts or heart or determination or anything else that ordinary fans, or their mothers, would love them for. The players were simply aware that some higher power guided their actions. They were also aware that the higher power was not, as on most teams, the field manager. Terrence Long complained that the A's front office didn't let him steal bases. Miguel Tejada said he was aware that Billy Beane wanted him to be a more patient hitter. "If I don't take twenty walks," he said, "Billy Beane send me to Mexico." Eric Chavez recalled, in an interview with *Baseball America*, how oddly the A's system, over which Billy had presided, trained him. "The A's started showing me these numbers," Chavez said, "how guys' on-base percentages are important. It was like they didn't want me to hit for average or for home runs, but walks would get me to the big leagues." Billy

Beane was a character in his players' imaginations—though not a terribly well drawn one.

The A's scored a run in the bottom of the third. Goliath 5, David 1. Finally I ask: "Where is Billy?"

"The weight room," says Paul, without looking up.

The weight room!

"Billy's a little strange during the games," says David.

IT WASN'T LONG after a player was traded to Oakland before he realized that his new team ran differently from any of his previous ones, although it generally took him some time to figure out why. At some point he grasped that his new general manager wasn't like his old one. Most GMs shook your hand when they signed you and phoned you when they got rid of you. Between your arrival and departure you might catch the odd glimpse of the boss, say, up in his luxury suite, but typically he was a remote figure. This GM wasn't like that. This GM, so far as anyone could tell, never set foot inside his luxury suite.

That is what the new player noticed right away: that Billy Beane hung around the clubhouse more than the other GMs. David Justice, who had spent fourteen years with the Braves, the Indians, and the Yankees, claimed he'd seen more of Billy in the first half of the 2002 season than he had all the other GMs put together. The new member of the team would see Billy in the locker room asking some shell-shocked pitcher why he'd thrown a certain pitch in a certain count. Or he'd see Billy chasing down the clubhouse hallway after the Panamanian pinch hitter, badgering him about some disparaging comment he'd made about the base on balls. Or he'd dash up the tunnel from the dugout in the middle of the game to watch tape of his previous at bat, and find Billy in shorts and a T-shirt, dripping sweat from a workout, at the other end; and, if the game wasn't going well, he might find Billy throwing stuff around the clubhouse. *Breaking things.*

It was hard to know which of Billy's qualities was most important to his team's success: his energy, his resourcefulness, his
intelligence, or his ability to scare the living shit out of even very
large professional baseball players. Most GMs hadn't played the
game and tended to be physically intimidated in the presence of
big league players. Billy had not only played, he might as well
wear a sign around his neck that said: *I've been here, so don't go
trying any of that big league bullshit on me.* He didn't want your
autograph. He wasn't looking to be your buddy. Seldom did the
player see Billy socially, away from the clubhouse. Billy kept his
distance, even when he was right in your face. Nevertheless, he
was a presence.

After a while the new player would start to wonder if there was
any place previously reserved for men in uniform that Billy didn't
invade. There was, just one. The dugout. Major League Baseball
rules forbade the general manager from sitting in the dugout. But
even there the GM was never very far away, because the manager,
Art Howe, walked around with a miniature Billy Beane perched on
his shoulder, hollering in his ear. In the Oakland A's dugout
occurred the most extraordinary acts of mind control; if Art had a
spoon in his head Billy could have bent it with his brain waves.
One time Adam Piatt, the spare outfielder, had gone up to the
plate in a tight game with a runner on first base with one out, and
bunted the guy over. Just like you were supposed to do. Just like
everyone in baseball did. Art hadn't exactly disapproved—at heart
Art was an old baseball guy. Instead, incredibly, he had wandered
down to where Piatt sat in the dugout and said, "You did that on
your own, right?"

The TV viewers saw only the wise old manager conferring with
his young player. They probably assumed they were witnessing
the manager making some fine point about the art of the sacrifice
bunt. The manager was more concerned with the politics of the
sacrifice bunt: Art Howe wanted to make sure that it wasn't him
who got yelled at by the GM after the game. Sure enough, in the

papers the next day Piatt confessed that he had bunted on his own—that Art hadn't given him the signal. Art, for his part, offered the reporters an impromptu lecture that might have been written by the GM himself on why the sacrifice bunt was a bad play. (Baseball players and coaches often used the newspapers to send memos to their general managers.)

Before long the new member of the Oakland A's realized: Billy Beane ran the whole show. He was like a Hollywood producer who insisted on meddling not only with the script but also the lights and camera and sets and wardrobes. He wasn't just making the trades and supervising scouts and getting his name in the papers and whatever else a GM did. He was deciding whether to bunt or steal; who played and who sat; who hit in which spot in the lineup; how the bullpen was used; even the manager's subtle psychological tactics. If you watched the games closely you noticed that Art Howe always stood on the dugout steps above the players, his chin raised and a philosophical expression upon his face. Art had a great chin. When he stood up and thrust it out, he looked like George Washington crossing the Delaware. No manager in baseball better conveyed, with the thrust of his chin, the idea that he was completely in control of any situation. They flashed up on the television screen that stoic image of Art ten times a game and at some point the announcers felt moved to mention Art's calming effect on young players. Art became known throughout baseball as the steady hand on the tiller. Why? Because he looked the part!

The whole thing was a piece of theatre. Billy had told Art how and where to stand during a game so that the players would be forced to look up to him, and take strength from his countenance, because when Art sat on the bench, as he preferred to do, he looked like a prisoner of war.

It was a different scene here in Oakland, and some players enjoyed it more than others. The thirty-nine-year-old utility infielder, Randy Velarde, complained often to reporters that the team was run from the front office and that the front office wouldn't let anyone bunt or steal. The twenty-three-year-old star pitcher, Barry Zito, said that it didn't matter who played for the Oakland A's or how much money the team had to spend: as long as Billy Beane ran the team, it had a shot at championships. A player who preferred to remain anonymous, asked how it would affect the team if Art Howe was fired, said that he couldn't see what difference it would make since "Billy runs the team from the weight room anyway." And it was true: before every home game Billy would put on his jock and head for the weight room. During the first couple of innings he'd run a few miles and lift a few weights and generally remind whichever pitchers and bench players who had sneaked out of the dugout to get in their workouts that they played for the only team in the history of baseball on which the general manager was also the best athlete. After that, what he did depended on the situation.

What he didn't do was watch the games. When he watched his team live, he became so upset he'd become a danger to baseball science. He'd become, as he put it, "subjective." His anger might lead him to do something unconsidered. The notion that he would huddle in his luxury suite with friends and family and visiting dignitaries—well, that just wasn't going to happen. Some visiting dignitary would hint he might like to see a game from Billy's box and Billy would say, "Fine, just don't think I'll be seeing it with you." His guest thought Billy was joking, until he discovered he had the suite to himself.

Billy couldn't bear to watch; on the other hand, he couldn't bear *not* to watch. He carried around in his pocket a little white box, resembling a pager, that received a satellite feed of live baseball scores. The white box was his chief source of real time information about the team he ran. He'd get into his SUV and drive in circles around the Coliseum, peeking every few minutes at the tiny white box. Or he'd set himself up in a place inside the clubhouse, white box in hand. He was like some tragic figure in Greek mythology whose offenses against the gods had caused them to design for him this exquisite torture: you must desperately need to see what you cannot bear to see.

Only every now and then Billy Beane did see. He'd permit himself a furtive glimpse of the action on live television, behind the closed door of Art Howe's office. And when he did, he usually wound up needing to complain to someone, whereupon he'd go find Paul and David in the video room.

Tonight happened to be one of those nights. In the middle of the fourth inning, with the A's still trailing 5–1, Billy appears in the doorway of the video room. He's wearing shorts and a T-shirt soaked with sweat. His cheeks are flushed. In his hand is his little white box. He hasn't watched the game exactly, but he has deduced its essence from his little white box.

"Fucking Hiljus," he says. "Why doesn't he just write them a note saying it'll be coming down the middle of the plate?"

He actually doesn't want to talk about the game. He wants to find a subject that will take his mind off the game. He turns to me. He's heard that I have just come back from living in Paris. He's never been to Paris.

"Is the Bastille still there," he asks, "or did they tear it down after the Revolution?"

"Still there," I say distractedly. I'm watching David Justice begin his second trip to the plate. I want to see what he does with whatever knowledge he acquired from watching himself cheated by the umpire. Who cares about the Bastille?

Billy Beane does. He's intensely curious about it. He's just now listening to some endless work of European history as he drives to and from the ballpark.

Justice quickly falls behind and Wells worries the outside corner of the plate. Wells knows what Justice knows, that the umpire will give the pitcher an outside strike he doesn't deserve. They're no longer playing a game; they're playing game theory. This time Justice doesn't take the outside pitches for the balls they are. He reaches out and fouls them off. Finally Wells makes a mistake, a pitch over the plate, and Justice lines a single to the opposite field.

"What's it look like?"

"What?"

"What's the Bastille look like?"

"It's just a pile of rocks, I think," I say.

"You mean you never went?"

I confess that I've never actually seen the Bastille. This kills Billy's interest. I'm a Bastille fraud. His mind, having no place else to go, returns to the action on the video screens. Justice is on first with nobody out and Miguel Tejada is coming to the plate. That simple fact, at this early point in the season, is enough to set Billy off.

"Oh great," he says, with real disgust. "Here comes Mister Swing at Everything."

I look down at David's chart. Mister Swing at Everything is who Tejada, on this night early in the 2002 season, seems to be. When I look up, Billy Beane is gone. For good. He's taken his white box into his car and will drive the long way home, listening to European history, to make certain the game is over before he is anywhere near a television set.

Mister Swing at Everything has thus far in the game lived up to his reputation. Miguel Tejada had grown up poor in the Dominican Republic, and in the Dominican Republic they had a saying, "You don't walk off the island." The Dominican hitters were notorious hackers because they had been told they had to be to survive. For years the A's had tried to beat out of Tejada his free-swinging ways, and they'd changed him a bit, though not as much as they'd hoped to change him. Still, their ideas are in his head. "Fucking Pitch!" Tejada screams to himself and the TV cameras each time he hacks away at some slider in the dirt or heater in his eyes. He's gotten himself out twice so far this game and he may have grown weary of the experience, because he just watches as Wells's first pitch passes across the heart of the plate. Wells, perhaps having decided that Tejada is beginning to worry about that one-way trip to Mexico, tries to come back to the same place, which he really shouldn't do. Tejada meets the pitch with a quick crude stroke and crushes it into the left field bleachers. Yankees 5, Oakland 3. Goliath, meet David.

Two innings later, in the bottom of the sixth, David Justice leads off the inning again, and this time draws a walk from Wells. Minutes later he crosses the plate, the score is 5–4 and the bases are loaded with two outs. The A's leadoff hitter, Jeremy Giambi, steps into the box. The one talent every fan and manager in the game associated with a leadoff hitter was the talent Jeremy Giambi most obviously lacked. "I'm the only manager in baseball," A's manager Art Howe complained, "who has to pinch-run for his leadoff man." Sticking the ice wagon in the leadoff slot had been another quixotic front office ploy. What Jeremy did have was a truly phenomenal ability to wear pitchers out, and get himself on base. In the first regard he was actually his brother's superior. He draws a walk from Mike Stanton and ties the game at 5–5.

Inside the video room, for the first time, we can hear the crowd. Fifty-five thousand fans are beside themselves. The pleasure of rooting for Goliath is that you can expect to win. The pleasure of rooting for David is that, while you don't know what to expect, you stand at least a chance of being inspired.

In the top of the seventh, the A's reliever Mike Magnante provides no relief. He gives up a double to Bernie Williams. Derek Jeter walks to the plate, Jason Giambi steps into the on-deck circle, and Art Howe brings in Jim Mecir. Mecir doesn't trot, he hobbles out of the A's bullpen. He really doesn't look like a professional ballplayer—which is to say, I am beginning to understand, he looks like he belongs on the Oakland A's. The Oakland A's are baseball's answer to the Island of Misfit Toys.

"What's wrong with him?" I ask.

"He's got a clubfoot," says Paul.

I think he's joking but he's not. Mecir was born with two clubfeet. As a child he'd had operations to correct them but he still walked with a limp. Somehow he had turned his deformity into an advantage. His strange delivery—he wasn't able to push off the mound with his right foot—put an unusually violent spin on his screwball. The pitch had proven to be ruthlessly effective against left-handed hitters.

Mecir walks Jeter. Giambi steps in. Mecir immediately attacks the hole in Giambi's swing, the waist-high inside pitch. Screwball after screwball dives over the inside part of the plate. The first is a ball but the second is a strike and Giambi doesn't even think of swinging at either one of them. The count is 1–1. The third pitch, Giambi takes for a ball. The odds shift dangerously toward him. Mecir defies them: another called strike on the inside corner. His fifth pitch should have been his last. It's a thing of beauty; Giambi flinches as it passes him on the inside corner of the plate. Strike three. A cheer erupts in the video room.

The umpire calls it a ball.

It's a terrible call, in a critical situation, bad enough to crack even Paul. "I'm sick of the fucking Yankees getting every call!" he shouts, then, looking for something to swat, settles on the wall. He leaves the video room. Even he doesn't want to watch what happens next: you can't give Jason Giambi four strikes and expect to live to tell about it. Giambi fouls off the next pitch and then drives the seventh pitch he sees into right field for a double, scoring two runs.

The A's fail to score again. A few minutes after he's done his impersonation of his boss, Paul returns to watch his team lose, wearing a mask of reason. After all, it was just one game. Nothing had happened to dissuade him that his original prediction for the A's season (ninety-five wins and a play-off spot) was wrong. Ninety-five wins meant sixty-seven losses; this was just one of those. Or so he says.

As he does, Scott Hatteberg appears in the video room. He's the
third and final defective part assembled by the A's front office to
replace Jason Giambi. He wants to see his videotape.

Hatteberg had spent the first six years of his career as a catcher
with the Boston Red Sox. He'd become a free agent at the end of
the 2001 season and the Red Sox had no interest in signing him.
He was, when Billy Beane signed him, a second string, washed-up
catcher. And so here he was: the final piece of a messy puzzle. I
watch him closely as he reviews his tape but can identify no deformity. He's six one, 215, and the weight looks more like muscle
than fat. He still has both arms, all ten fingers. He's not obviously
misshapen. His quick smile reveals a fine set of teeth. His hearing
is above average, too. He overhears me ask Paul why Billy had
eliminated the curious job created by Sandy Alderson: team
shrink. "Some teams need psychiatrists more than others," Hatteberg says. "In Boston we had an entire staff."

Above-average wit, too.

"So, what's wrong with *him*?" I ask, after he leaves.

"His catching career was over," said Paul. "He got hurt and
can't throw."

It turned out that Scott Hatteberg had been on the Oakland A's
wish list for several years. He'd never done anything flashy or sensational. He didn't hit an attention-getting number of home runs.
He had never hit much over or under .270. He had the same dull
virtues as David Justice and Jeremy Giambi: plate discipline and
an ability to get on base. He, like them, was a blackjack dealer
who understood never to hit on 19. The rest of baseball viewed
Hatteberg as a catcher who could hit some, rather than as an efficient device for creating runs who could also catch. When he'd
ruptured a nerve in his throwing elbow his catching days were finished, and so, in the eyes of most of baseball, was he. Therefore,
he came cheap.

That he had lost his defensive position meant little to the Oakland A's, who were forever looking for dirt-cheap opportunities to

accept bad defense for an ability to get on base. One trick of theirs was to pounce on a player just after he'd had what appeared to be a career-threatening injury. Billy Beane had a favorite saying, which he'd borrowed from the Wall Street investor Warren Buffett: the hardest thing to find is a good investment. Hatteberg wasn't like Jeremy Giambi, a minor leaguer they were hoping would cut it in the bigs. He wasn't like David Justice, an aging star in rapid decline. He was a commodity that shouldn't have existed: a big league player, in his prime, with stats that proved he had an unusual ability to create runs, and available at the new, low price of less than a million bucks a year. The only question Billy and Paul had about Scott Hatteberg was where on the baseball field to put him. Between Justice, who couldn't play in the field every day and stay healthy, and Jeremy Giambi, who couldn't play in the field every day and stay sane, they already had one full-time designated hitter. Hatteberg, to hit, would need to play some position in the field. Which one?

Chapter Eight

SCOTT HATTEBERG,
PICKIN' MACHINE

THE LIGHTS ON THE Christmas tree were off, his daughters were in bed, his wife was asleep—and he was up, walking around. His right hand still felt like it belonged to someone else. He'd played half a season for the Red Sox with a ruptured nerve in his elbow, that he crushed each time he straightened his throwing arm. He'd finally caved, and had the nerve moved back where it was meant to be; but when the operation was over he couldn't hold a baseball, much less throw one. He needed to reinstruct his hand how to be a part of a catcher's body; he needed to relearn how to do a simple thing he had done his entire life, the simple thing he now did for a living.

The Boston Red Sox had given up on him—just last week, had traded him to the Colorado Rockies for infielder Pokey Reese. He was in his sixth year in the big leagues and eligible for arbitration and the Rockies quickly made it clear to him that they weren't going to risk having some arbitrator say they had to pay Scott Hatteberg $1.5 million. A million and a half dollars actually wasn't much for a guy who'd spent five years in the big leagues, but the Rockies thought it was three times what he was worth. Thinking no one else would take an interest in a catcher who couldn't throw, they immediately granted Hatteberg his free agency. Then they proposed a deal: five hundred grand for one year. That was a 50 percent pay cut from the $950,000 he'd made in Boston the year before. Hatteberg refused. At midnight December 20, 2001, the Rockies' rights to Scott Hatteberg expired; one minute later, at 12:01 A.M., Paul DePodesta, assistant general manager of the Oakland A's, telephoned Hatteberg's agent.

This was truly odd. Hatteberg hadn't the slightest idea why the Oakland A's were so interested in him. All he saw was that one major league baseball team treated him like a used carpet in a Moroccan garage sale, twenty-eight other teams had no interest in him whatsoever, and one team was so wildly enthusiastic about him they couldn't wait till the morning to make him an offer. They pestered his agent on Christmas Day! When the Rockies heard that the Oakland A's had called Hatteberg's agent and initiated a bidding war, the team improved its offer. They wound up nearly matching Oakland's money. So what? They wanted him just in case. Just in case something happened to some other guy. Billy Beane wanted him to play. Billy Beane wanted him to *hit*. Hatteberg told his agent to cut a deal with Oakland: one year with a club option for a second, with a base salary of $950,000 plus a few incentive clauses. The moment he signed it, a few days after Christmas, he had a call from Billy Beane, who said how pleased he was to have him in the lineup.

And, oh yes, he'd be playing first base.

Baseball players share with airline pilots the desire, when they aren't working, to live in sensory deprivation chambers. In the off-season they can be found in clusters in central Florida, or the Phoenix suburbs. Hatteberg and his wife, Bitsy, had bought a house on a golf course just south of Tacoma, Washington. It wasn't their dream house—they'd have to wait until he finished playing ball for the place on the water. It was a real estate antidote to professional baseball. It would hold its value and could be quickly and tearlessly sold. When he was on the road, he knew that his girls were safe. Here a barking dog counted as crime.

Late at night, the dogs knew not to bark. Puttering around, surrounded by walls of silence, trying and failing to get comfortable with what Billy Beane had just said, he came across relics of his career. Old catcher's mitts, and old bats with his name branded into the barrel. Pictures of him at Washington State, where for three years he'd been the catcher. A framed jersey he'd worn as the catcher for Team USA in the 1990 Goodwill Games. Another he'd worn as the catcher for the Boston Red Sox. Catcher. He was a catcher. He'd been a catcher since he was ten years old. Two weeks ago he'd turned thirty-two. Twenty-two years behind the plate.

His living-room window looked out onto a blue-green fairway freshly carved out of a blameless Washington forest. Most guys golfed in the off-season; he preferred fly-fishing. The moisture on the fairway glistened in the artificial light. This time of year it was dark nearly half the time, and when it wasn't dark it was raining.

First base!

Billy Beane had promised not to tell the press that he'd hired Scott Hatteberg to replace Jason Giambi. He couldn't replace Giambi. Two guys couldn't do it. . . . First base!

Scott Hatteberg realized that he had to do something. He was going nuts. He thought of the pair of asphalt tennis courts down the road, built as a sop to the few prisoners of this gated community who didn't play golf. A few days after Christmas he strapped his daughters into their car seats, alongside his wife, his batting tee, a bucket of old baseballs, and a brand-new first baseman's mitt. The girls he dropped in the sandbox beside the courts, Bitsy he asked to hit grounders at him off the batting tee. Mrs. Scott Hatteberg listed herself at five foot one, 100 pounds. She wasn't built to hit in the big leagues. She didn't even look capable of grounding out to first base.

Bitsy had noticed something about her husband. Even though he'd been in the big leagues for five years, and had been the starting catcher for the Boston Red Sox, he had never really thought of himself as a big league ballplayer. The other players volunteered their autographs to fans before games. He never did, not because he didn't care to, but because he was worried they wouldn't know who he was. He doesn't admit this; she senses it's true all the same. And she doesn't particularly like it. It isn't that she wants baseball fans to know who her husband is. She wants *him* to know that they know who he is. And so, from the end of December to the start of spring training, in the drizzling rain, with her daughters wailing that they want to go home, she whacks big league ground balls at her husband.

Ron washington was the infield coach for the Oakland A's. He'd actually played with Billy Beane when Billy was with the Minnesota Twins, but that isn't why he was the infield coach. He was the infield coach because he had a gift for making players want to be better than they were—though he would never allow himself such a pretentious thought. Wash's job was to take the mess Billy Beane sent him during spring training and make sure that it didn't embarrass anyone by opening day. What Billy Beane sent him—well, Wash had some stories to tell. He was the one infield coach in baseball who could be certain that his general manager wouldn't be wasting any money on fielding ability. When you asked Wash what it was like to be the infield coach for a team that would have started a blind man if he had a talent for getting on base, he'd grimace and say, "I seen some shit. I can tell you that." There were times that Wash thought the players Billy sent him shouldn't even bother to bring their gloves; they should just take their bats with them into the field, and *hit* the ball back to the pitcher.

Wash had about six weeks to turn Scott Hatteberg into the Oakland A's starting first baseman. He took Hatty out onto the Arizona practice field, fed him grounders, and tried to teach him footwork. Reflecting on those grim times Wash would say, months later, "You could see he shouldn't be out there. He was on his heels. He didn't know where to go, what to do, how to do it. In the back of his mind he was saying, 'I don't want *nothin'* to happen in my area.' He'd do all the things that cause a fan in the stands to say, 'That kid is horseshit.' And what do he know? What do that fan know? He don't know *nuthin'*! But he'd be right. He'd be right about Hatty. That kid was horseshit."

Wash didn't ever say to Scott Hatteberg, or even give him the slightest non-verbal hint, what obscenities might cross the mind of the typical fan watching him play first base. The first thing Hatty needed was a feeling of confidence, even if he had no right to the feeling. But in the big meetings at the end of spring training, when the A's front office and his fellow coaches asked Wash whether Hatty was ready to be a big league first baseman, he'd said, "You can run him out there every three or four days but don't you go thinking you can put him out there every day."

From the first day of spring training Hatty experienced life at first base as a series of panic attacks. "There's this thing about first base," he says. "You can't drop balls: *any of them.*" It was nervewracking, in part because he had no idea what to do, but also because the stakes seemed so high. "I assumed if I was horrible at first, they'd release me," he said. He was horrible, but they didn't release him. Come opening day there was a temporary spot available for him in the lineup: designated hitter. The A's regular right fielder, Jermaine Dye, was taking longer than expected to recover from the leg he'd broken in a play-off game the previous year. That put David Justice in right field, and Jeremy Giambi in left, and opened up the DH slot for Hatteberg. To fill the hole at first base

Billy Beane had traded for Carlos Pena, a sensational young minor leaguer who appeared ready to make a splash in the big leagues. "Everyone said that Carlos was going to be the next Alex Rodriguez," said Hatteberg, "so once he arrived, I assumed I wouldn't be playing first base." When Dye came back, he further assumed, he'd be back on the bench.

That never happened. What happened instead is that, after starting out well enough, the team went into a tailspin. When the Yankees had come to town in late April the Oakland A's had been 11–8. Three weeks later they were four games under .500 and falling fast. In mid-May they'd gone into Toronto and been swept by the Blue Jays. The Blue Jays. Hatteberg thought he had seen it all with the Red Sox, but what happened immediately after the A's were swept by the Blue Jays was unique in his big league experience.

Like the other players, Scott Hatteberg sensed the Oakland A's were managed oddly, by big league standards. The team, even when it was on the field, appeared to be run not by the field manager but by the front office. And the front office were apparently pissed off. In what amounted to a purge, Billy Beane sent down to the minors the team's starting first baseman Carlos Pena, starting second baseman Frankie Menechino, starting pitcher Eric Hiljus, and right-handed setup man Jeff Tam. Jeremy Giambi, the starting left fielder, he traded to the Phillies for a bench player named John Mabry. In a matter of hours the A's front office had jettisoned three of their starting eight, including one guy everyone had tagged as Rookie of the Year (Pena) and another guy everyone thought was the front office's pet (Giambi). It was Scott Hatteberg's first real experience of Billy Beane. His first thought: *Oh my God, there is nothing this guy won't do.* Once again the team found itself without an everyday first baseman. By default, the job fell to him.

His performance, at the outset, lacked elegance. He labored over the most rudimentary task: getting into position to receive throws from other infielders. "It looks effortless when guys do it," he said, "but it's not. Trust me." At first base the game seemed faster than it ever had to him as a catcher. A ball would be grounded sharply to short or third and the throw would be on him before he was ready. Where was his back foot? Where was the bag? Was anyone laughing yet? Simple pop flies he'd lose in the air and they would drop ten yards away from him in the Coliseum's vast foul territory. "On a lot of the pop-ups I missed it wouldn't even look like an error," he said, "because I'd never get anywhere near the ball."

And then something happened: the more he went out to play first base, the more comfortable he felt there. By late June he could say, with a smile, that "the difference between spring training and now is that when a ground ball comes at me now, my blood pressure doesn't go through the roof." A large part of the change was due to Wash. Wash got inside your head because—well, because you wanted Wash inside your head. Every play Hatty made, including throws he took from other infielders, he came back to the dugout and discussed with Wash. His coach was creating an alternative scale on which Hatty could judge his performance. He might be an absolute D but on Wash's curve he felt like a B, and rising. "He knew that what looked like a routine play wasn't a routine play for me," said Hatty. Wash was helping him to fool himself, to make him feel better than he was, until he actually became better than he was. At the Coliseum it was a long way from the A's dugout to first base, but every time Hatty picked a throw out of the dirt—a play most first basemen made with their eyes closed—he'd hear Wash shout from the dugout:

"Pickin' Machine!"

He'd look over and see Wash with his fighting face on:

"Pickin' Machine!"

Hatty sensed that he was naturally more athletic than most guys management hid at first base, and he was right. He began to relax. He began to want the ball to be hit to him. He began to feel comfortable. He began to feel himself. One of the things he had always enjoyed as a catcher was the chance to talk to the other teams' players. First base was a far richer social opportunity. First base made catching feeling like a bad dinner party—what with the ump hanging on your shoulder and all the fans and cameras staring at you. At first base you could really *talk*. Posted on the bulletin board of the Oakland A's clubhouse was a memo, signed by Bob Watson, from Major League Baseball:

> Players of the opposing teams shall not fraternize at any time while in uniform.
> —Official Baseball Rule 3.09

By the summer of 2002, the memo might as well have been addressed directly to Scott Hatteberg. First base as he played it became a running social event. "Guys come to first," he said, "and they step into my little office. And I do like to chat." Rafael Palmeiro draws a walk and Hatty asks him which A's lefty is tougher to hit, Mark Mulder or Barry Zito. (Mulder, Raffy says.) Jeff Cirillo hits a single and, with only the tiniest prompting, starts to bitch and moan about hitting ninth in the Seattle lineup. Jeff Bagwell gets on by a fielder's error, and Hatty lets him know what a Bagwell fan he is, prompting Bagwell to go into this Eeyore-like dirge about what a poor natural hitter he actually is. "He keeps saying, 'I hate my swing I hate my swing,' and I'm like, 'Dude, you are unbelievable.'" Hatty encouraged all of it, and more. "The funny part is the etiquette," he said. "When a guy gets on, knowing when to break the ice. I try to be courteous. If a guy got a hit I might say, 'Nice piece of hitting there.' Before you know it, they're chattering away."

He was having fun. He began to make plays people didn't expect him to make; he began to make plays *Wash* didn't expect him to make. He still thought the whole Oakland experiment had been more than a tad unorthodox. "I think it's odd," he said, "the way they shove guys in on defense every which way." But by midsummer, he was overhearing people referring to him as an "above-average" first baseman. By the end of July, when you asked Wash what he made of the transformation of Scott Hatteberg into an above-average first baseman, he just shook his head and smiled. "He made a liar of me," he said. "Now he goes out and does what he does and he's a ballplayer, reacting." Then he'd think about it for a moment and say, "These are the kind of guys you go to war with. The Scott Hattebergs."

A knack for playing first base had little to do with the Oakland A's interest in Scott Hatteberg. It was a bonus that Hatty had made himself as good as he did but he could have played worse without wearing out his welcome. Hatty had been on a collision course with Oakland from the moment Paul DePodesta and Billy Beane had concluded that on-base percentage was three times more important than slugging percentage, and that certain secondary traits in a hitter, widely ignored by the rest of baseball, were also critically important to the success of the team. Hatty had some power, but what he really had was an approach to hitting that helped an offense to create runs. When he was with the Red Sox he had gotten on base at a rate about 25 points higher than the league average, and did so while (a) not playing regularly, and (b) being worn out behind home plate. Rested and playing regularly, he'd only get on base more.*

He'd do something else, too: wear out opposing pitching. Scott Hatteberg's at bats went on and on; they were nearly as drawn out as Jason Giambi's—this in spite of the fact that pitchers didn't

---

* Despite hitting in a pitcher's park, Hatteberg would finish the 2002 season tied—with A's teammate Ray Durham—for thirteen in the American League in on-base percentage. Behind him, in addition to the rest of the Oakland A's, were a lot of multimillionaires you might not expect to find there: Derek Jeter, Johnny Damon, Nomar Garciaparra.

have nearly so much reason to fear Hatteberg as they did Giambi.*
Hatteberg's was a more subtle, less visible strength. He was
unafraid of striking out and this absence of fear showed itself in
how often he hit with two strikes. The reason for his fearlessness
was how seldom he struck out. He consistently worked himself
into deep counts and yet, in spite of hitting often with two strikes,
routinely put the ball in play. The ratio of his walks to his strikeouts was among the highest in the league.†

His talent for avoiding strikeouts was another of his secondary
traits that, in the Oakland calculus, added value, subtly, to Scott
Hatteberg. The strikeout was the most expensive thing a hitter
routinely could do. There had been a lie at the heart of the system
to train A's minor league hitters. To persuade young men to be
patient, to work the count, to draw walks, to wait for the pitcher
to make a mistake that they could drive out of the park, the A's
hitting coaches had to drill into hitters' heads the idea that there
was nothing especially bad about striking out. "For a long time I
think they believed that a strikeout was no different from making
any other out," said Paul. "But it is."

Ideally what you wanted was for a hitter neither to strike out,
nor to adjust his approach to the task at hand simply to avoid
striking out. The ideal was hard to find. Most hitters had holes,
and knew it; most hitters hated to hit with two strikes. They
knew that if they got two strikes on them, they were especially
vulnerable. Paul had done some advance scouting of big league
teams. Most big league hitters, even very good ones, had some
glaring weakness. Paul could usually see quickly how a pitcher
should pitch to any given big league hitter, and how he could put
him away. Hatty, he couldn't figure. Hatty's at bats often didn't

---

* Hatteberg would finish the 2002 season third in the league in pitches seen per
plate appearance, behind Frank Thomas and Jason Giambi.

† Hatteberg's ratio of walks to strikeouts in the 2002 season was fourth in the
American League, behind John Olerud, Mike Sweeney, and Scott Spezio.

begin until he had two strikes on him. Hatty wasn't afraid to hit with two strikes; he seemed almost to welcome the opportunity. That was because Hatty had no hole. Obviously that couldn't be right: every hitter had a hole. But Paul had watched him plenty of times and he still couldn't find Hatteberg's weakness.

These secondary traits in a hitter, especially in the extreme form in which they were found in Scott Hatteberg, had real value to a baseball offense. And yet they were being priced by the market as if they were worth nothing at all.

Where did these traits come from? That was a big question the Oakland A's front office had asked themselves. Were they learned skills, or part of a guy's character? Nature or nurture? If nature, as they were coming to believe, physical gift or mental predisposition? Scott Hatteberg had something to say on these matters.

As far back as Hatteberg could remember—and he could remember Little League—two things were true about himself as a hitter. The first was that he had a preternatural ability to put a bat on a ball. Not necessarily to hit the ball out of the park; simply to make contact. ("Swinging and missing to me is like 'Jesus, what happened?'") The second was that it angered him far less to take a called strike than to swing at a pitch he couldn't do much with, and hit some lazy fly or weak grounder. Walks didn't particularly thrill him but they were far better than the usual alternative. "There was nothing I hated more," he said, "than swinging at the first pitch and grounding out. It struck me as a worthless experience."

It was also true that, as a boy, he had sought and found useful role models that encouraged his natural tendencies. The first and most important of these was Don Mattingly. Mattingly posters decorated his bedroom wall. He kept clips of old articles about Don Mattingly. On a trip to Florida he went to the Yankees' training facility and sneaked under a security rope to catch a glimpse of the great Mattingly. Security guards caught him and tossed him out of the Yankees' spring training Facility—though not until he had a good look at his hero in the batting cage. Whenever the Yankees played the Mariners he'd make the two-and-a-half-hour drive into Seattle from Yakima—where he mostly grew up—just to see Mattingly play. "He was a little guy," said Hatteberg, "and I was *tiny* growing up. So I was drawn to him. And I loved his swing. It was just poetic, his swing. It was similar to the way I swung—or wanted to swing. We both kind of squatted down a little bit." Mattingly was also, like him, a finicky hitter: he cared more than most what he swung at.

Hatteberg identified with this particular trait of Mattingly's though it was difficult to put into a single word. A baseball man might call it "patience" but it was more like "thoughtfulness." Mattingly, like him, but unlike a lot of the guys he played with, did not treat hitting a baseball as pure physical reaction. Hitting was something that you did better if you thought about it. Hatty owned a record of Mattingly talking about hitting. *The Art of Hitting .300*, it was called. He'd listened to it dozens of times. "One thing Mattingly said," Hatteberg recalled, "was that you could look at a guy's strikeouts and his walks and tell what kind of year he'd had. That stuck in my head." (The odd thing about Mattingly's sermon is that he himself never drew all that many walks.)

The trouble with Billy Beane had been that he couldn't find a way to get his whole self into a batter's box. Scott Hatteberg couldn't keep himself out of it; the pieces of his character fit too neatly together for him to leave any one of them outside the box. The outside world didn't fully understand this; it often tried to make him into something he was not. The Phillies had drafted him in the eighth round out of high school, for instance, when he himself didn't think he was ready. Scouts pressed him to sign, told him it was for his own good. Hatteberg had always been small, especially for a catcher, and when he graduated from high school he was only five ten and weighed 160 pounds. "I looked like I had pneumonia," he said. The Phillies ignored his objections. His own

high school coach—on retainer from the Phillies—told him he'd
be making the mistake of his life if he turned down the Phillies
eighty-five grand and went to college. He turned down the money
and went to college. "If I didn't make it in college," he said, "I
wasn't going to make it anyway."

He'd made it in college, and was taken in the first round of the
1991 draft by the Red Sox. Once in the minors, crude ability got
him as far as Double-A ball. There he encountered the two obsta-
cles that routinely ended professional hitting careers: pitchers
who had not only stuff but control too; and game theory. In
Double-A, as in the big leagues, a hitter saw the same pitchers
more than once. More to the point, the pitchers saw you more
than once, and invested some energy in trying to exploit what
they learned about you. He began to keep records of his at bats:
what pitchers threw him, how he responded. Keeping written
records, like seeing lots of pitches during each at bat, was a way to
gather information. The more information he had about a pitcher,
the better he hit against him. He didn't have the luxury of coast-
ing on raw talent; very few guys did. Sure, you might get to the big
leagues and even have a sensational month or two, but if you had
some fatal flaw you were found out. Kevin Maas! Maas comes up
in 1990 with the Yankees and hits ten home runs in his first
seventy-seven at bats. Had he kept hitting them out at that rate
for a full season he'd have broken Roger Maris's single-season
home run record as a rookie. He didn't. He stopped hitting home
runs; he stopped hitting period. After a couple of frustrating seasons, Kevin Maas was out of baseball.

Why do you think that happened? Hatteberg knew, or thought
he did: it happened because the big leagues was a ruthlessly efficient ecosystem. Every hitter had a weakness. Once he arrived in
the big leagues, teams saw him often enough to find that weakness, and exploit it. "Once your hole has been exposed," Hatteberg
said, "you have to make an adjustment or the whole league will
get you out. Any pitcher who can't exploit that hole isn't in the

big leagues." If you were unable to adapt, you were doomed. If you had a weakness for pitches out of the strike zone, without some extraordinary talent to compensate for it, you were doomed. Hatteberg took that logic one better: he believed that if he swung at *anything* he couldn't hit hard, even if the pitch was a strike, he was doomed. "If I just went up there and hacked," he said, "I'd have been weeded out well before the big leagues." He forced himself to look for a certain pitch from each pitcher, and then trained himself to see that pitch. He knew not just what he could do but what he couldn't do. He knew what pitches he couldn't hit well.

Billy Beane thought himself out of the big leagues. Scott Hatteberg thought himself into them. He'd been called up for the first time at the tail end of the 1995 season. With the division title in the bag, the team went into Yankee Stadium for a meaningless game—if any game between the Red Sox and the Yankees can be meaningless. Hatty was assigned to catch relievers in the bullpen, and didn't expect to play. He went out to Yankee Stadium early anyway because he didn't want to miss seeing the Yankees' first baseman, Don Mattingly, take batting practice. The game itself was a mess. The Red Sox quickly fell behind. In the top of the eighth inning the Yankee pitcher, David Cone, was working on a two-hit shutout. With the Red Sox down 9–0, the manager called the bullpen and told Hatteberg to pinch-hit. Hatteberg ran down from the pen, stepped into the batter's box, and stared down the first-base line. Don Mattingly was staring back.

Hatty took the first pitch, as he nearly always did, to get comfortable. Ball one. The second pitch was ball two. Cone had his best stuff that day. Hatteberg knew on the third pitch he'd see something in the strike zone, and he did. "I just about came out of my shoes," he said. Foul ball. Cone just missed with the next pitch and the count went to 3–1. A hitter's count. Hatteberg thought: *If I get a hit, I get the ball.* They always gave you the ball after your first big league hit. Then he had another thought: *I'm one ball away from meeting Don Mattingly.* It was Scott Hatte-

berg's first appearance in a big league batter's box and he was looking to draw a walk.

David Cone wasn't going to let him have it. Cone's next pitch
was less a pitch than an invitation, an inside fastball in what Hatteberg called his "happy zone," and he ripped it down the right
field line. It banged off the right field wall a few inches below the
top and bounded back crazily into the field of play. The Yankees
right fielder, Paul O'Neill, saw it for what it was, a clean double,
and gave up on it. Under a full head of steam Hatteberg rounded
first, picked up O'Neill jogging for the ball, and . . . Don Mattingly.
Mattingly stood directly in his line of vision. A twenty-five-year-
old making his major league debut might be forgiven for hearing a
soundtrack in his head: *My first big league hit! My first big league
hit!* Hatteberg heard another voice. It said: *Where am I going?*
Halfway toward second base he pulled up, and trotted back to his
childhood. "Hey Don, how you doin'?" he said.

The television announcers, Bob Costas and Bob Uecker, were,
at that moment, expressing their bewilderment at what they'd
just seen—this rookie who has decided he prefers a single to a double. They agreed that rookies all had a thing or two to learn before
they truly belonged in the big leagues. Mattingly just looked at
him strangely and said, "Hey, rookie, anyone show you where second base is?" The next few moments, before he was driven around
the bases to score the only Red Sox run of the game, etched themselves into Hatteberg's memory in Van Eyckian detail. Mattingly
standing behind him. Mattingly creeping in behind him, pretending to care if he ran. Mattingly razzing him. *Hey, rookie, you're
about as fast as me. Hey, rookie, you ought to get those brakes
checked.* A few weeks later Mattingly retired. Hatteberg never
saw him again.

Even in new, stressful situations, the quality at the center of
Scott Hatteberg—his compulsion to make himself at home in
the game, to slow the game down, to make it come to him, to

make it *his* game—was apparent. He was one of those people whose personality was inextricable from his performance. No: whose personality was *necessary* for his performance. The funny thing is that pro baseball took one look at that personality and decided it needed to be beaten out of him.

By late 1996 he was in the big leagues for good. Once he arrived, however, he faced another challenge: the idiocy of the Boston Red Sox. His cultivated approach to hitting—his thoughtfulness, his patience, his need for his decisions to be informed rather than reckless—was regarded by the Boston Red Sox as a deficiency. The Red Sox encouraged their players' mystical streaks. They brought into the clubhouse a parade of shrinks and motivational speakers to teach the players to harness their aggression. Be men! There was one in particular Hatteberg remembers who told the team that every man had a gland in his chest, called the thymus gland. "You were supposed to bang your chest before you hit," recalls Hatteberg, "to release all this untapped energy and aggression." (One former Red Sox player, Bill Selby, still does it.) Hatty sensed he might be in for trouble when he saw how the Red Sox management treated Wade Boggs. He'd spent a lot of time with Boggs in the batting cage during spring training, trying to learn whatever he could from the master. Boggs, a perennial All-Star, famously never swung at the first pitch—or any pitch after that he didn't love. Boggs was as efficient a machine as there ever was for acquiring information about opposing pitchers. By the time Wade Boggs was done with his first at bat, his team had seen everything the opposing pitcher had.

Boggs's refusal to exhibit the necessary aggression led to his ostracism by the Red Sox. "They would get on him for taking a walk when there was a guy on second," recalled Hatteberg. "They called him *selfish* for that."

If Wade Boggs wasn't allowed his patience, Hatteberg figured, he certainly wouldn't be, either. When Hatteberg let a pitch go by for a strike—because it was a strike he couldn't do much with—Red Sox managers would holler at him from the dugout. Coaches would try to tell him that he was hurting the team if he wasn't more inclined to swing with men on base, or in 2–0 counts. The hitting coach, former Rex Sox slugger Jim Rice, rode Hatty long and hard. Rice called him out in the clubhouse, in front of his teammates, and ridiculed him for having a batting average in the .270s when he hit .500 when he swung at the first pitch. "Jim Rice hit like a genetic freak and he wanted everyone else to hit the way he did," Hatteberg said. "He didn't understand that the reason I hit .500 when I swung at the first pitch was that I only swung at first pitches that were too good not to swing at." Hatty had a gift for tailoring the game to talents. It was completely ignored. The effect of Jim Rice on Scott Hatteberg was to convince him that "this is why poor hitters make the best hitting coaches. They don't try to make you like them, because they sucked."

Each time Scott Hatteberg came to bat for the Boston Red Sox he had, in effect, to take an intellectual stand against his own organization in order to do what was right for the team. Hitting, for him, was a considered act. He didn't know how to hit without thinking about it, and so he kept right on thinking about it. In retrospect, this was a striking act of self-determination; at the time it just seemed like an unpleasant experience. Not once in his ten years with the Red Sox did anyone in Boston suggest there was anything of value in his approach to hitting—in working the count, narrowing the strike zone, drawing walks, getting on base, in *not* making outs. "Never," he said. "No coach ever said anything. It was more, get up there and slug. Their philosophy was just to buy the best hitters money can buy, and set them loose." The Red Sox couldn't have cared less if he had waged some fierce battle at the plate. If he had, say, fought off the pitcher for eight straight pitches and lined out hard to center field. All that mattered was that he had made an out. At the same time, they praised him when he didn't deserve it. "I'd have games when I'd have two hits and I didn't take a good swing the whole game," he said, "and it was like 'Great game, Hatty.'"

Pro ball never made the slightest attempt to encourage what he did best: take precise measurements of the strike zone and fit his talents to it. The Boston Red Sox were obsessed with outcomes; he with process. That's what kept him sane. He didn't think of it quite this way, but what he'd been trying to do all along was tame a chaotic experience with reason. To an astonishing degree, he had succeeded.

To the Oakland A's front office, Hatteberg was a deeply satisfying scientific discovery. The things he did so peculiarly well at the plate were the things only science—or, at any rate, closer than normal scrutiny—could turn up. He was, in his approach to hitting, Billy Beane's opposite, but he was also Billy Beane's creation. The moment he arrived in Oakland, the friction in his hitting life vanished. In Oakland, he experienced something like the reverse of his Boston experience. "Here I go 0 for 3 with two lineouts and a walk and the *general manager* comes by my locker and says, 'Hey, great at bats.' For the first time in my career I've had people tell me, 'I love your approach.' I knew how I approached hitting but I never thought that it was anything anyone cared to think about." All these things he did just because that's how he had to do them if he was to succeed were, in Oakland, encouraged. The Oakland A's had put into words something he had only felt. "When you go to the plate," Hatty said, "it's about the only thing you do that is an individual thing or seems like an individual thing. When you go to the plate, it's about the only thing you do alone in baseball. Here they have turned it into a team thing."

That was a byproduct of the Oakland experiment. They were trying to subordinate the interest of the individual hitter to those of the team. Some hitters responded better than others to this approach. Hatteberg's response: "This is the most fun I've had since Triple-A."

Before and after games Hatteberg would go to the video room to study opposing pitchers and himself. On one of these nights the A's were playing the Seattle Mariners. The left-hander Jamie Moyer was scheduled to pitch for Seattle. Moyer had been a hugely successful big league pitcher, in spite of lacking conventional stuff. When he first came up, with the Chicago Cubs, Moyer threw as hard as the next guy. But he'd been hurt, and forced to adapt. Now, a few months before his fortieth birthday, he survived on his mastery of the strike zone and his knowledge of opposing hitters. He was the pitching equivalent of Scott Hatteberg. Had they taken a different approach to the game, neither would have lasted long in the big leagues.

Hatteberg hadn't had much chance to see Moyer, and so the tape was even more important to him than usual. "Don't think I've done too well against this guy," he said as he slammed the videotape into the machine. "Feiny, what am I lifetime against Moyer?"

Feiny doesn't look up from his seat at the center of the video room. "0 for 9," says Feiny.

"I'm 0 for 9," says Hatteberg, cheerily, and smacks the table in front of him. "That's not too promising, is it?"

Feiny doesn't say anything. He's busy cutting tape of the Texas Rangers, the A's next opponent. On his screen Alex Rodriguez waits for a pitch. "He's cheating," says Hatty. Feiny looks up; he's being drawn in by Hatteberg's desire for conversation. "Look at that," says Hatty. We all look up at the freeze-frame of A-Rod on Feiny's screen. Sure enough, just before the pitch comes to the plate, A-Rod, moving nothing but his eyeballs, glances back to see where the catcher behind him is set up.

"I used to hate it when I caught when guys did that," says Hatty. "I'd go, 'Dude, you're gonna get hit.'"

"Anyone else but A-Rod," agrees Feiny, "and he gets drilled."

Hatty turns back to the Jamie Moyer tapes. Moyer had beaten the A's several times already this season. Hatteberg had been in the lineup just once. Hatty has been a subplot in a running dispute between the front office and Art Howe. The front office want Hatteberg in the lineup all the time. Art Howe wants to do the usual thing, and keep lefties out of the lineup against lefties. The last two times the A's faced Moyer, Hatteberg hadn't been in the lineup. Moyer had shut out the A's both times, and given up a grand total of six hits. Now the front office were having their way. (The surprising thing is how long it took.) All this Hatteberg knows. He doesn't say it, but he wants badly to prove his manager wrong and his front office right.

He watches Jamie Moyer pitch against a series of left-handed hitters. Moyer's under six feet tall and narrow-shouldered, with the demeanor of a chartered accountant. When his fastball registers 82 miles per hour on the radar gun, he's having a good day. "I've faced guys who threw harder in high school," says Hatteberg. "This guy wouldn't get drafted. He could go out and try out for a team right now and if they didn't know who he was he wouldn't get signed."

That one of the best pitchers in the big leagues couldn't get beyond a tryout tells you something about the big leagues. It also tells you something about pitchers. A good pitcher, Hatteberg explained, creates a kind of parallel universe. It doesn't matter how hard he throws, in absolute terms, so long as he is able to distort the perception of the hitters. The reactions of the hitters on the tape reveal that when Moyer is on the mound, the batter's box feels like the Twilight Zone. We watch as Moyer renders the Yankees outfielder, John Vander Wal, helpless. He actually jams him with a fastball—that is, Vander Wal is unable to get his bat around quickly enough to hit it squarely.

"You know how many times Moyer jams guys with an eighty-mile-an-hour fastball?" says Hatteberg. "*All the time.* It's because he sets it up with a sixty-nine-mile-an-hour change-up." He fast-forwards to a slow curve, and an even slower change-up. "See," he says, "All this other shit is what makes his fastball look like ninety-four." He watches Moyer jam two more left-handed hitters with 82-mph fastballs and says, "He'll do this to me, too. If he gets two strikes on me, he'll try to get me pitching me inside." Then he reconsiders, and smiles, and says, "Unless he thinks I'm looking inside."

Moyer was one of the few pitchers in baseball who would think about Scott Hatteberg as much as Hatteberg thought about him. Moyer would know that Hatteberg never swung at the first pitch—except to keep a pitcher honest—and so Moyer might just throw a first-pitch strike. But Moyer would also know that Hatteberg knew that Moyer knew. Which brought Hatteberg back to square one.

He was knee-deep in game theory, and he had only an hour before he had to play the game. One of the big reasons he watched tape was to see if a pitcher "patterned himself"—that is, if you could count on seeing a certain pitch from him in a certain count. Moyer scrambled his pitches so thoroughly that looking for patterns was a waste of time. Moyer he watched just to imagine how it might go.

Then John Mabry walked into the video room.

"Hey, Hatty."

Hatty makes room for Mabry at the video screen. Hatty glances back at Feiny and says "I understand there's been some lipreading going on in here."

"Oh yeah?" says Mabry.

Feiny reddens and Mabry smiles—sort of. Mabry and Feiny have something like a running argument going, about why Mabry doesn't play more. Right after he came over from the Phillies, in exchange for Jeremy Giambi, Mabry had been torrid. Over the course of several weeks, playing irregularly, he'd hit over .400, with half a dozen homers, and still the manager seemed reluctant to write his name in the lineup. He'd asked Feiny why. The manager won't put him in the lineup, Feiny has explained, because the front office don't want him in the lineup.

What bothered Billy Beane about Mabry's approach to hitting was that it was the opposite of Scott Hatteberg's. When Mabry stepped into a batter's box, he intended to swing from the heels at the first pitch that looked tasty. Mabry made an enthusiastic case that a pinch hitter, to succeed, needs to be wildly aggressive, but it's not a case Billy cares to hear. Billy, for reasons he refuses to explain, is willing to have John Mabry in an A's uniform but he doesn't want to go so far as to let Mabry *play*. When Art Howe put Mabry in a few games, to give other guys a rest, and Mabry had started hitting homers, both Billy and Paul reacted as if they had walked into the casino, stuck a quarter into a slot machine, and hit the jackpot. They'd gotten lucky; it was now time to leave with their winnings. "Mabry's a great guy," Billy had said the other night, "but sooner or later Tattoo's going to show up and take him off the island."

A few days earlier Mabry had complained to Feiny about his lack of playing time, and Feiny had tried to help him out. "You know, John," he'd said, "maybe you want to try taking a few pitches."

That night Mabry had played—with Feiny's voice in his head. The first time he came to the plate he took the first five pitches he saw—till the count was full: 3–2. The next pitch he took a giant hack at, and struck out. The television camera read his lips as he walked back to the dugout. "Fucking Feinstein," he said. Mabry wound up walking twice and one of those walks led to a run that won the game; still, it was unclear whether he had forgiven Feiny—or even if he thought Feiny needed forgiving.

Mabry, too, is playing tonight. He sees the tape of Moyer, and wants to discuss him.

"This guy is hard to prepare for," Mabry says. "He chews up young guys because he feeds on their aggression."

"He's just so different from everyone else," says Hatty. "You're gauged for harder speeds. You almost have to remember your old high school swing."

"He preys on your aggression," says Mabry, making whatever Moyer does sound slightly vampirish. "He makes you think you can hit pitches you can't even reach."

"If it's not a strike, how hard it is to lay off?" asks Feiny. He's still staring into his own screen, watching Alex Rodriguez at bat.

"Oh, it's hard," says Mabry. On the screen Moyer doesn't seem to be pitching so much as tossing. I've seen less arc on ceremonial first pitches.

"Just lay off the bad pitches, John," says Feiny teasingly.

"Feiny," says Mabry testily. "You ever been in a major league batter's box?"

Feiny doesn't answer.

"I'm telling you," says Mabry, turning back. He points to the screen, on which Moyer tosses another cream puff. "You see that coming at you and it looks like you can hit it three miles."

"So just don't swing, John," says Feiny.

"Yeah," says Mabry, turning around again to glare at Feiny. "Well, the time you don't swing is the time he throws you three strikes."

"He is a really smart guy," agrees Hatty, looking to settle the dispute. "He's tough to plan for."

But Mabry is still staring at Feiny, who is refusing to stare back. "Feiny, have you ever faced a major league pitcher?"

"No, John," says Feiny, wearily, "I've never faced a major league pitcher."

"I didn't think so," says Mabry. "I didn't think Feiny had ever faced a major league pitcher."

That looked as if it might be a conversation-stopper. Then David Justice walks in. He sees that they've been watching the tape of Moyer and knows instantly what they're arguing about. They're arguing about the price of greed in the batter's box. Your only hope against a pitcher with Moyer's command of the strike zone, Justice says, is to give up on the idea that you are going to get rich and satisfy yourself with just making a living. "You think you can hit it out," says Justice, "but you can't hit it at all."

"Exactly," says Mabry.

"Which is why you don't swing at it," says Feiny.

Mabry just gets up and leaves. When he's gone, Hatteberg considers why everyone doesn't prepare for Jamie Moyer as he does—by watching tape, imagining what will happen, deciding what to look for, deciding what he will *never* swing at. "Some of the guys who are the best are the dumbest," he says. "I don't mean dumbest. I mean they don't have a thought. No system."

Stupidity is an asset?

"Absolutely. Guys can't set you up. You have no pattern. You can't even remember your last at bat." He laughs. "Arrogance is an asset, too. Stupidity and arrogance: I don't have either one. *And it taunts me.*"

He soon needs to stop thinking about playing and actually play. During the game he's as finicky as ever. He waits for pitches like a man picking through an apple bin at a grocery store, looking for the ripest. The first time up, the fruit's no good. He just stares at the first four pitches, all millimeters off the plate, and walks down to first base. His second time up, Moyer throws strikes. Hatteberg watches the first go by, and fouls off the second. With two strikes he thought Moyer would pitch him inside, and he does. He lines it into right field for a single, and knocks in what would prove to be the only run of the game. The third at bat he hits a shot to deep left that looked gone for a moment but wound up being caught on the warning track.

But none of those first three at bats stuck in Hatty's mind like the fourth. The fourth and final time he came to the plate, Moyer teased him with pitches on the edge of the strike zone and quickly got ahead 0–2. The next four pitches were either balls Hatty took or strikes he fouled off, because he couldn't do anything more with them. Six pitches into the at bat, with the count 2–2, Jamie

Moyer walks off the mound. He actually says something to Hatty, and stands there, as if waiting for an answer.

This is new. Hatty's at bats, inevitably, are conversations, but the non-verbal kind. The pitcher isn't supposed to stop in the middle of the game for a sociable chat. "I'd never had a pitcher talk to me while I was in the batter's box," he says. With Moyer just standing there, refusing to budge, Hatteberg steps out of the box: "What?" he shouts.

"Just tell me what you want," says Moyer wearily.

Hatty shrugs, as he doesn't know what to say.

"Tell me what you want and I'll throw it," says Moyer.

Hatty was always having to make a guess about what was coming next. His ability to do it depended on his knowing that the pitcher was trying to fool him. This more straightforward approach made him uneasy. It screwed up some inner calculation, threw him off-balance. He didn't feel comfortable. For once, he couldn't think of anything to say. And so he didn't say anything. He didn't want to know. He preferred to stick with his approach.

On the next pitch Moyer throws a change-up and Hatteberg hits right back at him. Just another out—and yet it wasn't. He did what he did so quietly that the market in general never perceived the value in it. Scott Hatteberg will finish the season at or near the top of a couple of odd statistical categories, and one not-so-odd one. He'll be first in the entire American League in not swinging at first pitches, and third in the percentage of pitches he doesn't swing at (64.5 percent). Trivial accomplishments, if they did not lead to another, less trivial one. At the end of the season Paul DePodesta will measure the performance of every A's hitter. He'll want to know how efficient each has been with his plate opportunities. He'll answer that question in an unorthodox way, by asking: how many runs would a lineup produce that consisted of nine perfect replicas of that hitter? If Scott Hatteberg, for example, had taken every single at bat for the Oakland A's in 2002, how many runs would he have generated? Nine Scott Hattebergs generate between 940 and 950 runs, tied for the Oakland A's lead with Miguel Tejada and Eric Chavez, obviously much flashier hitters. The offensively explosive 2002 New York Yankees, by comparison, scored 897 runs. Nine Scott Hattebergs are, by some measure, the best offense in baseball.

Chapter Nine

THE TRADING DESK

It's not like I'm making pitching changes
during the game.
—Billy Beane, quoted in the *Boston Herald*, January 16, 2003

IT WAS LATE JULY, which is to say that Mike Magnante had picked a bad time to pitch poorly. "Mags," as everyone called him, had come in against Cleveland in the top of the seventh with two runners on and a three-run lead. The first thing he did was to walk Jim Thome—no one could blame him for that. He then gave up a bloop single to Milton Bradley and the inherited runners scored—just plain bad luck, that. But then he threw three straight balls to Lee Stevens. Stevens dutifully took a strike, then waited for Mags to throw his fifth pitch.

The first question Billy Beane will ask Art Howe after the game is why the fuck he'd brought Magnante into a tight game. In tight situations Art was supposed to use Chad Bradford. Bradford was the ace of the pen. So that it would be clear in Art's head, Billy had instructed him to think of Bradford as "the closer before the ninth inning." Art's first answer about Magnante was that he thought Mags, the lefty, would be more effective than Bradford, the righty, against a left-handed slugger like Thome. Which is nuts, since

Mags hasn't gotten anyone out in weeks and Bradford has been good against lefties. Art's second answer is that Billy put Mags on the team, and if a guy is on the team, you need to use him. Art won't say this directly to Billy but he'll think it. The coaching staff had grown tired of hearing Billy holler at them for using Magnante. "The guy has got braces on both legs," says pitching coach Rick Peterson. "We're not going to use him as a pinch runner. If you don't want us to use him, trade him."

Mike Magnante goes into his stretch and looks in for the signal. He just last month turned thirty-seven, and is four days shy of the ten full years of big league service he needs to collect a full pension. It's not hard to see what's wrong with him, to discern the defect that makes him available to the Oakland A's. He is pear-shaped and slack-jawed and looks less like a professional baseball player than most of the beat reporters who cover the team. But he has a reason to hope: his history of pitching better in the second half than the first. The team opened the season with three lefties in the bullpen, which is two more than most clubs carried. A month ago they'd released one, Mike Holtz, and two days ago sent down the other, Mike Venafro. The story Mike Magnante told himself on the eve of July 29, 2002, was that he hadn't pitched often enough to find his rhythm. He'd go a week when he made only three pitches in a game. With the other Mikes gone, he finally had his chance to find his rhythm.

He makes an almost perfect pitch to Lee Stevens, a fastball low and away. The catcher is set up low and outside. When you saw the replay, you understood that he'd hit his spot. If he'd missed, it was only by half an inch. It's the pitch Mike Magnante wanted to make. Good pitch, bad count. The ball catches the fat part of the bat. It rises and rises and the two runners on base begin to circle ahead of the hitter. Mags can only stand and watch: an opposite field shot at night in Oakland is a rare, impressive sight. It is Lee Stevens's first home run as a Cleveland Indian. By the time the ball lands, the first and third basemen are closing in on the mound

like bailiffs, and Art Howe is on the top of the dugout steps. He's
given up five runs and gotten nobody out. It wasn't the first time
that he'd been knocked out of the game, but it wasn't often he'd
been knocked out on his pitch. That's what happens when you're
thirty-seven years old: you do the things you always did but the
result is somehow different.

The game is effectively over. Chad Bradford will come on and
get three quick outs, too late. The Indians' own left-handed relief
pitcher, Ricardo Rincon, strikes out David Justice on three pitches
and gets Eric Chavez to pop out on four. The contrast cast Mags in
unflattering light. The A's had the weakest left-handed relief
pitching in the league and the Indians had some of the strongest.
To see the difference, Billy Beane didn't even need to watch the
game.

H AVING JUST FINISHED an enthusiastic impersonation of a baseball owner pretending to be a farm animal receiving a beating,
Billy Beane rose back into his desk chair and waited, impatiently,
for Mark Shapiro to call. Mark Shapiro was the general manager of
the Cleveland Indians.

When Billy sat upright in his office, a few yards from the Coliseum, he faced a wall covered entirely by a white board and, on it,
the names of the several hundred players controlled by the Oakland A's. Mike Magnante's name was on that board. Swiveling
around to his rear he faced another white board with the names of
the nearly twelve hundred players on other major league rosters.
Ricardo Rincon's name was on that board. At this point in the year
Billy didn't really need to look at these boards to make connec-
tions; he knew every player on other teams that he wanted, and
every player in his own system that he didn't want. The trick was
to persuade other teams to buy his guys for more than they were
worth, and sell their guys for less than they were worth. He'd done
this so effectively the past few years that he was finding other

teams less eager to do business with him. The Cleveland Indians were not yet one of those teams.

Waiting for Shapiro to call him, Billy distracted himself by paying attention to several things at once. On his desk was the most recent issue of *Harvard Magazine*, containing an article about a Harvard professor of statistics named Carl Morris (the Bill James fan). The article explained how Morris had used statistical theory to determine the number of runs a team could expect to score in the different states of a baseball game. No outs with no one on base: 55. No outs with a runner on first base: 90. And so on for each of the twenty-four possible states of a baseball game. "We knew this three years ago," says Billy, "and Harvard thinks it's original."

He shoves a wad of tobacco into his upper lip, then turns back to his computer screen, which displays the Amazon.com home page. In his hand he's got a review he's ripped out of *Time* magazine, of a novel called *The Dream of Scipio*, a thriller with intellectual pretension. He reads the sentence of the review that has made him a buyer: "Civilization had made them men of learning, but in order to save it they must leave their studies and become men of action." As he taps on his computer keyboard, the television over his head replays Mike Magnante's home run ball of the night before. The Oakland A's announcers are trying to explain why the Oakland A's are still behind the Anaheim Angels and the Seattle Mariners in the division standings. "The main reason this team is trailing in the American League West," an announcer says, "is that they haven't hit in the clutch, they haven't hit with guys in scoring position." Billy drops the book review, forgets about Amazon, and reaches for the TV remote control. Of the many false beliefs peddled by the TV announcers, this fealty to "clutch hitting" was maybe the most maddening to Billy Beane. "It's fucking luck," he says, and faces around the dial until he finds *Moneyline* with Lou Dobbs. He prefers watching money shows to watching baseball anyway.

On the eve of the trading deadline, July 30, he was still pursuing two players, and one of them is the Cleveland Indians' left-hander, Ricardo Rincon. At that very moment, Rincon is still just a few yards away, inside the visitor's locker room, dressing to play the second game of the three-game series against the Oakland A's. The night before, he'd only thrown seven pitches. His arm, no doubt, felt good. The Cleveland Indians have given up any hope of winning this year, and are now busy selling off their parts. "The premier left-handed setup man is just a luxury we can't afford," said Indians' GM Shapiro. Shapiro has shopped Rincon around the league and told Billy that there is at least one other bidder. Billy has found out—he won't say how—that the other bidder is the San Francisco Giants and that the Giants' offer may be better than his. All Billy has offered the Indians is a minor league second baseman named Marshall MacDougal. MacDougal isn't that bad a player.

Anyone seeking to understand how this team with no money kept winning more and more games would do well to notice their phenomenal ability to improve in the middle of a season. Ever since 1999 the Oakland A's have played like a different team after the All-Star break than before it. Last year they had been almost bizarrely better: 44–43 before the break, 58–17 after it. Since the All-Star Game was created, in 1933, no other team had ever won so many of its final seventy-five games.*

The reason the Oakland A's, as run by Billy Beane, played as if they were a different team in the second half of the season is that they *were* a different team. As spring turned to summer the market allowed Billy to do things that he could do at no other time of the year. The bad teams lost hope. With the loss of hope came a

---

* Tom Ruane, a researcher associated with Retrosheet, which had evolved from Bill James's Project Scoresheet, offers this calculation: the only team since 1961 with a better second-half record over a four-year stretch than the Oakland A's in 1999–2002 were the 1991–94 Atlanta Braves, and *no* team over a four-year stretch has improved itself in midseason by so much.

desire to cut costs. With the desire to cut costs came the dumping of players. As the supply of players rose, their prices fell. By midsummer, Billy Beane was able to acquire players he could never have afforded at the start of the season. By the middle of June, six weeks before the trading deadline, he was walking into Paul DePodesta's office across the hall from his own and saying, "This is the time to make a fucking A trade." When asked what was meant by a "Fucking A trade," he said, "A Fucking A trade is one that causes everyone else in the business to say 'Fucking A.'"

By late July—the trade deadline was July 31—Billy's antennae for bargains quivered. Shopping for players just before the deadline was like shopping for used designer dresses on the day after the Oscars, or for secondhand engagement rings in Reno. His goal at the start of the season had been to build a team good enough to remain in contention until the end of June. On July 1, the American League West standings looked like this:

	Wins	Losses	Games Behind
Seattle	52	30	—
Anaheim	47	33	4
Oakland	46	36	6
Texas	35	45	16

Having kept the team close enough to hope, Billy could now go out and shop for whatever else he needed to get to the play-offs. When he set off on this shopping spree, he kept in mind five simple rules:

1. "No matter how successful you are, change is always good. There can never be a status quo. When you have no money you can't afford long-term solutions, only short-term ones. You have to always be upgrading. Otherwise you're fucked."

2. "The day you say you have to do something, you're screwed. Because you are going to make a bad deal. You can always

recover from the player you didn't sign. You may never recover from the player you signed at the wrong price."

3. "Know exactly what every player in baseball is worth to you. You can put a dollar figure on it."

4. "Know exactly who you want and go after him." (Never mind who they say they want to trade.)

5. "Every deal you do will be publicly scrutinized by subjective opinion. If I'm [IBM CEO] Lou Gerstner, I'm not worried that every personnel decision I make is going to wind up on the front page of the business section. Not everyone believes that they know everything about the personal computer. But everyone who ever picked up a bat thinks he knows baseball. To do this well, you have to ignore the newspapers."

His complete inability to heed Rule #5 Billy Beane compensated for by fanatically heeding the other four. His approach to the market for baseball players was by its nature unsystematic. Unsystematic—and yet incredibly effective.

The absence of cash is always a problem for a man on a shopping spree. Ricardo Rincon would be owed $508,000 for the rest of the season, and that is $508,000 the Oakland A's owners won't agree to spend. To get Rincon, Billy must not only persuade Indians GM Shapiro that his is the highest bid; he must find the money to pay Rincon's salary. Where? If he gets Rincon, he doesn't need Mike Magnante. No one else does either, so he's unlikely to save money there. No matter what he does, the A's will wind up eating Magnante's salary. But he might well be able to move Mike Venafro, the low-budget left-handed reliever he had just sent down to Triple-A. Venafro is a lot younger than Magnante. Other teams might be interested in him.

This gives Billy an idea: auction Mike Venafro to teams that might be competing with him for Ricardo Rincon.

He knows that the San Francisco Giants are after Rincon. He knows also that the Giants don't have much to spend, and that, if offered a cheaper option, they might be less inclined to stretch for Rincon. "Let's make them skinnier," he says, and picks up the phone and calls Brian Sabean, the GM of the Giants. He'll offer Venafro to the Giants for almost nothing. In a stroke he'll raise cash he needs to buy Rincon (because he won't have to pay Venafro's salary) and possibly also reduce his competitor's interest in Rincon, as they'll now see they have, in Venafro, an alternative.

Brian Sabean listens to Billy's magnanimous offer of Mike Venafro; all Billy wants in return is a minor league player. Sabean says he's interested. "Sabes," Billy says, after laying out his proposal, "I'm not asking for much here. Think it over and call me back."

The moment he hangs up he calls Mark Shapiro, current owner of Ricardo Rincon, and tells him that he has the impression that the market for Rincon is softening. Whoever the other bidder is, he says, Shapiro ought to make sure his offer is firm.

As he puts down the phone, Paul pokes his head into the office. "Billy, what about the Mets on Venafro? Just to have options." Sabean is the master of the dry hump. Sabean is always expressing what seems like serious interest in a player, but when it comes time to deal, he becomes less serious.

"The Mets could be after Rincon," says Billy.

The phone rings. It is Mark Shapiro, calling right back. He tells Billy that, by some amazing coincidence, the other buyer for Rincon has just called to lower his offer. Billy leans forward in his chair, chaw clenched in his upper lip, as if waiting to see if a fly ball hit by an Oakland A will clear the wall. He raises his fist as it does. "I just need to talk to my owner," he says. "Thanks, Mark."

He puts down the phone. "We have a two-hour window on Rincon," he says. He now has a purpose: two hours to find $508,000 from another team, or to somehow sell his owner on the deal. Never mind that his owner, Steve Schott, has already said that he won't spend the money to buy Rincon. He shouts across the hall. "Paul! What's left on Venafro's contract?"

"Two hundred and seventy thousand, eight hundred and thirty-three dollars."

He does the math. If he unloads Venafro, he'll still need to find another $233,000 to cover Rincon's salary, but he isn't thinking about that just yet. His owners have told him only that they won't eat 508 grand; they've said nothing about eating 233 grand. He has two hours to find someone who will take Venafro off his hands. The Mets are a good idea. Billy picks up the phone and dials the number for Steve Phillips, the general manager of the Mets. A secretary answers.

"Denise," says Billy, "Billy Beane, Vice President and General Manager of the Oakland Athletics. Denise, who is the best-looking GM in the game?" Pause. "Exactly right, Denise. Is Steve there?"

Steve isn't there but someone named Jimmy is. "Jimmy," says Billy." Hey, how you doin'? Got a question for you. You guys looking for a left-handed reliever?"

He raises his fist again. Yes! He tells Jimmy about Venafro. "I can make it real quick for you," he says. He knows he wants to trade Venafro, but he doesn't know who he wants in return.

How quick?

"Fifteen minutes?"

Fine.

"I can give you names in fifteen minutes," says Billy. "Yeah, look I'd do this if I were you. And I'm not shitting you here, Jimmy. I'm being honest with you."

Paul sees what is happening and walks out the door before Billy is finished. "I gotta find some more prospects," he says. He needs to find who they want from the Mets in exchange for Venafro.

Billy hangs up. "Paul! We got fifteen minutes to get names." He finds Paul already in his office flipping through various handbooks that list all players owned by the Mets. He takes the seat across from him and grabs one of the books and together they rifle through the entire Mets farm system, stat by stat. It's a new game:

maximize what you get from the Mets farm system inside of fifteen minutes. They're like a pair of shoppers who have been allowed into Costco before the official opening time and told that anything they can cart out the door in the next fifteen minutes they can have for free. The A's president, Mike Crowley, walks by and laughs. "What's the rush?" he says. "We don't need Rincon until the sixth or seventh inning."

"What about Bennett?" asks Paul.

"How old is he?" asks Billy.

"Twenty-six."

"Fuck, he's twenty-six and in Double-A. Forget it."

Billy stops at a name and laughs. "Virgil Chevalier? Who is that?"

"How about Eckert?" says Paul. "But he's twenty-five."

"How about this guy?" says Billy, and laughs. "Just for his name alone. *Furbush!*"

Anyone older than about twenty-three who is desirable will be too obviously desirable for the Mets to give up. They're looking for a player whose promise they have a better view of than the Mets. Someone very young. It will be someone they do not know, and have never seen, and have researched for thirty seconds.

"How about Garcia?" Paul finally asks.

"What's Garcia? Twenty-two?"

"Twenty-two," says Paul.

He shows Billy the stats for Garcia and Billy says, "Garcia's good. I'll ask for Garcia." He gets up and walks back to his office. "Fuck!" he says, on the way. "I know what I'll do. Why don't we go back to them and say, 'Give us cash too!' What's the difference between Rincon and Venafro?"

Paul punches numbers into his calculator: 232,923.

"I'll ask him for two hundred and thirty-three grand *plus* the prospect," says Billy. "The money doesn't mean anything to the Mets."

Being poor means treating rich teams as petty cash dispensers:

$233,000 is the difference between Venafro and Rincon's salaries for the rest of the season. If he can get the Mets to give him the $233,000, he doesn't even need to call his owner. He can just make the deal himself.

He pauses before he picks up the phone. "Should I call Sabean first?" He's asking himself; the answer, also provided by himself, is no. As Billy calls Steve Phillips, Paul reappears. "Billy," he says "you might also ask for Duncan. What can they say? He's hitting .217."

"Who would we rather have, Garcia or Duncan?" asks Billy.

The Mets' secretary answers before Paul. Billy leans back and smiles. "Denise," he says, "Billy Beane. Vice President and General Manager of the Oakland Athletics. Denise, who is the *coolest* GM in the game?" Pause. "Right again, Denise." Denise's laughter reaches the far end of Billy's office. "Billy has the gift of making people like him," said the man who had made Billy a general manager, Sandy Alderson. "It's a dangerous gift to have."

This time Steve Phillips is present, and ready to talk. "Look, I'm not going to ask you for a lot," says Billy generously, as if the whole thing had been Phillips's idea. "I need a player and two hundred and thirty-three grand. I'm not going to ask you for anyone really good. I have a couple of names I want to run by you. Garcia the second baseman and Duncan the outfielder who hit .217 last year."

Phillips, like every other GM who has just received a call from Billy Beane, assumes there must be some angle he isn't seeing. He asks why Billy sent Venafro down to Triple-A. He's worried about Venafro's health. He wonders why Billy is now asking for money, too.

"Venafro's *fine*, Steve," says Billy. He's back to selling used cars. "This is just a situation for us. I need the money for . . . something else I want to do later."

Phillips says he still wonders what's up with Venafro. The last few times he's pitched, he has been hammered. Billy sighs: it's

harder turning Mike Venafro into a New York Met than he supposed. "Steve, me and you both know that you don't judge a
pitcher by the last nine innings he threw. Art misused him. You
should use him for a whole inning. He's good against righties too!"

For whatever reason the fish refuses the bait. At that moment
Billy realizes: the Mets are hemming and hawing about Venafro
because they think *they* are going to get Rincon. "Look," says
Billy. "Here's the deal, Steve." He's no longer selling used cars.
He's organizing a high school fire drill, and tolerating no cutups.
"I'm going to get Rincon. It's a done deal. Yeah. It's *done*. The
Giants want Venafro. I've told them they can have him for a
player: Luke Robertson."

"Anderson," whispers Paul.

"Luke Anderson," says Billy, easing off. "We like Anderson. We
think he's going to be in the big leagues. But I'd like to deal with
you because Sabes doesn't have any money. You can win this
because you can give me two hundred thirty-three grand in cash,
and he can't. I don't have to have the two hundred thirty-three
grand in cash. But it makes enough of a difference to me that I'll
work with you." He's ceased to be the fire drill instructor and
become the personal trainer. You can do it, Steve! You can win!

Whatever place he's reached in the conversation, he likes.
"Yeah," he says. "It doesn't have to be Garcia or Duncan. I'll find
a player with you. If it makes you feel better." (*I want you, and
only you, to have Venafro.*) "Okay, Steve. Whoever calls me back
first gets Venafro." (*But if you drag your heels you'll regret it for
the rest of your life.*)

Billy's assistant tells him that Peter Gammons, the ESPN
reporter, is on the line. In the hours leading up to the trade deadline Billy refuses to take calls from several newspaper reporters.
One will get through to him by accident and he'll make her regret
that she did. Most reporters, in Billy's experience, are simply trying to be the first to find out something they'll all learn anyway
before their deadlines. "They all want scoops," he complains.

"There are no scoops. Whatever we do will be in every paper tomorrow. There's no such thing as a paper that comes out in an hour."

It's different when Peter Gammons calls. The difference between Gammons and the other reporters is that Gammons might actually tell him something he doesn't know. "Let's get some info," he says, and picks up the phone. Gammons asks about Rincon and Billy says, casually, "Yeah, I'm just finishing up Rincon," as if it's a done deal, which clearly it is not. He knows Gammons will tell others what he tells him. Then the quid pro quo: Gammons tells Billy that the Montreal Expos have decided to trade their slugging outfielder, Cliff Floyd, to the Boston Red Sox. Billy quickly promises Gammons that he'll be the first to know whatever he does, then hangs up the phone and says, "Shit."

Cliff Floyd was the other player Billy was trying to get. "There's more than one season," Billy often said. What he really meant was that, in the course of a single season, there was more than one team called the Oakland Athletics. There was, for a start, the team that had opened the season and that, on May 23, he'd booted out of town. Three eighths of his starting lineup, and a passel of pitchers. Players who just a couple of months earlier he'd sworn by he dumped, without so much as a wave good-bye. Jeremy Giambi, for instance. Back in April, Jeremy had been Exhibit A in Billy Beane's lecture on The New and Better Way to Think About Building a Baseball Team. Jeremy proved Billy's point that a chubby, slow unknown could be the league's best leadoff hitter. All Billy would now say about Jeremy is that walking over to the Coliseum to tell him he was fired was "like shooting Old Yeller."

There was a less sentimental story about Old Yeller, but it never got told. In mid-May, as the Oakland A's were being swept in Toronto by the Blue Jays, Billy's behavior became erratic. Driving home at night he'd miss his exit and wind up ten miles down the road before he'd realize what had happened. He'd phone Paul DePodesta all hours of the night and say, "Don't think I'm going to put up with this shit. Don't think I won't do something." When the team arrived back in Oakland, he detected what he felt was an overly upbeat tone in the clubhouse. He told the team's coaches, "Losing shouldn't be fun. It's not fun for me. If I'm going to be miserable, you're going to be miserable."

Just before the Toronto series the team had been in Boston, where Jeremy Giambi had made the mistake of being spotted by a newspaper reporter at a strip club. Jeremy, it should be said, already had a bit of a reputation. Before spring training he'd been caught with marijuana by the Las Vegas Police. Reports from coaches trickled in that Jeremy drank too much on team flights. When the reports from Boston reached Billy Beane, Jeremy ceased to be an on-base machine and efficient offensive weapon. He became a twenty-seven-year-old professional baseball player having too much fun on a losing team. In a silent rage, Billy called around the league to see who would take Jeremy off his hands. He didn't care what he got in return. Actually, that wasn't quite true: what he needed in return was something to tell the press. "We traded Jeremy for X because we think X will give us help on defense," or some such nonsense. The Phillies offered John Mabry. Billy hardly knew who Mabry was.

On the way to tell Jeremy Giambi that he was fired, Billy tried to sell what he was doing to Paul DePodesta. "This is the worst baseball decision I've ever made," he said, "but it's the best decision I've made as a GM." Paul knew it was crap, and said so. All the way to the clubhouse he tried to talk Billy down from his pique. He tried to explain to his boss how irrational he'd become. He wasn't thinking objectively. He was just looking for someone on whom to vent his anger.

Billy refused to listen. After he'd done the deal, he told reporters that he traded Jeremy Giambi because he was "concerned he was too one-dimensional" and that John Mabry would supply help on defense. He then leaned on Art Howe to keep Mabry out of the lineup. And Art, occasionally, ignored him. And Mabry proceeded to swat home runs and game-winning hits at a rate he had never before swatted them in his entire professional career. And the Oakland A's began to win. When Billy traded Jeremy Giambi, the A's were 20–25; they had lost 14 of their previous 17 games. Two months later, they were 60–46. Everyone now said what a genius Billy Beane was to have seen the talent hidden inside John Mabry. Shooting Old Yeller had paid off.

Neither his trading of Jeremy Giambi nor the other moves he had made had the flavor of a careful lab experiment. It felt more as if the scientist, infuriated that the results of his careful experiment weren't coming out as they were meant to, waded into his lab and began busting test tubes. Which made what happened now even more astonishing: as Billy Beane sat in his office in July, just a few months after he'd chucked out three eighths of the starting lineup, he insisted that the shake-up hadn't been the least bit necessary. Between phone calls to other general managers he explained how the purge he'd conducted back in May, in which he'd ditched players left and right, "probably had no effect. We were 21–26 at the time. That's a small sample size. We'd have been fine if I'd done nothing." The most he will admit is that perhaps his actions had some "placebo effect." And the most astonishing thing of all is that he almost believes it.

Two months later, he still didn't want to talk about Jeremy Giambi. All that mattered was that the Oakland A's were winning again. But they were still in third place in the absurdly strong American League West, and Billy worried that this year good might not be good enough. "We can win ninety games and have a nice little season," he said. "But sometimes you have to say 'fuck it' and swing for the fences."

And so he flailed about, seemingly at random, calling GMs and proposing this deal or that, trying to make a Fucking A trade. "Trawling" is what he called this activity. His constant chatter was a way of keeping tabs on the body of information critical to his trading success: the value the other GMs were assigning to

individual players. Trading players wasn't any different from trading stocks and bonds. A trader with better information could
make a killing, and Billy was fairly certain he had better information. He certainly had different information. In a short two months
with the Oakland A's, for instance, Carlos Pena had transformed
himself from a player Billy Beane coveted more than any other
minor leaguer into a player everyone valued more highly than
Billy did. He knew—or thought he knew—that Carlos was over-
valued. The only question was: how much could he get for him?

Dangling Carlos from a hook, Billy tried to lure the Pittsburgh
Pirates into giving him their slugging outfielder Brian Giles. When
the Pirates resisted, he offered to send Carlos and his fourth outfielder Adam Piatt to Boston for outfielder Trot Nixon, and then
send Trot Nixon and the A's flame-throwing Triple-A reliever,
Franklyn German, to Pittsburgh for Giles. Again, no luck. He then
gave up on Giles and tried and failed to talk Cleveland's GM,
Shapiro, into sending him both his ace, Bartolo Colon, and his best
hitter, Jim Thome, for Cory Lidle and Carlos Pena.

In all of this Billy Beane was bound to fail a lot more than he
succeeded: but he didn't mind! The failure wasn't public; the success it led to was. Trawling in late June, using Carlos Pena as
chum, he stumbled upon a new willingness of the Detroit Tigers
to trade their young but expensive ace, Jeff Weaver. Billy didn't
have much interest in Jeff Weaver (at $2.4 million a year, pricey)
but he knew that the Yankees would, and he had long coveted the
Yankees' only young, cheap, starting pitcher, Ted Lilly (as good as
Weaver, in Billy's view, and a bargain at $237,000). He sent Carlos
Pena to Detroit for Weaver, then passed Weaver to New York for
Lilly *plus* a pair of the Yankees' hottest prospects. Somehow, in
the bargain, he also extracted from Detroit $600,000. When Yan-
kees GM Brian Cashman asked him how on earth he'd done that,
Billy told him that it was "my brokerage fee."

That had happened on July 5. He wasn't finished; really he was
just getting started. He made a run at Tampa Bay's center fielder

Randy Winn and while Tampa Bay's management was willing to talk to Billy, they were too frightened of him to deal with him. One former Tampa executive says that "after the way Billy took [starting pitcher Cory] Lidle from them, they'll never deal with him again. He terrifies them." He came close to getting Kansas City outfielder Raul Ibanez, but then Ibanez went on a hitting tear that led Kansas City to reevaluate his merits and decide that Billy Beane was about to pick their pockets again. (The year before, at the trade deadline, Billy had given Kansas City nothing terribly useful for Jermaine Dye, just as, the year before, he'd given them next to nothing for Johnny Damon.)

With Carlos Pena gone, Billy re-baited his hook with Cory Lidle. Lidle had pitched poorly during the first half of the season but he was starting to look better. When Lidle went out to pitch, Billy rooted for him as he never had before—not simply for Lidle to win but for Lidle's stock to rise. Kenny Williams, GM of the Chicago White Sox, expressed an interest in Lidle. Billy suggested a package that would yield, in return, the White Sox's slugging outfielder Magglio Ordonez. The White Sox declined, but that conversation led to another, in which Billy discovered that the White Sox were willing to part with their All-Star second baseman and leadoff hitter, Ray Durham. To get Durham *and* the cash to pay the rest of Durham's 2002 salary, all Billy had to give up was one flame-throwing Triple-A pitcher named Jon Adkins. Over the past eighteen months Billy had traded every pitcher in the A's farm system whose fastball exceeded 95 miles per hour—except Adkins.

Ray Durham, acquired on July 15, had been a Fucking A trade. (It quickly inspired an article on baseballprospectus.com, the leading sabermetric Web site, with the title: "Kenny Williams, A's Fan.") In getting Durham, Billy got a lot more than just half of a season from a very fine player. Durham would be declared a Type A free agent at the end of the season. Lose a Type A free agent and you received a first-round draft pick plus a compensation pick at the end of the first round. If Kenny Williams valued those draft picks properly, he would have kept Durham on until the end of the season, and then let him walk. Those two draft picks alone were worth paying Ray Durham to play half a season; they were certainly worth more than the minor league pitcher the White Sox acquired for Durham.

This trading strategy came with a new risk, however. Baseball owners and players were, by the end of July, at work hammering out a new labor agreement. The players were threatening to strike; the owners were threatening to let them. *The Blue Ribbon Panel Report* had put oomph behind a movement, led by Milwaukee Brewer owner and baseball commissioner Bud Selig, to constrain players' salaries and share revenues among teams. One of Selig's proposals—tentatively agreed to by the players' union—was to eliminate compensation for free agents. No more draft picks. Billy Beane was making a bet: it wouldn't happen. The only way a new labor agreement occurs, he assumed, is if the players agree to some form of constraint on market forces, either through teams sharing revenues or some form of salary cap. And if they agree to that, the owners will be so relieved that they give the players what they want on every smaller issue.* "This is a small issue in the big picture," he says. "The history of the union negotiations tells you that they're never going to acquiesce to the slightest detail. If the owners do get revenue sharing, it's going to be, 'Grab your ankles.' It's going to be, 'Do what you want with me. Beat me like a farm animal.'"†

---

* You might think the players would want to eliminate the need for the rich teams that signed free agents to compensate the poor ones that had lost them. The practice was a tax on free agency. But the practice also gave the players' union veto power over any changes that the owners might want to make in the amateur draft, and this they valued even more highly.

† He was right about the draft picks.

Whereupon he bent over to illustrate what the owner of a baseball team might look like, were he to play the farm animal.

Cliff Floyd was Ray Durham all over again. Floyd would be a free agent at the end of the season and so, like Durham, a ticket for two more first-round draft picks. The trouble with Floyd, from the point of view of an impoverished team looking to acquire him, was that he was the only big star still left on the market. "His value will only fall so far," says Billy.

In the time he spent trying to nail down Rincon, he had lost Floyd. Or so it seemed. Now he notices he has a voice mail message. While he was talking to Gammons, someone else called. He's thinking it might be Sabean or Phillips calling to take Venafro's 270 grand paycheck off his hands. Money is what he needs, and he hits his telephone keypad as if there's money inside. There isn't. "Billy," says the soft, pleasant, recorded voice. "It's Omar Minaya. Call me back, okay?" Omar Minaya is the Montreal Expos' GM. Omar Minaya controls the fate of Cliff Floyd.

Billy puts his head in his hands and says, "Let me think." Which he does for about ten seconds, then calls Omar Minaya. He listens as Minaya tells him what he already knows from Peter Gammons; that his offer for Cliff Floyd is nowhere close to the Red Sox offer. In exchange for one of the best left-handed hitters in the game, Billy Beane had offered a Double-A pitcher who was promising but hardly a prized possession. The Red Sox, amazingly, have agreed to cover the $2 million or so left on Cliff Floyd's contract, and offered a smorgasbord of major and minor league players for Montreal to choose from—among them Red Sox pitcher Rolando Arrojo and a South Korean pitcher named Seung-jun Song. Plus, according to Cliff Floyd's agent, it is suddenly Cliff Floyd's dream to play for the Boston Red Sox (the Red Sox are likely to pay him even more than he is worth at the end of the year, when he becomes a free agent) and his distinct wish not to play for the Oakland A's (who will bill Cliff Floyd for the sodas he drinks in the clubhouse). Floyd has a clause in his contract that allows him to veto a trade to Oakland.

Billy listens to the many compelling reasons why Omar is about to trade Cliff Floyd to the Red Sox, and then says, in the polite tones of a man trying to hide his discovery of another's idiocy, "You really want to do that, Omar?"

Omar says he does.

"I mean, Omar, you really *like* those guys you're getting from Boston?"

Omar, a bit less certainly, says that he likes the guys he's getting from Boston.

"You like Arrojo that much, huh?" He speaks Arrojo's name with a question mark after it. Arrojo? The Toronto Blue Jays' GM, J. P. Ricciardi, said that watching Billy do a deal was "like watching the Wolf talk to Little Red Riding Hood."

It takes a full twenty seconds for Omar to apologize for his interest in Rolando Arrojo.

"So who is this other guy?" says Billy "This *Korean* pitcher. How do you say his name? Song Song?"

Omar knows how to say his name.

"Well, okay," says Billy. Yet another shift in tone. He's now an innocent, well-meaning passerby who has stopped to offer a bit of roadside assistance. "If you're going to send Floyd to Boston," he says, "why don't you send him through me?"

And Billy Beane now attempts to do what he has done so many times in the past: insert himself in the middle of a deal that is none of his business.

"Omar," he says. "You're in the catbird seat here. All you need to do is let the market come to you."

He then explains: Omar can have the Red Sox's money and he can have the Red Sox's players *plus* another player from the Oakland A's minor league system. Just about any player he wants, within reason. All he has to do is agree to give Cliff Floyd to Billy

Beane for a few minutes, and let Billy negotiate with the Red Sox. He is explaining, without putting too fine a point on it, that Omar is not getting all he could get out of the Red Sox for Cliff Floyd.

The Red Sox were in their usual undignified pant to make the play-offs. They had twisted themselves into a position in their own minds where they could not *not* get Cliff Floyd. They were among the many foolish teams that thought all their questions could be answered by a single player. Cliff Floyd was the answer. Cliff Floyd was a guy the Boston newspapers would praise them for acquiring. Cliff Floyd would bring false hope to Fenway Park. Cliff Floyd, in short, was a guy for whom the Red Sox simply had to overpay. And if Omar Minaya hasn't the stomach to extract every last hunk of flesh the Boston Red Sox are willing to part with in exchange for Floyd, Billy will do it for him. And once he's done it, he will give Omar the players he was going to get anyway *plus* a minor leaguer from the Oakland farm system.

Billy Beane never had the first hope of landing Cliff Floyd. For Cliff Floyd to become an Oakland A, the Montreal Expos would have had to agree to pay the rest of Floyd's 2002 salary. The Expos were now officially a failed enterprise, owned and operated by Major League Baseball. By Bud Selig. There is not the slightest chance that Bud Selig would pay a star to play for a team fighting for a spot in the play-offs. Billy had to have known that; what he'd been doing, all along, was making a place for himself in the conversation about Cliff Floyd. Everyone else in that conversation had money. All he had was chutzpah.

Omar's now curious. He wants to know exactly how this new deal would work. Billy spells it out: you give me Floyd and I will deliver to you Arrojo and Song Song—or whatever his name is—plus someone else. Some other minor leaguer from the Oakland A's system.

Omar still doesn't quite follow: how will he do that? Billy explains that he will use Floyd to get Arrojo and Song Song *and* some other things too, from the Boston Red Sox. It goes without saying that he will keep those other things.

Omar now follows. He says it sounds messy

"Okay, Omar," says Billy. "Let's do this. Here's what you do. Call them back and tell them that you want one other player, in addition to Arrojo and Song Song. His name is Youkilis."

Euclis.

The Greek god of walks.

Youkilis, an eighth-round draft choice the previous year. Youkilis, the first college player turned up by Paul DePodesta's computer, and ignored by the Oakland A's scouting department. Youkilis, a man who but for the last residue of old baseball wisdom in Billy's scouting department would have been taken by the Oakland A's in the third round of the 2001 draft. Youkilis was the Jeremy Brown of the 2001 draft. He was tearing up Double-A ball, and was on the fast track to the big leagues. He played as if he was trying to break the world record for walking, and for wearing out the arms of opposing pitchers.

From the moment he started to talk to Omar Minaya about Cliff Floyd, Billy Beane was after Youkilis.

Omar has no idea who Youkilis is. "*Kevin* Youkilis," says Billy, as if that helps. "Omar, he's nobody. He's just a fat Double-A third baseman." A fat Double-A third baseman who is *the Greek god of walks*. Who just happened to have walked into some power last year. Yes: the Greek god of walks was now hitting a few more home runs. Which is, of course, the true destiny of the Greek god of walks.

Omar doesn't understand how he can get Youkilis from the Red Sox, who have said they've made their best offer. "No, Omar," says Billy. "Here's how you do it. If I walk you through this, Omar, you can take it to the freaking bank. Trust me on this, Omar. He [Floyd's agent] wants him in Boston. You know why? Boston can pay him. You don't ask them for Youkilis. You just tell them

Youkilis is in the deal. You just call them and tell them that without Youkilis they don't have a deal. Then hang up. I guarantee you they'll call you right back and give you Youkilis. Who is *Youkilis*?"

He speaks the name as he has never before, as if he can summon only contempt for anyone with an interest in this *Youkilis*. "Youkilis for Cliff Floyd?" he says "It's ridiculous. Of course they'll do it. Fucking Larry Lucchino [the Red Sox president] doesn't know who the fuck Youkilis is. How are they going to explain to people that they didn't get Cliff Floyd because they wouldn't give up Youkilis?"

Poor teams enjoy one advantage over rich teams: immunity from public ridicule. Billy may not care for the Oakland press but it is really very tame next to the Boston press, and it certainly has no effect on his behavior, other than to infuriate him once a week or so. Oakland A's fans, too, were apathetic compared to the maniacs in Fenway Park and Yankee Stadium. He could safely ignore their howls.

Omar doesn't buy it. He thinks maybe Billy Beane is screwing up his deal.

"Omar, all I'm trying to do is give you a free player from me. And if they don't do it, what have you lost? You can still do the deal."

Omar says he's worried about losing his deal. He's got Bud Selig sitting on his shoulder. Omar, thanks to Bud Selig, is in violation of Billy Beane's Trading Rule #2: "The day you say you have to do something, you're screwed. Because you are going to make a bad deal."

"Omar," Billy says, "if they think they are going to get Floyd, Kevin Youkilis is not going to get in the way." Billy Beane helps Omar to imagine the Boston headlines. NEW RED SOX OWNERS LOSE PENNANT TO KEEP FAT MINOR LEAGUER.

Now Omar understands; now Omar very nearly believes. But Omar is also curious: who is this Youkilis fellow that has Billy

Beane so worked up? Perhaps Youkilis is someone who should be not an Oakland A, but a Montreal Expo.

"Youkilis?" says Billy, as if he's only just heard of the guy and very nearly forgot his name. "Just a fat kid in Double-A. Look at your reports. He's a 'no' for you. He's a 'maybe' for me. From our standpoint he's just a guy we like because he gets on base."

(Silly us!)

Now Omar wants to make it more complicated than it is.

"Omar, Omar," says Billy, "the point is I think you can get him in the deal and if you do I'm getting you something for nothing."

He puts down the phone. "He'll call Boston but I don't think he's going to push them," he says.

A's president Mike Crowley pokes his head into Billy's office. "Steve's on the phone." Steve in this case is Steve Schott, A's owner.

Billy's thoughts linger on Youkilis. He imagines, fairly accurately as it turns out, the next words he'll hear from the Red Sox. They'll know of course that it was he, and not Omar, who has dropped the stink bomb of Youkilis. They'll know because he, and no one else, has tried to get Youkilis from them in the past. They'll know, also, because the Red Sox assistant GM, Theo Epstein, talks to Billy Beane as often as he can. Epstein is a twenty-eight-year-old Yale graduate who has known for some time that he'd like to be the general manager of a big league team and, when he is, which general manager he'd most like to be. The Boston Red Sox are moments away from joining Billy Beane in his crusade to emancipate fat guys who don't make outs. All this Billy knows, and he still thinks Boston will give up Youkilis. What he doesn't know is that Theo Epstein has new powers—new Red Sox owner John Henry listens to everything he says—and has used them to establish Kevin Youkilis as the poster child for the Boston Red Sox farm system. ("Three months earlier," Epstein will later say, "and Billy would have had him.")

"Billy, Steve's still waiting to talk!" Mike Crowley again. His owner again. Billy looks around as if he's forgotten something; he's spent too much time on Youkilis. He needs to raise some cash. He goes back to his phone and calls Steve Phillips, the Mets GM, one last time. "Steve. Here's the deal. I don't want Rincon pitching against me tonight." He listens for a bit, and hears nothing that makes him happy. When he hangs up, he says, "He has no money. He needs what he has to sign Kazmir." (Kazmir is the high school pitcher—now the high school pitching holdout—drafted by the Mets nearly two months earlier.)

The Mets have no money to waste. This is new, too. The market for baseball players, like the market for stocks and bonds, is always changing. To trade it well you needed to be adaptable.

Every minute that passes is a minute Brian Sabean—or even Steve Phillips!—has to talk Mark Shapiro into backing out of the two-hour promise he's made Billy. Billy hollers to Mike Crowley: "Tell Schott that if we don't move Venafro, I'll sell Rincon for twice the price next year. No. Tell him that I'll make him a deal. If I don't do it, I'll cover it. But I keep anything over twice the savings."

Mike Crowley doesn't know what to do with this. His GM, who earns *400 grand* a year, is telling his owner that he'll take an equity stake in a single player. Go down this road and Billy Beane could make himself a very rich man, simply by dealing players as well as he has done. No reply comes back from the owner, and Billy assumes he is free to do what he wants with Rincon. (Later, and after the fact, the owners will indeed give him authority to do the deal.) He gives the Mets and Giants fifteen minutes more. Finally, he decides. He'll take the risk. He picks up the phone to call Mark Shapiro to acquire Rincon.

Phone in hand, almost casually, Billy says to Paul DePodesta, now seated on Billy's sofa, "Do you want to go down and release Magnante?"

"Do *I* want to?" says Paul. He looks right, then left, as if Billy must be talking to some other person, someone who enjoys telling a thirty-seven-year-old relief pitcher that he's washed up. When he looks left he can see the Coliseum a few yards away, through Billy's office window. It wasn't that Mags was just four days short of his ten-year goal. He'd get his pension. It was that, in all likelihood, Mags was finished in the big leagues.

"Someone's got to talk to him," says Billy. Now, suddenly, there is a difference between trading stocks and bonds and trading human beings. There's a discomfort. Billy never lets it affect what he does. He is able to think of players as pieces in a board game. That's why he trades them so well.

"Call Art," says Paul. "That's his job."

Billy starts to call Art and then remembers that he hasn't actually made the trade, and so reverses himself and calls Mark Shapiro in Cleveland. It's 6:30 P.M. The game against the Indians starts in thirty-five minutes.

"Mike Magnante has just thrown his last pitch in the big leagues," says Paul.

"Sorry I took so long, Mark," says Billy.

No problem, But since you did, do you want to wait until after the game to take Rincon?

"No, we want him now. We want to get him in our dugout tonight."

Why the rush?

"By and large Magnante cost us the game last night and Rincon won the game."

Okay. No big deal. We'll do it now.

"You feel comfortable with Ricardo's health, right?"

Right.

"We're going to have to release a guy before the game," says Billy. "In the spirit of speeding things up, you wanna call Joel?" Joel is Joel Skinner, the Indians manager. Panic rises on Billy's face. "Oh shit," he says. "McDougal. He has a little tweak in his leg. You know about that, right?" McDougal's the player Billy's giving up. McDougal's also been dogging it during workouts. He's conveyed to the A's minor league coaching staff a certain lack of commitment to the game. But these things the Cleveland Indians are required to learn the hard way.

No problem. I know about the tweak.

Billy hangs up and dials Art Howe's number. The A's manager has just returned to his office beside the clubhouse.

"Art. It's Billy. I have some good news and some bad news."

Art gives a little nervous chuckle. "Okay."

"The good news is you've got Rincon."

"Do I?"

"The bad news is you gotta release Magnante."

Silence on the other end of the line. "Okay," Art finally says.

"And you've got to do it before the game."

"Okay."

"I know it's not the best way to get rid of a guy but we got a good pitcher."

"Okay."

Billy hangs up and turns to Paul, "Can we designate Magnante for assignment?" This is a prettier way to release a player because it leaves open the possibility that some other club will claim him, and take his salary off Oakland's hands. When you designate a guy for assignment, Billy explains, "you put him in baseball purgatory. But he can't pray his way out."

He then makes several quick calls. He calls the A's equipment manager, Steve Vucinich. "Voos. We gotta get rid of Mags by game time. Yeah. You have twenty-five minutes to get him out of there." He calls the Mets' Steve Phillips. "Steve, I got the guy I wanted. Rincon." (For you, it's Venafro or nothing.) He calls the Giants' Brian Sabean. "Brian. Hey, Brian. Hey, it's Billy. I've made a deal for Rincon right now." (So don't think you can wait me out.) He calls Peter Gammons and tells him what he's done, and that he's not doing anything else.

Then he brings in the Oakland A's public relations man, Jim Young, who agrees he should have a press release ready before the game. He also says Billy should make himself available to the media. "Do I have to go talk to them?" Billy asks. He's already talked to everyone he wants to talk to.

"Yes."

After the final call, his phone rings. He looks at his caller ID and sees it's from the visitors' clubhouse. He picks it up.

"Oh, hi Ricardo." It's Ricardo Rincon, who is Mexican, and normally gives his interviews through an interpreter.

"Ricardo, I know it's a little bit shocking for you," says Billy. His syntax changes slightly, he's groping for a Mexican mode of expression and winds up saying whatever he can think of that Ricardo might understand. "But we have been trying to get you for a long time. You're going to love the guys on the team. They're fun."

Ricardo is trying to get it clear in his head that he's supposed to do what he's just been asked to do, take off his Cleveland Indians uniform, gather his personal belongings, and walk down the hall into the Oakland clubhouse and put on an Oakland uniform. He can't quite get his mind around it.

"Yes! Yes!" says Billy. "I don't know if you'll pitch tonight. But you're on *our* team tonight."

Whatever Ricardo says he means: *Oh my God, I might actually have to pitch tonight!*

"Yes. Yes. Possibly you'll punch out Jim Thome!" *Possibly you will punch out Jim Thome.* Billy is becoming, quickly, a Mexican immigrant.

"We'll have a uniform and everything ready for you." *And everything.* He's had just about enough touchy-feely for one evening. He tries to lead the conversation to a not horribly unnatural conclusion. "Where are you from, Ricardo?"

Ricardo says he's from Veracruz, Mexico.

"Well, Veracruz is closer to here than to Cleveland. You're closer to home!"

He finishes that one, hangs up, and says, "It's gotten to be a longer road trip for Ricardo than he expected." He looks absolutely spent. The wad of tobacco is gone from his upper lip and his mouth is dry. He gargles with the glass of water on his desk, and spits. "I've got to work out," he says.

At that moment Mike Magnante was removing his Oakland uniform and Ricardo Rincon was removing his Cleveland one. Mags quickly left the Oakland clubhouse; he'd come back for his things later when no one was around. His wife had brought the kids to the game so he couldn't just leave. Magnante watched the game with his family until the sixth inning, and then left so he wouldn't have to answer questions from the media. He had no desire to call further attention to his situation. In his youth he might have mouthed off. He would certainly have borne a grudge. But he was no longer young; the numbness had long since set in. He thought of himself the way the market thought of him, as an asset to be bought and sold. He'd long ago forgotten whatever it was he was meant to feel.

The main thing was that Mags was gone from the clubhouse before Billy walked across to change into his sweats. As Billy headed in, however, he bumped into Ricardo Rincon heading out, in street clothes. Ricardo remained confused. He had heard he was going to the San Francisco Giants, or maybe the Los Angeles Dodgers. He'd never imagined he might be an Oakland A. And he still doesn't understand the full implications of what's happened. The Oakland A's only left-handed relief pitcher is going out to find a seat in the stands to watch the game. Billy leads him back into the clubhouse where the staff has just finished steaming RINCON onto the back of an Oakland A's jersey. "You're on our team now," says Billy.

Ricardo Rincon walked back into his new clubhouse, put on his new uniform, and sat down and watched the entire game on television. "I was not ready," he said. "I couldn't concentrate." His left arm, however, felt great.

Chapter Ten

ANATOMY OF AN
UNDERVALUED PITCHER

Aᴠᴛᴇʀ ʙɪʟʟʏ ᴀᴄqᴜɪʀᴇᴅ Ricardo Rincon and Ray Durham, the team went from good to great. The only team in the past fifty years with a better second half record than the 2002 Oakland A's was the 2001 Oakland A's, and even they were just one game better. On the evening of September 4, the standings in the American League West were, with the exception of the Texas Rangers, an inversion of what they had been six weeks before.

	Wins	*Losses*	*Games Behind*
Oakland	87	51	—
Anaheim	83	54	3½
Seattle	81	57	6
Texas	62	75	24½

The Anaheim Angels were the second hottest team in baseball. They'd won thirteen of their last nineteen games, and yet lost ground in the race. The reason for this was that the Oakland A's had won *all* of their previous nineteen games—and tied the American League record for consecutive wins. On the night of September 4, 2002, before a crowd of 55,528, the largest ever to see an Oakland regular season game, they had set out to do what no other team had done in the 102-year history of the league: win their twentieth game in a row. By the top of the seventh inning, up 11–5 against the Kansas City Royals, with Tim Hudson still pitching, the game seemed all but over.

Then, suddenly, Hudson's in trouble. After two quick outs he gives up one single to Mike Sweeney and another, harder hit, to Raul Ibanez. Art Howe emerges from the dugout and glances at the bullpen.

What turned up in the A's bullpen seemed to vary from one night to the next. On this night the less important end of the bench held a cynical, short, lefty sidewinder Billy Beane had tried and failed to give away, Mike Venafro, and two guys newly arrived from Triple-A: Jeff Tam and Micah Bowie. On the more important end of the bench was a clubfooted screwball pitcher with knee problems; a short, squat Mexican left-hander who spoke so little English that he called everyone on the team "Poppy"; and a tempestuous flamethrower with uneven control of self and ball. Jim Mecir, Ricardo Rincon, Billy Koch. Of the entire bullpen, in the view of the Oakland A's front office, the most critical to the team's success was a mild-mannered Baptist whose delivery resembled no other pitcher in the major leagues: Chad Bradford. Billy has instructed Art Howe to bring in Bradford whenever the game is on the line. In most cases when Bradford came out of the pen, the game was tight and runners were on base. Tonight, the game isn't tight; tonight, history is calling Chad Bradford in from the pen.

Art Howe pulls his right hand out of his jacket and flips his fingers underhanded, like a lawn bowler. Taking his cue, Bradford steps off the bullpen mound and walks toward the field of play. Before reaching it, he pulls the bill of his cap down over his face and fixes his eyes on the ground three feet in front of him. He's six foot five but walks short. Really, it's a kind of vanishing act: by the time he steps furtively over the foul line, he's shed himself entirely of the interest of the crowd. If you didn't know who he was or what he was doing you would say he wasn't making an entrance but a getaway.

Baseball nourishes eccentricity and big league bullpens have seen their share of self-consciously colorful oddballs. Chad Bradford was the opposite. He didn't brush his teeth between innings, like Turk Wendell, or throw temper tantrums on the mound, like Al Hrabosky. He didn't stomp and glare and leap dramatically over the foul lines. His mother, back home in Mississippi, often complained about her son's on-field demeanor. Specifically, she complained that he never did anything to let people know how handsome and charming he actually was. For instance, he never allowed the television cameras to see his winsome smile, even when he sat in the dugout after a successful outing. Chad never smiled because he was mortified by the idea of the TV cameras catching him smiling—or, for that matter, doing anything at all.

None of it helps his cause of remaining inconspicuous. Once he's on the mound, nothing he does can wall him off from the crowd or the cameras. He makes his living on the baseball field's only raised platform, and in such a way as to call to mind a circus act. Sooner or later he needs to throw his warm-up pitches, and, when he does, fans who have never seen him pitch gawk and point. In their trailers outside the stadium TV producers scramble to assemble the tape the announcers will need to explain this curiosity. Pitching out of the stretch, he does not rear up and back, like other relief pitchers. He jackknifes at the waist, like a jitterbug dancer lurching for his partner. His throwing hand swoops out toward the plate and down toward the earth. Less than an inch off the ground, way out where the dirt meets the infield grass, he rolls the ball off his fingertips. When subjected to slow-motion replay, as this motion often is, it looks less like pitching than feeding pigeons or shooting craps. The announcers often call him a sidearm pitcher, but that hasn't been true of him for nearly four years. He's now, in baseball lingo, a "submariner," which is baseball's way of making a guy who throws underhand sound manly.

The truth is that there is no good word to describe Chad Bradford's pitching motion; "underhand" doesn't capture the full flavor of it. This year, for the first time in his career, Chad Bradford's knuckles have scraped the dirt as he throws. Once during warm-ups his hand bounced so violently off the ground that the baseball ricocheted over the startled head of Toronto Blue Jays' outfielder Vernon Wells, minding his own business in the on-deck circle. ESPN had replayed that one, over and over. Chad's new fear is that he'll do it again, in a game, and that the television cameras will catch him at it, and everyone will be paying him attention all over again.

The odd thing about Chad Bradford is that he wants so badly to be normal. Normal is what he's not. It's not just that he throws funny. His idiosyncratic streak runs straight down to the bottom of his character. Back in high school he had this shiny white rock he sneaked out with him to the mound. He'd noticed it one day when he was pitching. He was pitching especially well that day and the rock didn't look like any rock he'd ever seen on the mound. He attributed some part of his success to the presence of the shiny white rock. When he was done pitching, he picked up the rock and carried it home with him. For the next three years he never ventured to the pitcher's mound without his rock. He'd sneak it out with him in his pocket and put it on the mound, just so, and in such a way that no one ever noticed.

By the time he reached the big leagues, he'd weaned himself of his lucky rock but not of the frame of mind that created it. He had the tenacious sanity of the slightly mad. A big league pitcher who wishes to avoid attention, Chad Bradford has learned to disguise his superstitions as routines. There are things he always does—like throwing exactly the same number of pitches in the bullpen, in exactly the same order; or like telling his wife to leave the stadium the moment he enters a game. There are things he never does—like touch the rosin bag.

His twin desires—to succeed, and to remain unnoticed—grow less compatible by the day. Chad Bradford's 2002 statistics imply, to the A's front office, that he is not just the best pitcher in their bullpen but one of the most effective relief pitchers in all of baseball. The Oakland A's pay Chad Bradford $237,000 a year, but his performance justifies many multiples of that. At one point the Oakland A's front office says that if Bradford simply continues doing what he's done he'll one day be looking at a multi-year deal at $3 million plus per. The wonder isn't merely that they have him so cheaply, but that they have him at all. The wonder is that, until they snapped him up for next to nothing, nobody in the big leagues paid any attention at all to Chad Bradford.

In this respect, if no other, Chad Bradford resembled a lot of the Oakland A's pitchers. The A's had the best staff in the American League and yet of all their pitchers only Mark Mulder, one of the team's three brilliant starters, had failed to inspire serious doubts at some point in his career in the baseball scouting mind. The team's second ace, Tim Hudson, was a short right-handed pitcher who couldn't get himself drafted at all in 1996, after his junior year in college, and then not until the sixth round of the 1997 draft. The team's third ace, Barry Zito, had been spat upon by both the Texas Rangers, who took him in the third round of the 1998 draft but declined to pay him the $50,000 required to sign him, and the San Diego Padres, for whom Zito privately auditioned and badly wanted to play. The Padres told Zito that he didn't throw hard enough to make it in the big leagues. The Oakland A's disagreed and selected him with the ninth pick of the 1999 draft. Three years later a top executive for those same San Diego Padres would say that the reason the Oakland A's win so many games with so little money is that "Billy got lucky with those pitchers."

And he did. But if an explanation is where the mind comes to rest, the mind that stopped at "lucky" when it sought to explain the Oakland A's recent pitching success bordered on narcoleptic. His reduced circumstances had forced Billy Beane to embrace a different mental model of the Big League Pitcher. In Billy Beane's mind, pitchers were nothing like high-performance sports cars, or thoroughbred racehorses, or any other metaphor that implied a cool, inbuilt superiority. They were more like writers. Like writers, pitchers initiated action, and set the tone for their games. They had all sorts of ways of achieving their effects and they needed to be judged by those effects, rather than by their outward appearance, or their technique. To place a premium on velocity for its own sake was like placing a premium on a big vocabulary for its own sake. To say all pitchers should pitch like Nolan Ryan was as absurd as insisting that all writers should write like John Updike. Good pitchers were pitchers who got outs; how they did it was beside the point.

Pitchers were like writers in another way, too: their output was harder than it should have been to predict. A twenty-two-year-old phenom with superior command wakes up one morning in such a precarious mental state that he's hurling pitches over the catcher's head. Great prospects flame out, sleepers become stars. A thirty-year-old mediocrity develops a new pitch and becomes, overnight, an ace. There are pitchers whose major league statistics are much better than their minor league ones. How did *that* happen? It was an odd business, this getting of outs. Obviously a physical act, it was also, in part, an act of the imagination. In the minor leagues Tim Hudson develops a new pitch, a devastating change-up, that makes him look like a different pitcher from the one the A's drafted in the sixth round. Between junior and real college, Barry Zito refines the delivery of his curveball to the point where it is indistinguishable, as it leaves his hand, from his otherwise uninteresting fastball. The adjustments that lead to pitching success are mental as much as they are physical acts.

Of all the odd out-getters on the Oakland A's pitching staff,

Chad Bradford is the least orthodox. He has made it to the big leagues less on the strength of his arm than on the quality of his imagination. No one sees that now; because no one really knows who he is, or cares. When you know just a bit about him, you can see what powerful tricks a pitcher's imagination can play. But to do that you had to go back a ways, to before Chad Bradford became the man now making a spectacle of himself before 55,528 fans in Oakland's Coliseum.

CHAD BRADFORD grew up the youngest child of a lower-middle-class family in a small town called Byram, Mississippi, outside of the larger one called Jackson. "Country" is how he describes himself. Not long before Chad's second birthday his father suffered a stroke that nearly killed him, and left him paralyzed. The doctors had told his father that he'd never walk again. His father insisted that just wasn't true. He looked up from his bed, stone-faced, and announced his intention to raise his three boys and earn a living. Through an act of will, which he also thought of as an act of God, he did just that. By Chad's seventh birthday his father was able not only to walk but, in a fashion, to play catch with his son. He would never again be able to lift his arm over his shoulder, so he couldn't throw properly. But he could get a glove up to stop a ball. And after he caught the ball from Chad, he would toss it back to him underhanded. The strange throwing motion stuck in the little boy's mind.

Playing catch with his father was one of the things that made Chad happiest. His father didn't have any particular ambition for him, except that he should be happy, remain a Christian, and that his happiness and his Christianity should occur within the confines of Mississippi. The Bradfords didn't know any professional baseball players; they didn't know anyone who knew any professional baseball players. But twice Chad was asked by his school-teachers to write autobiographical essays, and both times he took professional baseball as his theme. At the age of eight he wrote: What I Want to Be When I Grow Up.

> If I were a A grown up
> I would be a baseball player
> And I would play for the Dodgers.
> I hope to play for the Cardinals too.
> I hope to play for the Oriole too
> And for all the teams I would
> Play shotestop.

"Shotestop" being the phonetic spelling, in Byram, Mississippi. Five years later, when Chad was thirteen, his teacher asked him and the other students to write the stories of their lives, as they looked back on them from their imagined old age. With the perspective of hindsight Chad Bradford could see that he had married right out of school, had two children, a son and a daughter, and become not a big league shortstop but a big league pitcher. He imagined no other future for himself and so it was lucky that no other future awaited him. Right after his high school graduation, at the age of eighteen, he married his girlfriend, Jenny Lack, who soon bore him a son, then a daughter. Between the two births, at the age of twenty-three, Chad Bradford made his debut in the major leagues with the Chicago White Sox. The power of an imagination can arise from what it refuses to foresee.

Between the eighth grade and the big leagues there was only one hitch: Chad wasn't any good. His ambition was a fantasy. Just about every baseball player who makes it to the big leagues was all-everything in high school; just about every big league pitcher dominated high school hitters. As a fifteen-year-old high school sophomore Chad Bradford was lucky just to make the team. He didn't play any sport other than baseball and didn't exhibit any particular athletic ability. Central Hinds Academy in Byram, Mississippi, had graduated hundreds of baseball players more promis-

ing than Chad Bradford and none of them had ever played profes-
sionally. Anyone Chad told he planned to become a professional
baseball pitcher looked at him with the same gawking awe as his
presence on a big league mound would later elicit. As a consequence he stopped telling people.

One of the people he didn't tell was his high school baseball
coach, Bill "Moose" Perry. Chad, like everyone he knew, was
raised Baptist. Moose wasn't just his coach but also his minister.
This curious blending of roles meant, in practice, that when
Moose needed to slap sense into one of his players, he felt sure he
did it with the hand of God. Moose looked at Chad Bradford, aged
fifteen, and saw a player who needed slapping. To Moose, Chad
Bradford was just a silly, lazy boy, who had come out for the baseball team not because he had any aptitude for, or interest in, the
game but because he wanted to hang around with his friends who
did. "The one thing Chad was, he was a good student," said
Moose, years later, looking for something nice to say. "And the
way it was at that school, if they showed any ability in *anything*,
you wanted to encourage them. But Chad's promise was basically
that he wanted to be there. That was it. It's horrible to say, but it's
true."

Chad told Moose that he wanted to pitch, but Moose couldn't
see how. "He might have been the type of guy who would pitch
games that were meaningless," said Moose, "but I wouldn't have
let him pitch any game that mattered. His curveball didn't do anything but spin. He didn't throw hard. His fastball, it was like setting it up there on a hittin' tee."

Moose had other jobs, aside from coaching and preaching to
high school baseball players. One of them was chapel leader for
the New York Mets' Double-A team in Jackson, Mississippi. In
that capacity, a few years earlier, he'd led Billy Beane in worship.
(Billy, a lapsed Catholic, says he went to hedge his bets.) The season before Chad Bradford's sophomore year, Moose preached to a
sidearm pitcher from a visiting team. After the service Moose

asked the pitcher how he got his effects, and the pitcher gave him a tutorial. One winter afternoon, before the season started, when the Central Hinds Academy baseball field was underwater and the team couldn't practice properly, Moose took Chad aside on the football field and asked him to try out this stuff the minor leaguer had shown him. Chad dropped his arm down just above a straight sidearm, from twelve to two o'clock, and, sure enough, his fastball moved. He still couldn't throw anything but a fastball, but now it tailed in on right-handed hitters and away from lefties. Chad could always throw the ball over the plate; now, thanks to his minister and coach, he could throw the ball over the plate in a way that hitters didn't enjoy.

All of a sudden Moose had a pitcher he could use, at least in theory. In practice Chad was still, as Moose put it, "silly." To make him less so, to toughen him up, Moose insisted that Chad cuss each time he threw a pitch. Anyone who wandered by Central Hinds Academy's baseball field of an evening in the early 1990s would see a gangly, peach-fuzzed young man sidearming pitches at his preacher, with each pitch booming out: "Shit!"

Throwing sidearm didn't come naturally to Chad. He'd leave practice every night and go home to the family's warm little brick house and play catch with his father, who remained unable to lift his partially paralyzed right arm over his shoulder and so still pitched the ball back to him underhand. His father remembers when Chad came home with his new sidearm delivery—and new movement on his ball. "I couldn't catch it!" he says. "It was whoosh. *Whoosh*. He like to have killed me. Right then I said, 'Uh-oh, no more pitch and catch.'"

Chad turned his attention to the side of the house. The gap between the two holly bushes in front was about the width of home plate. He'd practice sidearming the ball against the brick without hitting the bushes. He broke a few windows. His father announced he would build Chad a pitcher's mound. ("My dad can build anything.") His father hooked a piece of chain-link fence to a four-by-four post, tacked a carpet on top, and drew a strike zone on the carpet. He walked off sixty feet six inches, and, out of the Mississippi mud, sculpted a pitcher's mound. Every day after practice Chad threw off that mound. Years later, when he was in the minor leagues, he would come home to Byram, Mississippi, in the off-season, and throw off the mound his father had built for him.

The motion still wasn't comfortable but the more he worked at it the better he felt, and when he saw the misery his new trick caused he decided not to worry about his own personal discomfort. "I'd see the hitters kind of backing out against me and I thought: 'Hey, this is going to work.'" Still, he was never an all-star; no one imagined that he would amount to anything more than a good high school pitcher. Upon graduation, Chad was the only one who thought he might still play baseball. "I wasn't recruited by any Division I schools," he'd confess, and then laugh. "I wasn't recruited by any Division II schools either." He went over and talked to the coach at Hinds Community College, a few miles down the road. The coach there said he thought he might be able to use another pitcher, so there he went, pausing only long enough for Moose to perform his wedding ceremony.

At every level of baseball, including Little League, Chad Bradford might reasonably have decided that his baseball career was more trouble than it was worth. He couldn't explain it, he just loved playing the game. "I wish I could answer the question of where that love for the game comes from," he said, "but I don't know." He pitched well in junior college but never so well that anyone thought he had a future in the game. Or, rather, no one but Warren Hughes, a scout for the Chicago White Sox. Hughes was an odd duck, an Australian who had pitched for the Australian National team before landing a baseball scholarship at the University of South Alabama. When Hughes first saw Chad pitch, he'd only just started scouting for the White Sox, and he hadn't yet been dissuaded from scouting players who didn't fit professional baseball's various molds. "You didn't see many guys who threw from that angle who it looked natural to," said Hughes. "It just kind of intrigued me that from that arm slot he had such great command." It was a three-and-a-half-hour drive from Hughes's home in Mobile, Alabama, to Hinds Community College, but Hughes made it often.

At first, Chad didn't even know he was being scouted. He was shocked when, at the end of the 1994 season, he received a Western Union telegram from the Chicago White Sox, telling him that the team had drafted him in the thirty-fourth round. They didn't plan to offer him a contract, the telegram said, but they controlled his rights for the next year. They planned to keep an eye on him. The next year Warren Hughes, who never actually said much to Chad, kept turning up at Chad's games. "Pitchers that throw like that you have to see several times to appreciate," Hughes explained. "The more I'd see Chad, the more I'd appreciate him."

Hughes told Chad that the White Sox didn't have the money to sign him in 1995, and that he should continue with his education. That year Chad went completely undrafted—no other big league team had even noticed him—and set off for the University of Southern Mississippi. There he continued to pitch, to a big league scouting audience of one. The American South was crawling with baseball scouts but none of them had the slightest interest in Chad Bradford. No other White Sox scout came to see Chad—just this quirky Australian. The following year, 1996, Warren Hughes carted up to Chicago videotapes he'd made of Chad pitching, with a view to persuading the White Sox to draft Chad. But before he bothered, he called Chad to make sure he was willing to sign.

"Chad," he said. "How many other scouts have come to talk to you?"

"None."

"Well, Chad," he said. "It looks like I'm it. Looks like I'm your shot."

He told Chad that if he would agree in advance to sign, the White Sox would again take him in a lower round but this time offer him $12,500 to sign. Even then Chad sensed that the White Sox didn't take him seriously—that to them he was just a guy to fill out a minor league roster. The only evidence he had of their interest was this lone Australian fellow who for some reason kept turning up in rural Mississippi. He couldn't decide what to do: finish college or become a White Sox minor league pitcher. He did what he now always did when he couldn't decide what to do. He called Moose, and asked him what he should do.

"Chad," Moose asked, more minister than coach. "How bad you want to play pro baseball?"

"It's all I ever dreamed of."

"Then you're a fool not to take their money."

He spent his first full season in the minor leagues in high A ball. It didn't go well. In small-time college baseball his 86-mph fastball seemed respectable enough. Out here it looked faintly ridiculous. He had a wife and a son and couldn't help but wonder if he'd made a mistake not finishing school. They'd run through the signing bonus. He was making a thousand dollars a month in the minor leagues. In the off-season he drove a forklift and swept out trailers. "I'm looking at my numbers in the off-season," he said, "and I'm thinking: should I be doing this?" When he turned up in spring training for the 1998 season, the White Sox asked him the same question. The pitching coaches informed him that he'd been officially classified a "fringe prospect." "They said, 'If you have a good season, you can stay around. If not, you're on your way out.'"

His goal at the start of the 1998 season was simply to keep his job. Late that spring several people noticed that he seemed to be approaching that job differently. He'd changed his delivery, so that he came at the hitter from a lower angle. In college he had drifted, unthinkingly, from two o clock to three o clock, from a three-quarters delivery to straight sidearm. That's where he was at the end of his dismal first season in the minor leagues. Now, for the first time in his career, he found his point of release well below his

waist. But until he watched tape of himself Chad had no idea that
he'd changed anything at all. He never did: his development into
a pitcher who looked like he belonged in a slow-pitch softball
game was unconscious. Feeling himself falling, he had reached
back blindly for something to grab hold of; the curious motion was
the first stable object he found. "Moose took me from twelve to
two," he said. "But I honestly don't know how I went down lower
from there. I have no idea what happened. I can't explain it." All
he knew was that when he threw it from lower down, his ball had
a new movement to it that flummoxed hitters during minor
league spring training, and continued to flummox them in
Double-A ball.

In late June, the Chicago White Sox promoted Chad from
Double-A to its Triple-A team in Calgary. When he arrived, he
found out why: his new home field was high in the foothills of the
Canadian Rockies, wind blowing out. The place was famously
hellish on pitching careers: the guy he'd come to replace had simply quit and skipped town. The first game after Chad arrived, his
team's starter gave up six runs in the first two thirds of an inning.
The first reliever came on and gave up another seven runs without
getting an out. What should have been ordinary fly balls rocketed
through the thin mountain air every which way out of the park.
Still in the top of the first inning, and his team already down 13–0,
the Calgary manager pointed to Chad. "When I see I'm next," said
Chad, "I'm thinking, 'what the hell am I doing here?'" He went
into the game and found the answer waiting for him. When he left
the game two hours later, it was the top of the eighth and the score
was 14–12. He'd gone six and a third innings and given up a single
run. The pitcher who replaced him promptly gave up five more
runs and the final score was 19–12.

An obscure, soft-tossing Double-A pitcher, who had never gone
more than a couple of innings in a minor league game, had thrown
six and a third merciless innings in maybe the toughest ballpark
in Triple-A. As astonishing as the performance had been, the

really curious thing was how he'd done it: by dropping down even further. As usual, Chad didn't realize what had happened until afterward. Maybe it was the thinness of the air, maybe the pressure, but some invisible force, or some distant memory, had willed his arm earthward. For the first time in his life he was attacking hitters underhanded. He only knew one other guy who threw like that.

When asked how he explained his miraculous success, all Chad could say is that "the Good Lord had a plan for me." The Good Lord's plan, it would seem, was to illustrate to baseball players the teachings of Charles Darwin. Each time Chad Bradford was thrust into a new and more challenging environment he adapted, unconsciously, albeit not as the White Sox, or he, hoped he would adapt. When he'd been scouted by Warren Hughes, Chad's fastball came in at around 86 mph. Hughes had sold Chad to his White Sox bosses as a guy who would grow stronger, and one day pitch sidearm, with control, at 90 mph plus. Chad himself adored the thought that he might one day throw as hard as most guys—that he would be normal. Instead, Chad came to throw underhand at between 81 and 84 mph.

Dropping his release point had various effects, but the most obvious was to reduce the distance between his hand, when the ball left it, and the catcher's mitt. His 84-mile-per-hour fastball took about as much time to reach the plate as a more conventionally delivered 94-mile-per-hour one. Underhanded, his sinker rose before it fell, like a tennis serve with vicious topspin. Ditto his slider, which made straight for a right-handed hitter's eye before swooping down and away. Even hitters who had faced him before fought the instinct to flinch, and found it nearly impossible to get under his pitches and lift them into the mountain air. They'd start their swing at a rising ball and finish it at a falling one. The best they could usually do with any of his pitches was to beat them into the ground. As miserable as the Canadian Rockies were for most pitchers, they might as well have been created for

Chad Bradford to pitch in. No matter how thin the air, no matter how strong the outgoing breeze, it remained impossible to hit a ground ball over the wall.

Guided by some combination of the survival instinct and the failure to imagine any earthly role for himself other than Big League Pitcher, Chad Bradford dominated Triple-A hitters, even as every other pitcher on the Calgary team struggled. In a ballpark built for sluggers, he pitched fifty-one innings with an earned run average of 1.94, and gave up only three home runs. Hitters routinely complained how uncomfortable they felt against him, how hard Chad was to read, how *deceptive* he was. This was funny. Off the pitcher's mound, Chad had no ability to deceive anyone about anything. He was who he was. Country. Every now and then he might try to get away with something at home—like not cleaning out the garage when he'd told his wife that he would. He simply couldn't do it. "I'll all but gotten away with something and then I'll come clean," he said. "I just hate the guilt." On the pitcher's mound, he had no guilt. The moment he scuffed the rubber with his foot he became a pitiless con artist, a sinister magician. He sawed pretty ladies in two, and made rabbits vanish.

He assumed, in a vague sort of way, that if he kept getting hitters out, the White Sox front office would have no choice but to call him up. He was right. Tossing a ball around with an older minor leaguer one day, he was called into the Calgary manager's office. His new assignment: catch the first plane to Dallas. He'd join the White Sox bullpen in their upcoming series with the Texas Rangers. He went right back on the field and resumed tossing the ball around. The older player he'd been tossing with, a pitcher named Larry Casian who would retire at the end of the year, asked what the manager had wanted; and Chad told him. Casian asked why on earth Chad was out playing catch on a Triple-A field when he was meant to be flying to the big leagues. Chad said he didn't know, and kept throwing. "I think I was in shock," he said. Eight years after his minister and coach had showed him a trick to spare him the embarrassment of being cut from his high school team, he was getting a chance to practice it in the major leagues.

They called him into the second game of the three-game series at The Ballpark in Arlington. He didn't feel he belonged; he felt out of his depth. "You think: how'm I gonna do this? You think it's like a totally different game than the one you played your whole life." He retired the first seven batters he faced, in order. The last two months of the season he pitched thirty and two-thirds innings in relief for the White Sox, and finished with an earned run average of 3.23. At one point he'd made a dozen consecutive scoreless appearances. In a season justly famous for the number of home runs hit, none were hit off Chad Bradford.

In the off-season he went back, as he always did, and always would, to Byram, Mississippi. For the first time, though he didn't know why, he did not work out on the pitching mound his father had built, and rebuilt, for him. Dropping down and throwing sidearm had ended their games of catch. Making the big leagues severed this final dependency. He didn't think anything of it; leaving the old mound behind was just the next thing to do. When he turned up for camp in the spring of 1999, he thought, "Great. I'm in the big leagues."

He wasn't. The White Sox didn't trust Chad Bradford's success. The White Sox front office didn't trust his statistics. Unwilling to trust his statistics, they fell back on more subjective evaluation. Chad didn't look like a big leaguer. Chad didn't act like a big leaguer. Chad's success seemed sort of flukey. He was a trickster that big league hitters were certain to figure out. The White Sox brass didn't say any of this to Chad's face, of course. During 1999 spring training the White Sox GM, a former big league pitcher named Ron Schueler, told Chad that his pitches weren't moving like they used to move. He was sending Chad down to Triple-A. Chad didn't have the nerve to say what he thought but he thought it all the same: *My ball doesn't move? But all I have is movement!* When he got to Triple-A, a coach assured him that his ball moved as it always had, and that the GM just needed something to tell him other than the truth, that the White Sox front office viewed him as a "Triple-A guy."

The Good Lord might have had a plan for Chad Bradford but apparently even He was required to respect the mystery of life behind the big league clubhouse door. For the next two years Chad pitched mainly in the minor leagues, bouncing up only briefly, and usually successfully, to the big league team. For two years he simply dominated Triple-A hitters and watched pitchers with much less impressive statistics leapfrog him. "I watched guys get called up from Double-A. I realized I was a just-in-case guy. Just in case somebody got hurt. Just in case somebody got traded. That no matter how well I did, I wasn't going to get called up." He talked to his wife about quitting the White Sox and going to pitch in Japan, where he might make a good living. He found that the only way he could get himself out of bed in the morning and to the ballpark was to remind himself that he wasn't pitching only for the White Sox. "By the middle of the 1999 season I was pitching for every other big league team that might be watching," he said. "I'm just sitting there hoping someone's watching."

Someone was.

THE POOL OF PEOPLE Chad Bradford didn't know who had nevertheless found him worthy of their attention had tripled. When he was an amateur, one big league scout had taken an interest in him. As a professional, he had two more distant admirers. One was Paul DePodesta, who couldn't quite believe that the White Sox were keeping this deadly pitching force in Triple-A, and had mentioned to Billy Beane how nice it would be if he somehow could talk the Chicago White Sox into making Chad Bradford an Oakland A. The other was a bored paralegal in Chicago named

Voros McCracken. Looking for a way to ignore whatever he was meant to be doing for the Chicago law firm that he loathed working for, Voros McCracken had taken up fantasy baseball. He didn't know it, but he was about to explain why the Chicago White Sox had so much trouble grasping the true value of Chad Bradford—and why the Oakland A's did not.

Voros was thinking of drafting Chad Bradford for his fantasy baseball team. But before he did, he wanted to achieve a better understanding of major league pitching. Specifically, he wanted to know how you could tell if a pitcher was any good.

Voros had played baseball as a kid, and there had been a time when he had been obsessively interested in it. The moment his interest became an intellectual obsession was in 1986 when, at the age of fourteen, he picked up the most recent Bill James *Abstract*. He was astonished by what he found inside. "Basically, everything you know about baseball when you are fourteen years old, you know from baseball announcers," said Voros. "Here was this guy who was telling me that at least eighty percent of what baseball announcers told me was complete bullshit, and then explained very convincingly why it was." Voros's interest in baseball waned in his late teens and early twenties; but when he rediscovered it, in the form of fantasy leagues on the Internet, it was in the spirit of Bill James.

The Internet of course had consequences for the search for new baseball knowledge. One of the things the Internet was good for was gathering together people in different places who shared a common interest. Internet discussion groups, and Web sites like baseballprimer and baseballprospectus, sprung up, created by young men who, as boys, had been seduced by the writings of Bill James. In one of the discussion groups, where he went to discuss what to do with his fantasy baseball team, Voros saw someone say that no matter how much research was done, no one would be able to distinguish pitching from defense. That is, no one would ever come up with good fielding statistics or, therefore, good pitching statistics. If you don't know how to credit the fielder for what happens after a ball gets put into play, you also, by definition, don't know how to debit the pitcher. And, therefore, you would never be able to say with real certainty how good any given pitcher was. Or, for that matter, any given fielder.

When Voros read that, "I thought, 'That's a stupid attitude. Can't you do *something*?' It didn't make any sense to me that the way to approach the problem was to give up." He tried to think about it logically. He divided the stats a pitcher had that the defense behind him could affect (hits and earned runs) from the stats a pitcher did all by himself (walks, strikeouts, and home runs). He then ranked all the pitchers in the big leagues by this second category. When he ran the stats for the 1999 season, he wound up with a list topped by these five: Randy Johnson, Kevin Brown, Pedro Martinez, Greg Maddux, and Mike Mussina. "I looked at that list," said Voros, "and said, 'Damn, that looks like the five best pitchers in baseball.'" He then asked the question: if his reductive approach of looking at just walks, strikeouts, and homers identified the five best pitchers in baseball, how important could all the other stuff be?

As it happened, 1999 was supposedly an "off" year for Greg Maddux. His earned run average had risen from 2.22 in 1998 to 3.57 in 1999, mainly because he gave up fifty-seven more hits in thirty-two fewer innings. Several times during the season Maddux himself mentioned that he was astonished by how many cheap hits he was giving up; but of course no one paid any attention to that. What Voros noticed was that Maddux's hits allowed per balls put in play was far above what it usually was—in fact, it was among the highest in the big leagues. As it happened, the same year, Maddux's teammate, pitcher Kevin Millwood, had one of the lowest hits allowed per balls in play. Even stranger, their statistics the following year were reversed. Millwood had one of the highest ratios of hits per balls in play, Maddux one of the lowest. It didn't make any sense.

Voros asked himself another question: from year to year is there *any* correlation in a pitcher's statistics? There was. The number of walks and home runs he gave up, and the number of strikeouts he recorded were, if not predictable, at least understandable. A guy who struck out a lot of hitters one year tended to strike out a lot of hitters the next year. Ditto a guy who gave up a lot of home runs. But when it came to the number of hits per balls in play a pitcher gave up, there was no correlation whatsoever.

It was then that a radical thought struck Voros McCracken:

> *What if the pitcher has no control of whether a ball falls for a hit, once it gets put into play?*

Obviously some pitchers give up fewer hits than others, but that might be because some pitchers had more strikeouts than others, and, therefore, allowed fewer balls to be put into play. But it was generally assumed that pitchers could affect the way in which a ball was put into play. It was generally assumed that a great pitcher, like Randy Johnson or Greg Maddux, coaxed hitters into hitting the ball in a way that was less likely to become a hit. The trouble with that general assumption is that it didn't square with the record books. There were years when Maddux and Johnson were among the worst in baseball in this regard.

If Voros McCracken was right, then what had heretofore been attributed to the skill of the pitcher was in fact caused by defense, or ballpark, or luck. But the examples of Greg Maddux and Kevin Millwood suggested that defense and ballparks might be of secondary importance. They pitched in front of the same group of fielders, and, usually, in the same ballparks. That led Voros to a second radical thought:

What if what was heretofore regarded as the pitcher's responsibility is simply luck?

For a century and a half pitchers have been evaluated, in part, on their ability to prevent hits once the ball is put in play. A pitcher who suffered a lot of balls falling for hits gave up more earned runs and lost more games than one who didn't. He was thought less well of than a pitcher against whom balls in play were caught by fielders. A soon-to-be unemployed young man, soon to be back living with his parents in Phoenix, Arizona, begged to differ. He was coming to the conclusion that pitchers had no ability to prevent hits, once the ball was put into play. They could prevent home runs, prevent walks, and prevent balls from ever being put into play by striking out batters. And that, in essence, is all they could do.

Voros McCracken had a radical theory. And he was staring at a lot of hard evidence supporting it.

What happened next bolsters one's faith in the American educational system: Voros McCracken set out to prove himself wrong. He wrote a computer program that paired major league pitchers who had very similar walks, strikeouts, and home runs—but had given up very different number of hits. He located ninety such "pairs" from the 1999 season. If hits per ball in play were indeed something a pitcher could control, Voros reasoned, then the pitchers who had given up the fewer number of hits in 1999 would proceed to give up fewer hits in 2000. They didn't. There was, in fact, no correlation from one year to the next in any given pitcher's ability to prevent hits per balls in play.

Instead, baseball kept thrusting before Voros beguiling situations explained by his theory. A couple of months into the 2000 season, for instance, the newspapers were full of stuff about how heretofore mediocre White Sox pitcher James Baldwin, off to a great start, had somehow become the next Pedro Martinez. Voros looked more deeply at the numbers and saw that Baldwin had extremely low number of hits for the number of balls he'd put in play. His earned run average was sensational—because he'd been lucky. Sure enough, the hits started falling and Baldwin regressed to mediocrity and people stopped putting his name in the same sentence with Pedro Martinez.

For pretty much the whole of 2000 Voros McCracken, as he put it, "went looking for a reason Maddux got hit in 1999, and to this day I'm still looking for it." At length, he penned an article revealing his findings for baseballprospectus.com. Its conclusion: "There is little if any difference among major league pitchers in their ability to prevent hits on balls hit into the field of play." ESPN columnist Rob Neyer saw Voros's piece and, stunned by both the quality of the thought and the force of the argument, wrote an article about Voros's article. Several thousand amateur baseball analysts wrote in to say that Voros's argument, on the face of it, sounded nuts. Several suggested that "Voros McCracken" might be a pseudonym for Aaron Sele, a well-hit pitcher then playing for the Seattle Mariners.

Bill James also read Rob Neyer's article. James wrote in, and said Voros McCracken's theory, if true, was obviously important, but that he couldn't believe it was true. He—and about three thousand other people—then went off to disprove it himself. He couldn't do it, and the three thousand other guys couldn't either. About the most they could suggest was that there was a slight tendency for knuckleballers to control hits per balls in play. Nine months later, on page 885 of his mammoth *Bill James Historical Baseball Abstract*, James laid out Voros McCracken's argument, noted that Voros McCracken "is NekcarCcM Sorov spelled backwards," then went on to make four points:

1. *Like most things, McCracken's argument can be taken too literally. A pitcher does have some input into the hits/ innings ratio behind him, other than that which is reflected in the home run and strikeout column.*

2. With that qualification, I am quite certain that McCracken is correct.

3. This knowledge is significant, very useful.

4. I feel stupid for not having realized it 30 years ago.

One of the minor consequences of Voros McCracken's analysis of pitching was to lead him to Chad Bradford, Triple-A pitcher for the Chicago White Sox. Voros had developed a statistic he could trust—what he called DIPS, for defense independent pitching statistic. It might also have been called LIPS, for luck independent pitching statistic, because the luck it stripped out of a pitcher's bottom line had, at times, a more warping effect than defense on the perception of a pitcher's true merits. At any rate, Chad Bradford's Triple-A defense independent stats were even better than his astonishingly impressive defense dependent ones. (Chad pitched a total of 202⅔ innings in Triple-A, with an earned run average of 1.64.) And so Voros McCracken snapped up Bradford for his fantasy team, even though a player did a fantasy team no good unless he accumulated big league innings. "Basically," said Voros, "I was waiting for someone to see what I'd seen in Bradford and put him to use."

He waited nearly a year. Inadvertently, Voros McCracken had helped to explain why the White Sox thought of Chad Bradford as a "Triple-A guy." There was a reason that, in judging young pitchers, the White Sox front office, like nearly every big league front office, preferred their own subjective opinion to minor league pitching statistics. Pitching statistics were flawed. Maybe not quite so deeply as hitting statistics but enough to encourage uncertainty. Baseball executives' preference for their own opinions over hard data was, at least in part, due to a lifetime of experience of fishy data. They'd seen one too many guys with a low earned run average in Triple-A who flamed out in the big leagues. And when a guy looked as funny, and threw as slow, as Chad Bradford—well, you just knew he was doomed.

If one didn't already know better, one might think that Voros McCracken's article on baseballprospectus.com would be cause for celebration everywhere inside big league baseball. One knew better. *Voros* knew better. "The problem with major league baseball," he said, "is that it's a self-populating institution. Knowledge is institutionalized. The people involved with baseball who aren't players are ex-players. In their defense, their structure is not set up along corporate lines. They aren't equipped to evaluate their own systems. They don't have the mechanism to let in the good and get rid of the bad. They either keep everything or get rid of everything, and they rarely do the latter." He sympathized with baseball owners who didn't know what to think, or even if they should think. "If you're an owner and you never played, do you believe Voros McCracken or Larry Bowa?" The unemployed former paralegal living with his parents, or the former All-Star shortstop and current manager who no doubt owned at least one home of his own?

Voros McCracken's astonishing discovery about major league pitchers had no apparent effect on the management, or evaluation, of actual pitchers. No one on the inside called Voros to discuss his findings; so far as he knew, no one on the inside had even read it. But Paul DePodesta had read it. Paul's considered reaction: "If you want to talk about a guy who might be the next Bill James, Voros McCracken could be it." Paul's unconsidered reaction: "The first thing I thought of was Chad Bradford."

VOROS McCRACKEN had provided the theory to explain what the Oakland A's front office already had come to believe: you could create reliable pitching statistics. It was true that the further you got from the big leagues, the less reliably stats predicted big league performance. But if you focused on the right statistics you could certainly project a guy based on his Triple-A, and even his Double-A, numbers. The right numbers were walks, home runs, and strikeouts plus a few others. If you trusted those, you didn't have to give two minutes' thought to how a guy looked, or how hard he threw. You could judge a pitcher's performance objectively, *by what he had accomplished.*

Chad Bradford was, to the Oakland A's front office, a no-brainer. "It wasn't that he was doing it differently," said Paul DePodesta. "It was that the efficiency with which he was recording outs was astounding." Chad Bradford had set off several different sets of bells inside Paul's computer. He hardly ever walked a batter; he gave up virtually no home runs; and he struck out nearly a batter an inning. Paul, like Bill James, thought it was possible to take Voros's theory too literally. He thought there was one big thing, in addition to walks, strikeouts, and home runs, that a pitcher could control: extra base hits. Chad Bradford gave up his share of hits per balls in play but, more than any pitcher in baseball, they were ground ball hits. His minor league ground ball to fly ball ratio was 5:1. The big league average was more like 1.2:1. Ground balls were not only hard to hit over the wall; they were hard to hit for doubles and triples.

That raised an obvious question: why weren't there more successful ground ball pitchers like Chad Bradford in the big leagues? There was an equally obvious answer: there were no ground ball pitchers like Chad Bradford. Ground ball pitchers who threw overhand tended to be sinker ball pitchers and they tended to have control problems and also tended not to strike out a lot of guys. Chad Bradford was, statistically and humanly, an outlier.

The best thing of all was that the scouts didn't like him. The Greek Chorus disapproved of what they called "tricksters." Paul thought it was ridiculous when the White Sox sent Chad back down to Triple-A, but he could guess why they had done it. Once upon a time he had sat behind home plate while Chad Bradford pitched; he'd listened to the scouts make fun of Chad, even as Chad made fools of hitters. The guy looked funny when he threw, no question about it, and his fastball came in at between 81 and

85 mph. Chad Bradford didn't know it, but as he dropped his arm slot, and took heat off his fastball, he was becoming an Oakland A. "Because of the way he looked, we thought he might be available to us," said Paul. "Usually the guys who are setting off bells in my office are the guys everybody knows about. But nobody knew about this guy, because of the way he threw. If he had those identical stats in Triple-A but he threw ninety-four, there is *no way* they'd have traded him."

Already Billy Beane was finding that guys he wanted magically became less available the moment he expressed an interest in them. At the end of the 2000 season he finally called the new White Sox GM, Kenny Williams, who had replaced the old White Sox GM, Ron Schueler, and said, very casually, that he was looking for "a guy who could be a twelfth or thirteenth pitcher on the staff." Someone in the White Sox farm system. Someone maybe in Triple-A. He was willing to give up this minor league catcher in exchange for a Triple-A arm, Billy said, and he didn't much care which one. He asked the White Sox to suggest a few names. It took Kenny Williams a while to get around to him, but finally he mentioned Chad Bradford. Said he hated to even bring Bradford up because the young man had just called in from Mississippi and said his back was hurting, and he might need surgery. "He'll do," said Billy.

Chapter Eleven

THE HUMAN ELEMENT

ARLIER THAT HISTORIC September evening, before Chad
Bradford took the mound, a traffic jam extraordinary even
by Northern California standards stretched as far as the
eye could see. The Oakland A's ticket office had never experienced anything quite like the crush of the previous two days.
When the Kansas City Royals came to town, the A's sales department expected about ten thousand fans to turn up. In just the last
twenty-four hours more than twenty thousand people had stopped
by, in the flesh, to buy seats in advance. Before the game, an aer-
ial view of Oakland would reveal nearly everyone in sight heading
toward the Coliseum. Billy Beane alone was heading away from it.

Billy hadn't the slightest intention of watching his team make
history. It was just another game, he said, and he didn't watch
games. "All they provide me with is subjective emotion," he said,
"and that can be counterproductive." He figured he could give a
few press interviews, and then slip away in his Range Rover to
Modesto. In Modesto, on the same night the Oakland A's were try-

ing to win their twentieth game in a row, the Visalia Oaks were playing the Modesto A's. Both teams were Single-A affiliates of Oakland. Most of the players the A's had drafted a few months before played for one or the other. Billy could stand to watch young men who still had time and space to fail: Nick Swisher, Steve Stanley, Mark Teahen, and Jeremy Brown. Especially Brown, the bad body catcher from Hueytown, Alabama. Everyone had laughed when the Oakland A's drafted Brown in the first round. Every day Brown was more interesting to Billy.

And so the only moment that Billy Beane looked forward to, on a day he should have gloated through, was when he'd make his getaway. On his way out of the office, however, he'd been cut off by the team's stunned marketing department. The people who sold the Oakland A's couldn't quite believe that the guy who'd built them was taking off. They explained to Billy that if he left, he might as well pile a bunch of money in the street and set it on fire: he'd be blowing the biggest chance they'd had in years to promote the Oakland A's to the wider world. The winning streak had become a national news story. And so Billy, slightly miffed, stayed. He sat still for CBS Evening News, CNN, Fox Sports News, ESPN, and a few others, then went down to the weight room and hid, from the media and the game.

At some point between the treadmill and the stationary bicycle he noticed on his little white box that it was the bottom of the third inning and his team was ahead 11–0. For the first time in a very long while, he relaxed. Still dripping sweat, he set himself up in manager Art Howe's empty office, with the television switched on. Nineteen games into a winning streak, up eleven–zip against one of the worst teams in baseball, with one of the best pitchers in baseball still on the mound for the Oakland A's—this one game appeared safe to watch. It wasn't going to violate the laws of probability; it wasn't going to drive him mad, and cause him to do something he might later regret. At that moment, Billy Beane was so at peace with his world that he let me into it.

His feet were up on Art Howe's Formica desk. He was feeling detached. Expansive. Delighted and delightful. This was the way he felt most of the time; this was the way he almost always handled himself away from baseball. He had, he confessed, expressed his concern when he saw that Art Howe had written John Mabry's name on the lineup card, where Scott Hatteberg's should have been. It was a shame for Hatteberg, I thought. Here he's been performing these valuable and rather selfless services to the Oakland A's offense, and the one game the world will watch, he isn't allowed to play. Art explained to Billy that Hatteberg had never faced Kansas City's ace, Paul Byrd. Mabry, on the other hand, not only had hit Byrd hard but claimed to be able to see him tipping his pitches—that is, Mabry could guess what Byrd was about to throw. Billy now says he deferred to Art's judgment, as if deferring to Art's judgment comes naturally to him. Mabry promptly made Art Howe look like a genius. He'd driven in one run with a single up the middle in the six-run first inning—and helped to chase Byrd from the game. Then, in the second inning, he'd whacked a solo home run.

With the score 11–0, and Tim Hudson still carving up the Royals lineup, the absence of Scott Hatteberg from the lineup is a distant memory. Billy Beane is right to feel his usual self: the odds of something going wrong are ridiculously small. He calls his daughter Casey, now twelve years old, and still living in Southern California.

"Hey Casey, you watching the game?"

Pause.

"*American Idol*? You're watching *American Idol*??"

Casey is watching *American Idol*.

He tells Casey the news—the team is winning big, a nation of baseball fans is watching—teases her a bit, and lets her go.

Billy Beane should always be so calm during his team's games. If he believes what he claims to believe—that the game can be reduced to a social science; that it is simply a matter of figuring out the odds, and exploiting the laws of probability; that baseball players follow strikingly predictable patterns—then there is no point in being anything but calm. To get worked up over plays, or even games, is as unproductive as a casino manager worrying over the outcomes of individual pulls of the slot machines. Billy as good as makes this point now by pointing at the TV, where Eric Chavez, having just made a difficult defensive play look routine, sheepishly starts kicking the dirt in front of him. "He's almost afraid to acknowledge how good he really is," says Billy. "And here's the thing. He's twenty-four years old. You know if he's here now"—he holds his hand at his chest—"he'll wind up here"—he raises his hand over his head. "You could make a case that Chavvy is the most naturally gifted player in the game."

I ask him to make the case, and, in his current, detached mood, he's more than happy to. Up eleven–zip against a sorry club, he's reveling in the objective, scientific spirit.

"Age is such a critical factor in evaluating guys," he says, then plucks the Oakland A's media guide off Art Howe's bookshelf. "Here. Chavvy is twenty–four. The season isn't over. He's got 31 homers, 28 doubles, 55 walks, a .283 batting average, and a .353 on-base percentage. Who do you want to compare him to?"

"Jason Giambi," I say.

"All right," as he pulls out the New York Yankees media guide. "But I know the answer to this already, because I already did it." He finds Giambi's career statistics. "When Jason was twenty-four years old, he spent half the year in Edmonton—on a Triple-A team. In the half he was in the big leagues he hit 6 homers, drew 28 walks, and hit .256. Who else?"

"Barry Bonds," I say. Across the Bay, Bonds is making the argument every night that he is the finest hitter who ever played the game.

"That's hard," he says. "Bonds has reached that level where

even talent can't take you. But okay, let's take Bonds." He grabs the San Francisco Giants media guide. "I know what it's going to show because I did this with him, too. Bonds was born in 1964. In 1988, he hit .283, with 24 homers, 72 walks, and 30 doubles. That gives you some idea of how good Chavvy is."

"Who else?" he asks. But before I can think of anyone else, he says, "Let's try A-Rod [Alex Rodriguez]. No one had a quicker start than A-Rod." He pulls the Texas Rangers media guide. "A-Rod was 24 in 1999. In 1999, he hit .285, with 25 doubles, 42 homers, and 111 runs batted in." He looks up. "That compares well enough, but then there's defense. Chavvy is the best fielding third baseman in the game. A-Rod isn't the best fielding shortstop."

I'm still having trouble getting my mind around the notion of making such forecasts about human beings, and I say as much. My problem can be simply put: every player is different. Every player must be viewed as a special case. The sample size is always one. His answer is equally simple: baseball players follow similar patterns, and these patterns are etched in the record books. Of course, every so often some player may fail to embrace his statistical destiny, but on a team of twenty-five players the statistical aberrations will tend to cancel each other out. And most of them will conform fairly exactly to his expectations. About Eric Chavez's career, for instance, he has not the slightest doubt. "The only thing that will stop Chavvy is if he gets bored," he says. "People don't understand that. He continues to frustrate people who take him out of context. He is *twenty-four years old*. What he's done at twenty-four no one has done. Health permitted, his whole career is a lock."

I mention that there are times when Billy is one of the people Chavvy frustrates. Chavvy, like Miguel Tejada, is Mister Swing at Everything. In his current mood, Billy waves the objection aside. He can't understand how I can be so intolerant. "Chavvy's young," he says. "He's good-looking. He's a millionaire. He kind of owes it to himself to swing at everything. What were *you* like when you were twenty-four?"

This was the character whose behavior was consistent with the way he said he wanted to run his baseball team: rationally. Scientifically. This was the "objective" Billy Beane, the general manager who was certain that "you don't change guys; they are who they are." Who will describe his job as "a soap box derby. You build the car in the beginning of the year and after that all you do is push it down the hill." To this Billy Beane's way of thinking there was no point in meddling with the science experiment. There was no point in trying to get inside players' heads, for instance, to reshape their approach to the game. They will be who they will be. When you listen to the "objective" Billy Beane talk about his players, you begin to wonder if baseball players have free will.

But there is another, less objective Billy Beane. And in the top of the fourth inning, when Miguel Tejada drops a routine, inning-ending double-play throw from second baseman Mark Ellis, the other Billy Beane awakens from his slumber. Even as the Royals score five runs they shouldn't have, Billy remains calm—after all, it's still 11–5, and Tim Hudson is still pitching—but he's on alert. He begins to talk about his players in a different way. And he allows me to see that the science experiment is messier than the chief scientist usually is willing to admit.

In the Oakland fourth, center fielder Terrence Long hits a grounder back to the pitcher, and runs hard down the first-base line. This is new. Heretofore, when Terrence Long has grounded out, he has trotted down the line with supreme indifference to public opinion. Too young to know that you are what you pretend to be, Terrence Long has nearly perfected the art of seeming not to care. As it happens, a few days ago, Terrence walked out into the players' parking lot and discovered that someone had egged his car. Hearing of the incident, Billy stopped by Terrence's locker and told him that he'd had an e-mail from the culprit, an A's fan, who said he was furious that he'd paid money to watch Terrence Long jog the bases. The effect on Terrence Long was immediate. He went from jogging to first on a routine ground out to running as fast as he can until the first moment he can stop without pissing off Billy Beane. As he sprints down the line, Billy says that Terrence's real problem is "his own self-doubt, exacerbated by the media. That's one of the mistakes that young players make—they actually read the papers."

In the Oakland fifth, with the score still 11–5, Ramon Hernandez leads off. Twice in the first four innings the Oakland catcher has taken outside fastballs and driven doubles to the opposite field. This is new. All season long Ramon Hernandez has been trying and failing to pull outside fastballs. He's been a complete bust on offense, and failed to conform to the Oakland A's front office's greater expectations of him. As it happens, the other day, Billy stopped by Ramon Hernandez's locker and made a bet with him: each time he went the opposite way with an outside pitch, Billy would pay him fifty bucks; each time he tried to pull an outside pitch, he'd pay Billy fifty bucks. The point of the exercise, Billy now says, is "it gives me an excuse to henpeck Ramon. It's a subversive way for me to keep nagging the shit out of him without him knowing it."

Most of the players who pass across the television screen on this historic evening have been on the receiving end of Billy Beane's subtle attempts to manipulate their behavior. He claims there is no point in trying to change people, and then he goes ahead and tries to change them anyway. He knows most of his players better than he would ever allow himself to be known by them, and while that is not saying very much, it's still says something. "Look at Miggy's face," he says, at the end of the sixth inning. The television camera is on Tejada, in the dugout, looking surprisingly glum. "He's the only guy in the lineup without a hit. This is what happens with younger players: they want to do too much. Watch him: he'll try to do more than he should." And sure enough, after Tim Hudson gets into trouble, and Chad Bradford is called in from the bullpen, he does.

W HEN CHAD BRADFORD is in the bullpen, he often thinks about his father. It helps put whatever pressure he's feeling into perspective. The doctors had told his father he'd never walk again and the man had not only walked, he'd worked, and not only worked, but played catch. If his father could do *that*, how hard was this?

The thought usually made him feel better, but tonight, with so much on the line, it doesn't. He's feeling like a different pitcher than he was just a few weeks ago. Before the trouble started, he'd been exactly as effective as Paul DePodesta's computer had predicted he would be. For nearly two full seasons he's been living his dream. Chad himself had not quite believed it when, before the 2001 season, just after his back surgery, Billy Beane called him to tell him that he had traded for him with a view to his becoming the critical middle reliever in the Oakland A's big league bullpen. Billy told Chad the statistics he thought he was capable of generating, and even Chad thought they were a stretch. Amazingly, to Chad, he'd done almost exactly what Billy Beane predicted he would do. "It's like the guy knows what's going to happen before it happens," said Chad.

Now he's unsure that Billy Beane's faith in him is justified. He pulls his cap down over his eyes and walks briskly toward the mound, reaching it in exactly the same number of steps he always does. Outside, everything looked the same; inside, everything felt different. A few weeks ago, when he looked in to take the signal from the catcher, he was oblivious to his surroundings. He'd be repeating to himself his usual phrase, to shut down his mind to the pressure.

Make your pitch.

Make your pitch.

Make your pitch.

Tonight, he wasn't oblivious; tonight, as he leaned in, he was aware of everything. The crowd noise. The signs. The national audience. And a new mantra, now running through his head:

Don't Fuck This Up!

Don't Fuck This Up!

Don't Fuck This Up!

He's having the worst slump in his entire professional career and while it isn't actually all that bad a slump—one bad outing in Yankee Stadium, another in Fenway Park—he has no ability to put it into perspective. On his bookshelf at home there were two books, side by side, tattered by his constant use of them. One was *The Mental Game of Baseball*. The other was the Bible. He has a favorite passage, Philippians 4:13: *I can do all things through Christ who strengthens me.* It's giving him no solace. A few nights before, after another nerve-wracking outing, he'd called his wife, Jenny, who had taken the kids back to Byram for the start of the school year, and said, "I don't think I can do this anymore."

The Oakland A's pitching coach, Rick Peterson, thinks that Chad's problems began in early August, when ESPN announcer Jeff Brantley had come into Oakland and done a piece on him, identifying Chad on national television as one of the premier setup men in the game. Attention disturbed Chad's concentration. Peterson had been critical to Oakland's pitching success. He kept the Oakland pitchers healthy; and, in some cases, he also kept them focused. He was fond of saying that "if you have twelve different pitchers, you've got to speak twelve different languages." The difference between Chad and the other pitchers was that the others' language had words for the phrase "I belong in the big leagues." Chad's language lacked the vocabulary of personal defiance. Of self-confidence. Throughout his career, Chad had responded to trouble not by looking inside himself to see what was there, but by dropping his point of release lower to the ground. His knuckles now scrape the dirt when he throws. "He's got nowhere to go," said Peterson, "unless he throws upside down."

His pitching coach is trying to teach Chad how to go inside. After one of his weak outings, when he was looking lost, Peterson had made him sit down and watch tape of himself slicing and dicing big league hitters for the first five months of the season. As Chad watched the tape of his old self, Peterson made his point.

"You're a Christian, right, Chad?"

"Yeah."

"You believe in Jesus?"

"Yeah."

"Have you ever seen him?"

"No, I've never seen him."

"Ever seen yourself get hitters out?"

"Yeah."

"So why the fuck do you have faith in Jesus when you never seen him, but you don't have faith in your ability to get hitters out when you get hitters out all the time?"

His coach left him with that thought. Chad sat there and said to himself: "Okay. That makes sense." But a little while later the doubts returned. For his entire career hardly anyone has believed in him and now that they do, he can't quite believe in himself. "It's my greatest weakness," he said. "I have zero self-confidence. The only way I can explain it is that I'm not the guy who throws ninety-five miles an hour. The guy who throws ninety-five can always see his talent. But I don't have that. My stuff depends on deception. For it to work, there's so much that has to go right. When it starts not going right, I think, 'Oh my gosh, I hope I can keep foolin 'em. Then I start to ask, 'How much longer can I keep foolin em?'"

He's having—with him, there isn't a more accurate way to put it—a crisis of faith. When he knows, he always hits his spots; when he hopes, he never does; and he's now just hoping. Oblivious to how good he is, he is susceptible to the argument that his success is a trick, or a fluke, or a spell that at any moment might break. He doesn't much care that he is, for the first time in his miraculous career, the only one still making this argument.

That night in early September he's fighting himself more fiercely than ever before. Billy Beane knows it. His cheap out-getting machine has a programming glitch. He has no idea how to fix it—how to get inside Chad Bradford's head. Sloth, indolence, a lack of discipline, an insufficient fear of management—these problems Billy knows how to attack. Insecurity is beyond him. If he knew how to solve the problem, he might be finishing up his playing career and preparing himself for election to the Hall of Fame. But he still doesn't know; and it worries him. Chad doesn't know that he will retire batters at such a predictable rate, in such a predictable way, that he might as well be a robot. As a result, he might not do it.

B ILLY BEANE only watches all of what happens next because he's somehow allowed himself to be trapped into watching the game with me. What happens next is that Chad Bradford shows the world how quickly a big lead in baseball can be lost. He gets the final out in the seventh inning, on a ground ball. The eighth inning is the problem. Art Howe allows Chad to return to the mound to face a series of left-handed hitters.

"I'm glad Art's leaving him in," says Billy. "He's wasted if you only use him to get an out."

I ask if it worries him that Chad relies so heavily on faith. That Chad's genuine, understandable belief that the Good Lord must be responsible for his fantastic ability to get big league hitters out leaves him open to the suspicion that the Good Lord might have changed His mind.

"No," says Billy. "I'm a believer, too. I just happen to believe in the power of the ground ball."

In nearly seventy relief appearances this year Chad Bradford has walked exactly ten batters, about one every thirty he has faced. He opens the eighth inning by walking Brent Mayne.

As Mayne trots down to first base, the Oakland crowd stirs and hollers. Someone from the center field bleachers hurls a roll of toilet paper onto the field. It takes a minute to clear, leaving Chad time with his hellish thoughts. When play resumes, fifty-five thousand people rise up and bang and shout, perhaps thinking this will help Chad to settle down.

"Why should noise have any more effect on the hitter than the pitcher?" says Billy, a bit testily. "If you're playing away, you just pretend they are cheering for you."

Chad walks the second hitter, Dee Brown. It's the first time all year he's walked two batters in a row. The TV cameras pan to Miguel Tejada and second baseman Mark Ellis, conferring behind their gloves.

"In the last ten years guys started covering their lips with their gloves," snaps Billy. "I've never known a single lip-reader in baseball. What, has there been a rash of lipreading I don't know about?"

The third batter, Neifi Perez, hits a slow ground ball to the second baseman. John Mabry, playing first, races across and cuts it off. Chad just stands on the mound and watches the play develop. By the time it has, it's too late for him to cover first base. The bases are now loaded, with nobody out. Another roll of toilet paper streams from the bleachers into center field. The crowd is on its feet, making more noise than ever, still thinking, Lord knows why, that their attention is what Chad Bradford needs to get him through his troubles.

Billy stares at the television with disgust, like a theatre critic being forced to watch a mangled interpretation of *Hamlet*. "I can't believe I have to sit here and watch this shit," he says. He pulls his little white box onto the desk in front of him. Its plastic shine has been rubbed dull. "I would be dying right now if I was walking around watching this," he says. He's fantasizing: if I hadn't trapped him with the TV inside this office he would be out in the parking lot, marching around glancing every five seconds at the white box. He'd rather be dying out there than whatever he's doing in here.

The next batter, Luis Ordaz, is the one who makes good on Billy's prediction about Miguel Tejada ("Watch him: he'll try to do more than he should"). Ordaz hits a routine ground ball to Tejada's right. Instead of making the routine play, the force at third, Tejada tries to make the acrobatic one, the force at home. His leaping throw bounces in the dirt in front of Ramon Hernandez and all runners are safe: 11–6. Bases still loaded, nobody yet out.

Art Howe virtually leaps out of the dugout to yank Chad from the game. On his way to his seat on the bench Chad stares at the ground, and works to remain expressionless. He came in with a six-run lead. He leaves with the tying run in the on-deck circle. The ball never left the infield.

"Jesus Christ, what a fucking embarrassment," says Billy. He reaches under the desk and extracts a canister of Copenhagen. He jams the chaw into his upper lip. "Why am I even watching this shit?"

The new pitcher, Ricardo Rincon, gets two quick outs, and gives up just one run on a sacrifice fly: 11–7. With two outs and runners on first and third, Art Howe walks out yet again. This time he calls for right-hander Jeff Tam, newly arrived from Triple-A, to face the right-handed Mike Sweeney, who is, at the moment, leading the American League in hitting.

"Fuck," says Billy. "Why? They all take this lefty-righty shit too far. What's wrong with leaving Rincon in?"

Tam had two years in the A's bullpen where he played the role now played by Chad Bradford. There was a time when Ron Washington, the infield coach, took to calling Tam "Toilet Paper" ("Because he's always cleanin' up everybody else's shit"). But something happened, either in Tam's head or his delivery, and for the past two years he hasn't been the same guy. "Relievers are like volatile stocks," Billy says. "They're the one asset you need to watch closely, and trade for quick profits."

As his manager and reliever confer, Billy Beane looks at me apologetically. In under forty-five minutes he's passed from detachment to interest, from interest to irritation, from irritation to anger, and is now, obviously, on the brink of rage. He's embarrassed by his emotions but not enough to control them. "All right," he finally says, "you'll have to excuse me, I'm going to have to pace around here."

With that, he walks out into the clubhouse, closing the door behind him, and begins to storm around. Past the trainer's room where poor Tim Hudson, who must be wondering what he needs to do to get a win, is having heat applied to his shoulder. Past Scott Hatteberg and Greg Myers, the two lefties on the bench who had thought they had the night off, rushing back through the clubhouse to the batting cage to take some practice swings, in case they are asked to pinch-hit. And, finally, past the video room where Paul DePodesta stews on the improbability of the evening. Paul already has calculated the odds of winning twenty games in a row. (He puts them at fourteen in a million.) Now he's calculating the odds of losing an eleven-run lead. ("It may not be fourteen in a million but it's close.")

In his *1983 Abstract*, Bill James had contemplated tonight's game. James had observed in baseball what he called a "law of competitive balance." "There exists in the world a negative momentum," he wrote,

which acts constantly to reduce the differences between strong teams and weak teams, teams which are ahead and teams which are behind, or good players and poor players. The corollaries are:

1. Every form of strength covers one weakness and creates another, and therefore every form of strength is also a form of weakness and every weakness a strength.

2. The balance of strategies always favors the team which is behind.

3. Psychology tends to pull the winners down and push the losers upwards.

More metaphysics than physics, it was as true of people as it was of baseball teams. People who want very badly to win, and to be seen to have won, enjoy a tactical advantage over people who don't. That very desire, tantamount to a need, is also a weakness. In Billy Beane, the trait is so pronounced that it is not merely a weakness. It is a curse.

When play resumes, Jeff Tam and Mike Sweeney fight a great battle. On the tenth pitch of the at bat, after fouling off four pitches with Superman swings, Sweeney takes a slider from Tam and golfs it off the 1-800-BAR-NONE sign, just over the left field wall.

11–10.

Something big crashes in the clubhouse.

On the TV over Art Howe's desk, Art himself is again on his way to the mound, to replace Jeff Tam with a lefty named Micah Bowie. Mike Sweeney enthusiastically explains to his teammates in the Kansas City dugout how he thought his home run was a foul ball. The announcers say what a pity it is that Miguel Tejada "tried to do too much" with the routine ground ball to third. Had he not, the A's would be out of the inning. Billy bursts back in the room—cheeks red, teeth black. "Fucking Tam," he says. "He thinks he's going to fool the best hitter in the league with his slider." He mutes the television, grabs his tin of Copenhagen, and vanishes, leaving me to watch the game alone in his manager's office.

The manager's office is now completely silent. The fifty-five thousand people outside are making about as much noise as fifty-five thousand people can make, but none of it reaches this benighted place. Pity Art Howe. What little he has done to make the office a home suggests a view of the world so different from Billy Beane's that it's a wonder he's kept his job as long as he has. There's a framed aphorism, called "The Optimist's Creed." There is a plaque containing the wisdom of Vince Lombardi. There is an empty coffee pot, with a canister of non-dairy creamer. Behind the manager's white Formica desk is a sign that says *Thank You For Not Smoking*. There are photos that hint at a fealty to baseball's mystique: one of Art standing on the dugout steps, another of Art and Cal Ripken, Jr. (signed by Ripken). On the television, Art maintains his stoical expression. Beneath him flashes the news that no Athletics team has lost an eleven-run lead since the Philadelphia A's lost one to the St. Louis Browns in 1936. Baseball has so much history and tradition. You can respect it, or you can exploit it for profit, but it's still being made all over the place, all the time.

Micah Bowie gets the final out in the Kansas City eighth, and the A's go quickly in their half. In the top of the ninth, facing closer Billy Koch, the Royals get a man as far as second base. With two outs and two strikes against a weak hitter, Luis Alicea, the game, once again, looks over. Then Alicea lines a single into left center.

11–11.

From somewhere in the clubhouse I hear a sharp cry, then the clatter of metal on metal. I open Art Howe's door to sneak a peek, and spot Scott Hatteberg running from the batting cage to the tunnel that leads to the Oakland dugout.

Hatteberg isn't particularly ready to play. He's in the wrong state of mind, and carrying the wrong bat. After Art Howe told him he wasn't playing tonight, he'd poured himself a cup of coffee, then another. He'd sat down briefly and chatted with some guy he'd never met, and whose name he couldn't remember, who wanted to show him some bats he had handcrafted. Hatteberg had picked out one of the guy's bats, a shiny black maple one with a white ring around its neck. He liked the feel of it.

Like most of the players, Hatteberg, as a minor leaguer, had signed a contract with the Louisville Slugger company, in which he agreed to use only the company's bats. All but certain that he would not play tonight, he had taken his contraband bat with him to the dugout. By the time the score was 11–0, certain that he would never play, he had the bat between his knees and four cups of coffee in his bloodstream. He is, by the bottom of the ninth, chemically altered. He's also holding a bat he's never hit with.

The score remains 11–11. The Kansas City closer, Jason Grimsley, is on the mound, throwing his usual blazing sinkers. Jermaine Dye flies to right for the first out. The television camera pans the A's dugout and from their expressions you can see that a lot of the players think the game is as good as lost. In losing an eleven-run lead, they'd lost more than that. They look as if they know the last good thing already has happened to them.

Art Howe tells Scott Hatteberg to grab a bat. He's pinch-hitting. Hatteberg grabs the bat given to him by the anonymous craftsman. It violates the contract he signed as a minor leaguer with the Louisville Slugger company, but what the hell.

He had faced Grimsley just two days before, in a similar situation. Tie game, bottom of the ninth, but that time there were men on base. He didn't need to watch tape tonight. With a pitcher like Grimsley you always know what you'll be getting: 96-mph heat. You also, usually, know where you'll be getting it: at the bottom of, or just below, the strike zone. Two days ago Grimsley had thrown him six straight sinking fastballs, down and away. With two strikes on him, Hatteberg had swung at the last of them and hit a weak ground ball to second base. (Miguel Tejada had followed him with a game-winning single up the middle.) As disappointing as that experience had been, it now served a purpose. He'd seen six pitches from Jason Grimsley. He's gathered his information. He knew that, if at all possible, he shouldn't fool around with Grimsley's low sinkers.

Tonight, as he steps into the box, he promises himself that he won't swing at anything down in the zone until he has two strikes. He'll wait for what he wants until he has no choice but to accept whatever happens to be coming. He's looking for something up—something he can drive for a double, and get himself in scoring position.

He settles into his usual open stance, and waggles the shiny black contraband bat back and forth through the zone, like a golfer on the first tee. As Grimsley comes into the stretch, his face contorts in the most unsettling way. He actually grins as he pitches, and it's not a friendly grin. It's the grin of a man who enjoys pulling wings off flies. The effect on the TV viewer is unnerving. But Hatty doesn't see Grimsley's face. He's gazing at the general area where he expects the ball to leave Grimsley's hand. He needs to see just one pitch, to get his timing down. He's thinking: *if I can lay off the first pitch I might get a pitch up in the zone.* Over and over he's telling himself: *lay off the first pitch.* The man who will this year lead the entire American League in laying off first pitches feels he needs to give himself a pep talk to lay off the first pitch. It must be the caffeine.

He lays off the first pitch. It's a ball, just low. Another round of horrible facial expressions, and Grimsley's ready again. The second pitch is another fastball, but it's high in the strike zone. Hatty takes his short swing; the ball finds the barrel of his bat, and rockets into deep right center field.

He leaves the batter's box in a crouching run. He's moving just as fast as he does when he hits a slow roller to the third baseman. He doesn't see Grimsley raging. He doesn't hear fifty-five thousand fans erupting. He doesn't notice the first baseman turning to leave the field. He doesn't know that there's a fellow from Cooperstown following him around the bases, picking them up, and will soon come looking for his bat. The only one in the entire Coliseum who does not know where the ball is going is the man who hit it. Scott Hatteberg alone watches the ball soar through the late night air with something like detachment.

The ball doesn't just leave the park; it lands high up in the stands, fifty feet or so beyond the 362 sign in deep right center field. When he's finally certain that the ball is gone for good, Scott Hatteberg raises both hands over his head, less in triumph than disbelief. Rounding first, he looks into the Oakland dugout. But there's no one left inside—the players are all rushing onto the field. Elation transforms him. He shouts at his teammates. He's not saying: *Look what I just did.* He's saying: *Look what we just did! We won!* As he runs, he sheds years at the rate of about one every twenty feet. By the time he touches home plate, he's less man than boy.

And, not five minutes later, Billy Beane was able to look me in the eye and say that it was just another win.

Chapter Twelve

THE SPEED OF THE IDEA

B
ILLY BEANE never allowed himself sentimental feelings about a game, or a player, or his own experiences. He'd walled himself off from his finer feelings, or tried to. He defined himself by his distaste for, rather than his romance with, his ballplaying past. This set him apart from most people who made their living in the game. Former big league ballplayers usually have friendly ghosts.

The sympathy most former ballplayers had for their own professional experiences—for the way they played the game—was nevertheless a problem for the anti-traditional Oakland A's. They needed to employ men with experience, but with that experience came the usual feelings and hunches and instincts. Billy often felt as if he were having to fight the past in his players and coaches—that Paul DePodesta was the only person in the entire organization who drew the same conclusions from the same data as he did. And, as the play-offs approached, this problem always intensified.

One day before the end of the regular season, Ron Washington and Thad Bosley, the A's infield and hitting coaches, came together in a batting cage, just off the visitors' clubhouse in The Ballpark in Arlington. Their talk began innocently enough. The team was about to play its second to last game of the regular season, against the Texas Rangers. Ray Durham was getting in some extra hacks, with Wash and Boz looking on, less coaches than connoisseurs.

Crack!

Wash and Boz were having one last, soulful look at Ray Durham before Durham went the way of all of Billy Beane's rent-a-stars. There was little chance Billy would re-sign Ray Durham for next season. There wasn't enough wrong with him. There wasn't *anything* wrong with him. Durham had what every general manager in the game had always prized: pop in the leadoff slot, speed on the base paths, and a reputation, less deserved now than five years ago, as a good second baseman. In the free market Durham probably would be overpriced; but even if he was fairly priced, Billy wouldn't keep him. There was nothing inefficient about the market for Ray Durham's services.

"Look at Ray," says Wash.

Crack!

"That little sonofabitch got some *juice* in that body," says Wash. "He will *hurt* you, you throw the ball in the wrong place."

"Swings like a man," says Boz. "And that man's a menace."

"He stands up there like some little Punch and Judy," says Wash. "But he can hurt you."

Crack! It's unclear whether Ray is listening to any of this.

"You know what impressed me the most about Ray when he first came over?" says Boz. "The way he runs down the first-base line."

"He's the only base stealer we got," says Wash. "You know what a base stealer is?"

I assumed I didn't.

"A base stealer is a guy who when everyone in the goddamn yard know he gonna get the bag, he gets the bag."

Crack!

Wash had been recruited to play baseball by the Kansas City Royals in the early seventies, at a time when the Royals were trying to take track stars and turn them into baseball players. Those Royals had made a fetish of speed, and Wash, a speedster, was the beneficiary. The way Wash tells it, with the first pitch of every game he and his teammates started running, and they didn't stop until the last. "There was sometimes you didn't run," he says, but then he has to think hard about what times those might be. "You didn't run on Nolan Ryan," he finally says, "because when you ran on Nolan Ryan all you did was piss Nolan Ryan off. You'da kept your ass on first base, the hitter might have done something."

Not thinking where it might lead, I ask Wash how many bases he stole in his youth.

"I stole fifty-seven one year," he says.

Ray Durham turns, slightly, and cocks his head in mock amazement: *no shit!*

Wash is looking straight at Ray when he says, "Boz stole ninety."

Boz just nods.

Ray drops his bat in wonder. "You stole *ninety*?" he says.

Boz just nods again, like it's no big deal.

"Damn!" Ray's now engaged. He's like an American tourist who has just discovered the German on the train next to him is a long-lost cousin. "It's different here, huh?" he says.

The question is rhetorical. Ray Durham knows firsthand just how different it is here. Two months ago, freshly plucked for next to nothing by Billy Beane from the Chicago White Sox, Durham was seated in a dugout before his first game with his new team. The Oakland beat reporters swarmed around him. Their second question was, "How do you feel about Billy Beane putting you in center field?" That was the first Ray Durham had heard of Billy's quixotic plans for him. He hadn't played in the outfield since high school. Durham dutifully said that he was willing to consider anything to help the team, a statement his saucer eyes translated beautifully into a question: *Are you fucking kidding me?* In nanoseconds Durham's agent was on the phone to Billy to explain that his client, an *All-Star* second baseman, was a free agent at the end of the year. While happy to perform the usual offensive services for this low-rent team that, by some miracle, had got their sweaty peasant hands on him for half a season, Ray Durham did not intend to jeopardize his financial future by making a spectacle of himself in center field for the Oakland A's.

Ray had put an end to that particular stab at baseball efficiency. But when the A's coaches told him to stop trying to steal bases, he had stopped. His whole career Ray Durham had been hired to steal bases; the moment he arrived in Oakland, his coaches told him to stay put wherever he was until the ball was hit. Billy had traded for Ray not because Ray stole bases but because Ray had a talent for getting on base—for not making outs. And so, for the first time in his career, Ray mostly played it safe on the bases. From the aesthetic point of view, this was a pity. Let Ray Durham do what he pleased on the base paths and he became a human thrill ride. The other night in Seattle, after a passed ball, he went from second to third in a heartbeat and then, instead of stopping like a sane person, just flew around the bag and headed toward home. The entire stadium suffered a little panic attack. The Seattle catcher dove and spun, the Seattle pitcher felt his sphincter in his throat, and forty thousand Seattle fans gasped like they'd just reached the first crest on a giant roller coaster. A millisecond later Ray screeched to a halt, trotted back to third, and chuckled. Ray knew how to use his legs to fuck with people's minds.

Not running is about as natural to Ray as not breathing, but until now he's bottled up not just his speed but his feelings. Now he says, "It's different here, huh?"

Wash snorts. "It's the shit," he says. "We have twenty-five stolen bases all year. Eight were guys going on their own and getting it. Ten were 3–2 counts. Seven, Art gave the green light." One hundred and sixty games into the season Art Howe has given base runners the green light a grand total of seven times. It's got to be some kind of record.

"Ray, how many bags you got this season?" asks Wash.

"Twenty-five," says Ray.

"When he came over, he had twenty-two," says Wash. "So he got three bags here. Two of those he took on his own."

"You run on this team and you're on your own," says Boz, ominously.

"Yeah," says Wash. "There's a rule on this club. It's okay if you get it. If you don't, you got hell to pay." That would cast Billy Beane as Satan.

Ray shakes his head in wonder, and goes back to taking his cuts. *Crack!*

"If you say base-running isn't important, you forget how to run the bases," says Boz.

"You wanna see something funny," Wash says. "Come sit with me in the third-base box and watch that shit comin' at me. Nobody on this club know how to go from first to third." In addition to being the infield coach on a team that can't afford to waste money on defense, Wash is the third-base coach on a team that can't afford to waste money on speed. Whenever a ball goes to the wall, he's required to make these weirdly elaborate calculations to take into account the base-running talents Billy Beane has provided him with. He doesn't want to hear that foot speed is overpriced.

Ray can no longer concentrate on his hitting. "Cautious doesn't work in the play-offs," he says.

Wash and Boz don't say anything to that. Ray's got three weeks, at most, before he's a free agent deciding which multi-million-dollar offer to accept: Ray can say whatever he wants about Billy

Beane's approach to baseball. In a few days the Oakland A's will face the Minnesota Twins in the first round of the play-offs, and all the noise on the television and in the papers is about how the play-offs are different from the regular season. How the play-offs are about "manufacturing" runs. The play-offs were all about street cred, and science didn't have any.

"I don't see a lot of play-off games where the score is 8–5," says Ray. "It's always 1–0 and 2–1."

"The fact of it is," says Wash, "Billy Beane *hates* to make outs on the base paths."

Ray shakes his head sadly and resumes taking his cuts.

I've stumbled upon a revolutionary cell within the Oakland A's, three men who still believe in the need for speed. These aren't stupid men. Ray's obviously as shrewd as a loan shark. Ron Washington can't open his mouth without saying something that belongs in *Bartlett's*. Boz had succeeded in more than just baseball. After thirteen seasons in the big leagues, he'd spent seven more writing and producing music. Boz had something of the outsider's perspective—which is why Billy had hired him. Boz embraced his unusual role with the Oakland A's, not "hitting coach," but "on-base instructor." He didn't mind the front office's indifference to batting average. Their indifference to the running game was another matter.

"Ray was *bred* on being aggressive running the bases," says Wash. "Until he got here he *never* got chastised for being aggressive on the base paths."

Crack! Ray lines a pitch off the foot of bullpen catcher Brandon Buckley, who has been pitching to him from behind a screen. As Brandon hops around and tries to figure out if he's broken something, Ray turns and says, "The White Sox always told us an aggressive mistake is not really a mistake."

Wash is overcome with fellow feeling. Here they have this specimen of base-running prowess *and no one gives a shit*. He says, "Ray, what you thinkin' about when you put the ball in play?"

"Second base."

"As long as the ball is rolling?"

"I'm runnin'."

"You runnin'."

"A single is a double," says Ray.

"A double is a triple," says Wash.

Nobody says anything for a minute. Then Wash says, "Different situation here. Somebody on this team runs and get his ass thrown out and you got all kinds of *gurus* who tell you that you just took yourself out of the inning."

"I never seen anything like it," says Ray.

TWO THINGS happened toward the end of every season, after Billy Beane's Oakland A's have secured a play-off spot. The first was a slightly unseemly attempt by a small handful of staff members to use the newspapers to create pressure on the GM to improve their standard of living. The most transparent of these was an interview given by manager Art Howe to the *San Jose Mercury News*, on the subject of a long-term contract for himself. "With all the years I've been here and with what we've accomplished," he said, "I would think I deserve it. My thinking is, if I don't get it here, I'll get it somewhere else." After Art's wife confessed that she, too, was befuddled by Billy Beane's unwillingness to secure their retirement years, Art mentioned how struck he was by how different baseball teams arrange their pecking order. "Down in Anaheim," he said, "all they talked about is the manager. I don't think most people even know who the general manager is down there."

The other thing that invariably happened was an unsystematic rethink in the engine room about this quixotic course the captain has set all season long. Coaches, players, reporters: everyone at once starts to worry that the Oakland A's don't bunt or run. Especially run. Billy Beane's total lack of interest in the stolen base—

which has served the team so well for the previous 162 games—is regarded, in the postseason, as sheer folly. Even people who don't run very fast start saying that "you need to make things happen" in the postseason. Take the action to your opponent. "The atavistic need to run," Billy Beane calls it.

The regular season is all but forgotten, but it shouldn't be. Any way you looked at it, it had been a miracle. In all of Major League Baseball only the New York Yankees won as many games as the Oakland A's. All but written off when they let Jason Giambi leave for greener pastures, the A's had won 103 games, one more than they had the year before. Maybe more astonishingly, at least for economic determinists, the teams in baseball's best division, the American League West, finished in inverse order to their payrolls.

	Wins	Losses	Games Behind	Payroll*
Oakland	103	59	—	$41,942,665
Anaheim	99	63	4	$62,757,041
Seattle	93	69	10	$86,084,710
Texas	72	90	31	$106,915,180

The more money the teams spent on players, at least in the American League West, the less able those players were to win baseball games. The same wasn't exactly true in every other division, but there had been plenty of other astonishing endings: big-budget disasters (the Mets, the Dodgers, the Orioles) and low-budget successes (the Twins).

---

* The payroll figures are Major League Baseball's on August 31, 2002. The wacky funhouse mirror quality of the 2002 season, in which several poor teams made the play-offs and no very rich teams made the World Series, had no discernable effect on Major League Baseball's view of the role of money in baseball success. Commissioner Bud Selig continued to insist that the Oakland A's—who also had turned a slight profit—were doomed. "We're asking them [the Oakland A's] to compete in a stadium they can't compete in," he said, in February 2003. "They're not viable without a new stadium."

In spite of the Oakland A's fantastic success, there was a subtle pressure to change the way they did business. Most of it came from the media. About the fifteenth time he heard some TV pundit say that the Oakland A's couldn't win because they didn't "manufacture runs," Billy began to worry his coaches and players might actually believe it. He printed out the 2002 offensive statistics for the Oakland A's and the Minnesota Twins and sat down with the coaches. The Twins team batting average was 11 points higher than the A's, and their slugging percentage was 5 points higher. And yet they had scored thirty-two fewer runs. Why? Their team on-base percentage was a shade lower, and they'd been caught stealing sixty-two times, to Oakland's twenty, and had twice as many sacrifice bunts. That is, they'd squandered outs. "They were trying to manipulate the game instead of letting the game come to them," said Billy. "The math works. But no matter how many times you prove it, you always have to prove it again."

The moment the play-offs began, you could feel the world of baseball insiders rising up to swat down the possibility that the Oakland A's front office actually might be onto something. The man who spoke for all insiders was Joe Morgan, the Hall of Fame second baseman, who was in the broadcast booth for the entire five-game series between the A's and the Twins. At some point during each game Morgan explained to the audience the flaw in the A's thinking—not that he had any deep understanding of what that thinking entailed. But he was absolutely certain that their strategy made no sense. When the A's lost the first game, 7–5, it gave Morgan his opening to explain, in the first inning of the second game, why the Oakland A's were in trouble. "You have to manufacture runs in the postseason," he said, meaning bunt and steal and in general treat outs as something other than a scarce resource. Incredibly, he then went on to explain that "manufacturing runs" was how the New York Yankees had beaten the Anaheim Angels the night before.

I had seen that game. Down 5–4 in the eighth inning, Yankees second baseman Alfonso Soriano had gotten himself on base and stolen second. Derek Jeter then walked, and Jason Giambi singled in Soriano. Bernie Williams then hit a three-run homer. A reasonable person, examining that sequence of events, says, "Whew, thank God Soriano didn't get caught stealing; it was, in retrospect, a stupid risk that could have killed the whole rally." Joe Morgan looked at it and announced that Soriano stealing second, the only bit of "manufacturing" in the production line, was the *cause*. Amazingly, Morgan concluded that day's lesson about baseball strategy by saying, "You sit and wait for a three-run homer, you're still going to be sitting there."

But the wonderful thing about this little lecture was what happened right under Joe Morgan's nose, as he was giving it. Ray Durham led off the game for Oakland with a walk. He didn't attempt to steal, as Morgan would have him do. Scott Hatteberg followed Durham and he didn't bunt, as Morgan would have him do. He smashed a double. A few moments later, Eric Chavez hit a three-run homer. And Joe Morgan's lecture on the need to avoid playing for the three-run homer just rolled right along, as if the play on the field had not dramatically contradicted every word that had just come out of his mouth. That day the A's walked and swatted their way to nine runs, and a win—in which Chad Bradford, returned to form, pitched two scoreless innings. Two days later in Minnesota, before the third game, Joe Morgan made the same speech all over again.

As it turned out, the A's did everyone in baseball a favor and lost to the Twins, in the fifth game.* The two games they won the

---

* In the five-game series, Scott Hatteberg went 7–14 with three walks, no strikeouts, a home run, and a pair of doubles. He scored five runs and knocked in three. Chad Bradford faced ten batters and got nine of them out, seven on ground balls. The tenth batter hit a bloop single. Bradford snapped out of his slump after the twentieth win. His confidence returned about the same time Scott Hatteberg started telling him what the hitters said on the rare occasions they got to first base

scores were 9–1 and 8–3. The three games they lost the scores were 7–5, 11–2, and 5–4. These were not the low-scoring games of Ray Durham's play-off imagination. And yet virtually all of the noisy second-guessing after their defeat followed the line of reasoning laid down by Ray Durham and Joe Morgan. One of the leading Bay Area baseball columnists, Glenn Dickey of the *San Francisco Chronicle*, explained to his readers that "The A's don't know how to 'manufacture' runs, which kills them in close games in the postseason. Manager Art Howe, who believed in 'little ball' before he came to the A's, has become so accustomed to the walk/homer approach that he can't adjust in the postseason." In late October, Joe Morgan will summarize the Oakland A's problems in print: "The A's lose because they are two-dimensional. They have good pitching and try to hit home runs. They don't use speed and don't try to manufacture runs. They wait for the home run. They are still waiting."

All of the commentary struck the Oakland A's front office as just more of the same. "Base-stealing," said Paul DePodesta, after the dust had settled. "That's the one thing everyone points to that we do. Or don't. So when we lose, that's why." He then punched some numbers into his calculator. The Oakland A's scored 4.9 runs per game during the season. They scored 5.5 runs per game in the five-game series against the Twins. They hadn't "manufactured" runs and yet they had scored more of them in the play-offs than they had during the regular season. "The real problem," said Paul, "was that during the season we allowed 4.0 runs per game, and during the play-offs we allowed 5.4. The small sample size makes that insignificant, but it also punctuates the absurdity of the critiques of our offensive philosophy." The real problem was that Tim Hudson, heretofore flawless in big games, and perfect

---

against him. After Anaheim's second baseman, Adam Kennedy, blooped a single off Bradford, he turned to Hatty and said, "Jesus Christ, there's no way that's eighty-four miles an hour."

against the Minnesota Twins, had two horrendous outings. No one could have predicted that.

The postseason partially explained why baseball was so uniquely resistant to the fruits of scientific research: to *any* purely rational idea about how to run a baseball team. It wasn't just that the game was run by old baseball men who insisted on doing things as they had always been done. It was that the season ended in a giant crapshoot. The play-offs frustrate rational management because, unlike the long regular season, they suffer from the sample size problem. Pete Palmer, the sabermetrician and author of *The Hidden Game of Baseball*, once calculated that the average difference in baseball due to skill is about one run a game, while the average difference due to luck is about four runs a game. Over a long season the luck evens out, and the skill shines through. But in a series of three out of five, or even four out of seven, anything can happen. In a five-game series, the worst team in baseball will beat the best about 15 percent of the time; the Devil Rays have a prayer against the Yankees. Baseball science may still give a team a slight edge, but that edge is overwhelmed by chance. The baseball season is structured to mock reason.

Because science doesn't work in the games that matter most, the people who play them are given one more excuse to revert to barbarism. The game is structured, psychologically (though not financially), as a winner-take-all affair. There isn't much place for the notion that a team that falls short of the World Series has had a great season. At the end of what was now widely viewed as a failed season, all Paul DePodesta could say was, "I hope they continue to believe that our way doesn't work. It buys us a few more years."

Billy beane had been surprisingly calm throughout his team's play-off debacle. Before the second game against the Twins, when I'd asked him why he seemed so detached—why he wasn't walking around the parking lot with his white box—he said, "My shit doesn't work in the play-offs. My job is to get us to the play-offs. What happens after that is fucking luck." It was Paul who took a bat to the chair in the video room, late at night after the fifth game, after everyone else had gone home for good. Billy's attitude seemed to be, all that management can produce is a team good enough to triumph in a long season. There are no secret recipes for the postseason, except maybe having three great starting pitchers, and he had that.

His objective spirit survived his team's defeat a week. The fact that his team had lost to the clearly inferior Minnesota Twins festered. He never said it, but it was nonetheless evident that he couldn't quite believe how little appreciation there was for what he'd done. Even his owner, who was getting multiples more for his money than any owner in baseball, complained. The public reaction to the thing ate at Billy. In these situations, when his mind was disturbed, he often went looking to make a trade. But there was no player on whom his mind naturally fixed; the only person in the organization whose riddance would make him happier was his manager, Art Howe. It wasn't long before he had a novel idea: trade Art.

It took him about a week to do it. He called New York Mets GM Steve Phillips and told him that Art was a superb manager but his latest one-year contract called for a big raise, and Oakland couldn't really afford to pay it. Phillips had just fired his own manager, Bobby Valentine, and was in a bit of a fix. Billy had thought he might even get a player from the Mets for Art but in the end settled on moving Art's salary. Art signed a five-year deal for $2 million a year to manage the New York Mets. In Art's place Billy installed Ken Macha, the A's bench coach.

That made him feel better for a bit. Then it didn't. He had the feeling he'd come to the end of some line. Here they had run this low-budget franchise as efficiently as a low-budget franchise could be run and no one had even noticed. No one cared if you found radically better ways to run a big league baseball team. All anyone cared about was how you fared in the postseason crapshoot. For his work he'd been paid about as well as a third-year relief pitcher, and Paul had been paid less than the major league minimum. Billy was worth, easily, more than any player; his services were more dramatically undervalued than those of any player he'd ever acquired. He could see only one way to exploit this grotesque market inefficiency: trade himself.

His timing was about perfect. The market for Billy Beane's services was changing rapidly. What appeared to be a new trend had started a year ago, in Toronto. Rogers Communications, the Blue Jays' new owner, had made it clear that the team, which had been losing more money than any in baseball, had to be self-sustaining. After the 2001 season the Blue Jays' new CEO Paul Godfrey, formerly the metro chairman of Toronto (i.e., mayor) and a man with no baseball experience, set out to run the business along rational lines. He started by firing his general manager. He then piled up on his desk the media guides for the other twenty-nine teams in baseball, and went looking for a replacement. He called just about everyone in baseball, and interviewed most of them. Buck Showalter, who had run the Diamondbacks and was now a TV announcer. Dave Dombrowski, who ran the Detroit Tigers. Pat Gillick, who had been the Blue Jays' GM during the glory years and was now the GM of the Seattle Mariners. Doug Melvin, who just had been fired by the Rangers. John Hart, the GM of the Cleveland Indians, who would wind up replacing Melvin at the Rangers. "They all said the same thing to me," says Godfrey. "It always came back to: give me the bucks to compete with the Yankees and I'll do it. They didn't understand what I was even talking about when I said I wanted someone who had a strategy going forward. I didn't want a guy who said, 'Give me a hundred fifty million bucks and I'll give you a winner.'"

In all of baseball Godfrey found one exception to the general money madness: Billy Beane's Oakland A's. He concluded that the

A's were playing a different game than everyone else. He decided that, whatever game they were playing, he wanted to play it too. He assumed that Billy Beane, who had a long-term contract in Oakland, was off-limits. So he'd offered the Blue Jays' top job to Paul DePodesta—but Paul didn't want it. And so Godfrey went back into the Oakland A's media guide and found the picture of the guy under DePodesta. His name was J. P. Ricciardi, the A's director of player development. J.P. flew to Toronto for the interview—and had the job in about five minutes. "He had a reason for everything," said Godfrey. "Of all the people I'd talked to, J.P. was the only one with a business plan and the only one who told me, 'You are spending too much money.' He basically went through the lineup and said, 'These people are all replaceable by people you've never heard of.' And I said, 'You sure?' And he said, 'Look, if you can stand the heat in the media, I can make you cheaper and better. It'll take a couple of months to make you cheaper and a couple of years to make you better. But you'll be a lot better.'"

The first thing J. P. Ricciardi did after he took the job was hire Keith Law, a twenty-eight-year-old Harvard graduate who had never played baseball, but who wrote lots of interesting articles about it for baseballprospectus.com. That was partly Billy's idea. Billy had told J.P. that, in order to find the fool at the poker table, "you need your Paul." The second thing J.P. did was fire twenty-five Blue Jays scouts. Then, over the next few months, he proceeded to get rid of just about every highly paid, established big league player and replace them with minor leaguers no one had ever heard of. By the end of the 2002 season J.P. had taken to watching every Blue Jays game with Keith Law. By then he could turn to his pet sabermetrician in the middle of a game and gleefully shout, "Rain Man, we got a $1.8 million team out there on the field right now!"

That superior management armed with science could be had so cheaply was easily the greatest inefficiency in all of baseball, and the owner with the keenest sense of markets, and their follies, saw this. John Henry had just purchased the Boston Red Sox, and he was looking to overhaul his franchise in the image of the Oakland A's. In late October he hired Bill James as "Senior Consultant, Baseball Operations." ("I don't understand how it took so long for somebody to hire this guy," Henry said.) Just to be sure, he also hired Voros McCracken as a special adviser on pitching. Then he went looking for someone to run the show.

Only one guy had ever actually proved he could impose reason on a big league clubhouse, and that guy, two weeks after his team had been bounced from the play-offs, was now dissatisfied with his job. One thing led to another, and before long Billy Beane had agreed to run the Boston Red Sox. He would be guaranteed $12.5 million over five years, the most anyone had ever been paid to run a baseball team. Billy hadn't yet signed the contract, but that was just a formality. He had already persuaded his owner to let him out of his contract, and started to overhaul the Red Sox. In his mind's eye he had traded Red Sox third baseman Shea Hillenbrand to some team that didn't understand that a .293 batting average was a blow to the offense when it came attached to a .330 on-base percentage. He'd signed Edgardo Alfonzo to play second base, and Bill Mueller to play third. Red Sox catcher Jason Varitek was gone and White Sox backup Mark Johnson was in his place. Manny Ramirez's glove was requisitioned by general management, and the slugger would spend the rest of his Red Sox career as a designated hitter. All in his mind's eye.

In Oakland, Billy Beane's imminent departure quickly rippled through the organization. Paul DePodesta had agreed to become the new general manager of the Oakland A's. He'd promoted his fellow Harvard graduate, David Forst, to be his assistant. Paul's main concern was just how much Billy Beane's Boston Red Sox should pay the Oakland A's for poaching their general manager. Billy came to work one day to face a new situation. As he put it, "I've now got two Harvard guys on my sofa trying to figure out how they're going to screw me." It looked like the beginning of a new relationship. He and Paul argued back and forth until they settled on the player Paul would get in exchange for Billy Beane: Kevin Youkilis. The Greek god of walks. The player who, but for the A's old scouting department, should have been an Oakland A. The player with the highest on-base percentage in all of professional baseball, after Barry Bonds. Paul wanted another minor leaguer too, but Youkilis was the real prize.

All that remained was for Billy to sign the Red Sox contract. And he couldn't do it. In the forty-eight hours after he accepted John Henry's job offer, Billy became as manic and irrational and incapable of sleep as he had been back in May, after the A's had been swept by the Blue Jays. As decisive as he was about most things, he was paralyzed when the decision involved himself. He loved the idea of working for John Henry, with his understanding of markets and their inefficiencies. But you didn't up and move three thousand miles and start a new life just to work for a different owner. Five days before, Billy had convinced himself he wasn't taking the job just for the money. Since it was pretty clear he wasn't doing it for the love of the Red Sox, it raised a question of why he was doing it at all. He decided he was doing it just to show that he could do it. To prove that his own peculiar talents had concrete value. Dollar value. And that in any sane world he'd be paid a fortune for them.

Now he had a problem: he'd just proved that. Baseball columns everywhere were abuzz with the news that Billy Beane was about to become the highest paid general manager in the history of the game. Now that everyone knew his true value, Billy didn't need to prove it anymore. Now the only reason to take the job was for the money.

The next morning, he called John Henry and told him he couldn't do it.* A few hours later, he blurted to a reporter some-

---

* The job went to Theo Epstein, the twenty-eight-year-old Yale graduate with no experience playing professional baseball.

thing he wished he hadn't said but was nevertheless the truth: "I made one decision based on money in my life—when I signed with the Mets rather than go to Stanford—and I promised I'd never do it again." After that, Billy confined himself to the usual blather about personal reasons. None of what he said was terribly rational or "objective"—but then, neither was he. Within a week, he was back to scheming how to get the Oakland A's back to the play-offs, and Paul DePodesta was back to being on his side. And he was left with his single greatest fear: that no one would ever *really* know. That he and Paul might find ever more clever ways to build great ball clubs with no money, but that, unless they brought home a World Series ring or two, no one would know. And even then— even if they did win a ring—where did that leave him? He'd be just one more general manager among many who were celebrated for a day, then forgotten. People would never know that, for a brief moment, he was right and the world was wrong.

About that I think he may have been mistaken. He'd been the perfect vessel for an oddly shaped idea, and that idea was on the move, like an Oakland A's base runner, station to station. The idea had led Billy Beane to take action, and his actions had conse- quences. He had changed the lives of ballplayers whose hidden virtues otherwise might never have been seen. And those players who had been on the receiving end of the idea were now busy returning the favor.

EPILOGUE: THE BADGER

THE JEREMY BROWN who steps into the batter's box in early October is, and is not, the fat catcher from Hueytown, Alabama, that the Oakland A's had made the least likely first-round draft choice in recent memory. He was still about five foot eight and 215 pounds. He still wasn't much use to anyone hoping to sell jeans. But in other ways, the important ways, experience had reshaped him.

Three months earlier, just after the June draft, he'd arrived in Vancouver, Canada, to play for the A's rookie ball team. Waiting for him there was a seemingly endless number of jokes to be had at his expense. The most widely read magazine in the locker room, *Baseball America*, kept writing all these rude things about his appearance. They quoted unnamed scouts from other teams saying things like, "He never met a pizza he didn't like." They pressed the A's own scouting director, Erik Kubota, to acknowledge the perversity of selecting a young man who looked like Jeremy Brown with a first-round draft choice. "He's not the most physically fit," Kubota had said, sounding distinctly apologetic. "It's not a pretty body. . . . This guy's a great baseball player trapped in a bad body." The magazine ran Jeremy's college year-book picture over the caption: "Bad Body Rap." His mother back in Hueytown read all of it, and every time someone made fun of the shape of her son, she got upset all over again. His dad just laughed.

The other guys on the rookie ball team thought it was a riot. They couldn't wait for the next issue of *Baseball America* to see what they'd write about Jeremy this time. Jeremy's new friend, Nick Swisher, was always the first to find whatever they'd writ-ten, but Swish approached the thing with defiance. Nick Swisher, son of former major league player Steve Swisher, and consensus first-round draft pick, took shit from no one. Swish didn't wait for other people to tell him what he was worth; he told them. He was trying to instill the same attitude, without much luck, in Jeremy Brown. One night over dinner with a few of the guys, Swish had said to him, "All that stuff they write in *Baseball America*—that's bullshit. You can play. That's all that matters. You can play. You think Babe Ruth was a stud? Hell no, he was a fat piece of shit." Jeremy was slow to take offense and it took him a second or two to register the double-edged nature of Swish's pep talk. "Babe Ruth was a fat piece of shit," he said. "Just like Brown." And everyone at the table laughed.

A few weeks after he'd arrived in Vancouver, Jeremy Brown and Nick Swisher were told by the team's trainer that the coaches wanted to see them in their office. Jeremy's first thought was "Oh man, I know I musta done something dumb." That was Jeremy's instinctive reaction when the authorities paid special attention to him: he'd done something wrong. What he'd done, in this case, was get on base an astonishing half the time he came to the plate. Jeremy Brown was making rookie ball look too easy. Billy Beane wanted to test him against stiffer competition; Billy wanted to see what he had. The coach handed Jeremy and Nick Swisher plane tickets and told them that they were the first guys from Oakland's 2002 draft to get promoted to Single-A ball.

It took them forever to get from Vancouver, Canada, to Visalia, California. They arrived just before a game, having not slept in thirty-one hours. No one said anything to them; no one wanted to have anything to do with them. That's the way it was as you climbed in the minors: your new teammates were never happy to see you. "Everybody just kind of looks at you and doesn't say anything," said Jeremy. "You just try to be nice. You don't want to get off on the wrong foot."

That first night in Visalia, he and Swish dressed and sat on the end of the bench. They might as well have been on the visiting team. No one even came down to say hello; if Swish hadn't been on hand to confirm the fact Jeremy might have wondered if he still existed. In the third inning the team's regular catcher, a hulk named Jorge Soto, came to the plate. Jeremy had never heard of Soto but he assumed, rightly, that he was competing with Soto for the catching job. On the first pitch Soto hit a shot the likes of which neither Jeremy nor Swish had ever seen. It was still rising as it flew over the light tower in left center field. It cleared the parking lot and also the skate park on the other side of the parking lot. It was the farthest ball Jeremy had ever seen hit live. Five hundred and fifty feet, maybe more. As Soto trotted around the bases, Jeremy turned to Swish and said, "I don't think I'm ever going to catch here."

If it was up to his new teammates, he wouldn't have. They locked the door; if Jeremy Brown and Nick Swisher wanted in, they'd have to break it down. One day he was walking through the Visalia clubhouse when someone shouted in a mocking tone, "Hey, Badger." Jeremy had no clue what the guy was talking about. He soon learned. His teammates, who still weren't saying much to him, had nicknamed him "The Badger." "It was 'cause when I get into the shower I kind of got a lot of hair on my body," Jeremy explained. Behind his back, they were all still having fun

.at his expense. Jeremy just did what he always did, smiled and got along.

Along with most of the other players drafted by the Oakland A's in 2002, Jeremy Brown had been invited to the Instructional League in Arizona at the end of the season. By then, three months after he'd been promoted to Visalia, no one was laughing at him. In Visalia, he'd quickly seized the starting catching job from Jorge Soto, and led the team in batting average (.310), on-base percentage (.444) and slugging percentage (.545). In fifty-five games, he'd knocked in forty runs. So artfully had he ripped through the pitching in high Single-A ball that Billy Beane had invited him to the 2003 big league spring training camp—the only player from the 2002 draft so honored. Every other player in the Oakland A's 2002 draft—even Nick Swisher—had experienced what the A's minor league director Keith Lieppman called "reality." Reality, Lieppman said, "is when you learn that you are going to have to change the way you play baseball if you are going to survive." Jeremy alone didn't need to change a thing about himself; it was the world around him that needed to change. And it did. The running commentary about him in *Baseball America* hung a U-turn. When the magazine named him one of the top three hitters from the entire 2002 draft, and one of the four top prospects in the Oakland A's minor league system, his mom called to tell him: someone had finally written something nice about him. His teammates in Visalia no longer called him "The Badger." Everyone now just called him "Badge."

When Jeremy Brown comes to the plate on this mid-October afternoon in Scottsdale, Arizona, it's the bottom of the second inning. There's no score, and there's no one on base. The big left-hander on the other team has made short work of the A's first three hitters. He throws Jeremy a fastball off the plate. Jeremy just looks at it. Ball one. Pitch number two is a change-up on the outside corner, where Jeremy can't do much with it anyway, so he just lets it be. Strike one. Jeremy Brown knows something about pitchers: "They almost always make a mistake," he says. "All you have to do is wait for it." Give the game a chance to come to you and often enough it will. When he takes the change-up for a called strike, he notices the possibility of a future mistake. The pitcher's arm motion, when he throws his change-up, is noticeably slower than it is when he throws his fastball.

The pitcher's next pitch is a fastball off the plate. Ball two. It's 2–1: a hitter's count.

The fourth pitch is the mistake: the pitcher goes back to his change-up. Jeremy sees his arm coming through slowly again, and this time he knows to wait on it. The change-up arrives waist-high over the middle of the plate. The line drive Jeremy hits screams over the pitcher's right ear and into the gap in left center field.

As he leaves the batter's box, Jeremy sees the left and center fielders converging fast. The left fielder, thinking he might make the catch, is already running himself out of position to play the ball off the wall. Jeremy knows he hit it hard, and so he knows what's going to happen next—or imagines he does. The ball is going to hit the wall and ricochet back into the field. The left fielder, having overrun it, will have to turn around and chase after it. Halfway down the first-base line, Jeremy Brown has one thought in his mind: *I'm gonna get a triple.*

It's a new thought for him. He isn't built for triples. He hasn't hit a triple in years. He thrills to the new idea: Jeremy Brown, hitter of triples. A funny thing has happened since he became, by some miracle, the most upwardly mobile hitter in the Oakland A's minor league system. Surrounded by people who keep telling him he's capable of almost anything, he's coming to believe it himself.

He races around first ("I'm haulin' ass now") and picks up the left fielder, running with his back to him, but not the ball. He's running as hard as he's ever run—and then he's not. Between first and second base his feet go out from under him and he backflops into the dirt, like Charlie Brown. He notices, first, a shooting pain in his hand: he's jammed his finger. He picks himself up, to scramble back to the safety of first base, when he sees his teammates in the dugout. The guys are falling all over each other, laughing. Swish. Stanley. Teahen. Kiger. Everybody's laughing at him again. But their laughter has a different tone; it's not the sniggering laughter of the people who made fun of his body. It's something else. He looks out into the gap in left center field. The outfielders are just standing there: they've stopped chasing the ball. The ball's gone. The triple of Jeremy Brown's imagination, in reality, is a home run.

AFTERWORD: INSIDE BASEBALL'S RELIGIOUS WAR

ANYONE WHO WANDERS into Major League Baseball can't help but notice the stark contrast between the field of play and the uneasy space just off it, where the executives and the scouts make their livings. The game itself is a ruthless competition. Unless you're very good, you don't survive in it. But in the space just off the field of play there really is no level of incompetence that won't be tolerated. There are many reasons for this, but the big one is that baseball has structured itself less as a business than as a social club. The Club includes not only the people who manage the team but also, in a kind of Women's Auxiliary, many of the writers and the commentators who follow it, and purport to explain it. The Club is selective, but the criteria for admission and retention are nebulous. There are many ways to embarrass the Club, but being bad at your job isn't one of them. The greatest offense a Club member can commit is not ineptitude but disloyalty. Had he not been an indiscreet writer, Jim Bouton might have made a second career scouting and coaching big league prospects. But because he wrote *Ball Four* he was as good as banished from the Club.

That's not to say that there are not good baseball executives and bad baseball executives, or good baseball scouts and bad baseball scouts. It's just that they aren't very well sorted out. Baseball doesn't subject its executives to anything like the pressures of playing baseball, or even of running a business. When a big league baseball team spends huge sums of money and loses, heads may roll, but they don't roll very far. Club insiders have a remarkable talent for hanging around, scouting young players, opining on the game, until some other high-level job opens up. Whereupon, with genuine hope in their hearts, they go for their interview with all the other Club members who were fired the last time around. There are no real standards, because no one wants to put too fine a point on the question: what qualifies these people for this job? Taking into account any quality other than clubability would make everyone's membership a little less secure.

This book, as I've said many pages ago, began with a simple, obvious observation: some baseball executives seemed to be much better than others at getting wins out of dollars. The idea didn't begin with me—an excellent baseball writer named Doug Pappas had long hammered on this idea of efficiency. Pappas had pointed out that one team, the Oakland A's, had been consistently so much more efficient than anyone else that they appeared to be in a different business. I have tried to explain how this could be.

To fully appreciate the response to *Moneyball* from inside the Club you need a bit of otherwise irrelevant background. When I began my reporting I didn't know anyone inside the Oakland A's; I'd never even heard of Billy Beane, the Oakland GM. In the year I spent studying his organization the only explicit interest Beane took in my project—the only time he mentioned it—were the few times he said I shouldn't focus too much on him. He and the other critical character in the Oakland front office, assistant GM Paul DePodesta, were never exactly rude to me but they made it pretty clear that they had more interesting things to do than talk to me. The only power they ever had over my project was to throw me out of their office or clubhouse—which they did, on occasion. But the sad truth is that I was a matter of some indifference to them. As far as they knew I wasn't even writing a book about the Oakland A's. I was writing a book about the collision of reason and baseball. (They weren't the only ones whose eyes glazed over when I tried to explain what I was up to.) They would be in it but so would other teams. So, for that matter, would players whose lives had been changed by the new value system they were introducing. A long section of the book would be devoted to the spiritual father of their enterprise, the baseball writer Bill James.

It was only after I had spoken with other teams, and found they didn't have much to add to this particular story, that I came to focus on the A's management and players. By that time the baseball season was over, and I had my material. As always happens when the material is strong, the story became telescoped in the writing. I felt compelled to jettison everything that didn't have to do with putting together a baseball team. The result wasn't anything like a biography of a man; it was more like a biography of an idea—that left its main character, Billy Beane, for thirty-five pages at a time.

Until they saw it, the Oakland front office had only the faintest notion of what my book would be like. Oakland's staff read the book when reviewers read it, about a month before the hardcover hit the stores. Each member of that staff had a slightly different reaction to it. Beane's was something like horror. He was surprised that so much of the thing was about him and disturbed that I'd portrayed him as a maniac. I probably should have felt more guilt about this than I did. I assumed most readers understood that this wasn't the whole man, and that I had my own agenda. I wanted to capture Beane doing what he did so well and interestingly: value, acquire, and manage baseball players. And when he did this, in his most intense moments, he was a bit of a maniac.

That's the background to what happened next, which was something new in my experience as a writer. The Club of people who made their living just off the field of play—GMs and scouts, along with some of the noisier members of the Women's Auxiliary, the writers and commentators—flipped out. Not at me, mind you: at *Billy Beane*. For the six months of the 2003 baseball season, the sun did not set without some professional blowhard—half of the radio guys seemed to think it was clever to call themselves "Mad Dog"—spouting off about Beane's outsized ego. To catalog the scorn heaped on the poor man—whose only crime was not throwing me out of his office often enough—would take too long. But it's worth citing a few examples:

> It was Beane who had a best-selling book, *Moneyball*, written mostly about him, in which he bragged endlessly about outsmarting wealthy clubs by reinventing the way players are evaluated. —Art Thiel, *Seattle Post Intelligencer*

> . . . the other person being mentioned as Evans' possible successor, Oakland's Billy Beane, has done a terrific job with modest funds with the A's, but he's also a shameless self-promoter who wrote a book about his imagined genius and is despised by scouts around baseball. —Doug Krikorian, *Long Beach Press Telegram*

> Two things are apparent in the recently released book *Moneyball, The Art of Winning an Unfair Game.* Oakland general manager Billy Beane's ego has exploded. . . . —Tracy Ringolsby, *The Rocky Mountain News*

I'll return later to the second thing apparent to Mr. Ringolsby, because he speaks for a big faction of the Club. What seemed apparent to me, terrifyingly so, was that baseball insiders were going to compel my subjects to recant—to say that this book about their organization was laughably off-target and could safely be ignored. If the Oakland A's had a dollar for every journalist who asked Billy Beane or Paul DePodesta if they'd been "misquoted," they could have gone out and bought a proper center fielder. The public pressure on Beane, especially, was intense: no man was ever accused of saying more things he never said, or doing more things he never did. A few insiders took the novel approach of accusing Beane of lying that he'd been misquoted, when he'd never said he'd been misquoted in the first place. "He was not misquoted for two hundred and some pages," thundered an outraged Seattle GM, Pat Gillick, just before swearing he would never read the book, and just after his expensive Mariners, once again, had been left in the dust by the low-budget A's.

But the Oakland A's didn't recant, and a phony debate soon heated up. It wasn't as interesting as a real debate, in that there was no chance for an exchange of ideas. It was more like a religious war—or like the endless, fruitless dispute between creationists and evolutionary theorists. On one side, parrying half-baked questions and insults, was the community of baseball fans who thought hard about the use and abuse of baseball statistics. On the other side, hurling the half-baked questions and insults, were the Club members, who felt a deep, inchoate desire to preserve their status.

Q: If Billy Beane thinks he's such a goddamn genius, how come he didn't draft (fill in the high school phenom)? How come he's paying Jermaine Dye $11 million a year?

A: The point is not that Billy Beane is infallible; the point is that he has seized upon a system of thought to make what is an inherently uncertain judgment, the future performance of a baseball player, a little less uncertain. He's not a fortune-teller. He's a card counter in a casino.

Q: If Billy Beane's so smart, and he says that on-base percentage is so important, how come the A's don't score more runs?

A: They don't score more runs because their on-base percentage is not that great—much worse than it used to be. The market for on-base percentage has changed, thanks in large part to the success of the Oakland A's. Still, the A's on-base percentage retains one important trait: it's good for the money. And the point is not to have the highest on-base percentage, but to win games as cheaply as possible. And the way to win games cheaply is to buy the qualities in a baseball player that the market undervalues, and sell the ones that the market overvalues.

Q: What kind of egomaniac claims that he discovered all these statistics? On-base percentage! My old buddy (fill in the name of old buddy) has known about on-base percentage since 1873.

A: The Oakland's A's never claimed to have discovered sophisticated statistical analysis. They claim to be ramming it down the throat of an actual big league baseball team.

I had gone to some trouble to show that all the ideas Beane slapped together were hatched by someone else's brain. Indeed, any reader of *Moneyball* who had read Bill James or followed the work of some of the best baseball writers (Peter Gammons, Rob Neyer, Alan Schwarz) or the two leading Web sites, baseballprospectus and baseballprimer, might fairly wonder what all the fuss was about: *We knew this already.* The fuss, so far as I was concerned, was that the rubber had finally met the road, and, for putting it there, Billy Beane deserved a lot of credit. (Or blame, depending on your point of view.) Intellectual courage was his contribution. He'd had the nerve to seize upon ideas rejected, or at least not taken too seriously, by his fellow Club members, and put them into practice. But I'd never thought of Beane as a genius. He was more like a gifted Wall Street trader with no talent for research.

Over and over again during the 2003 season I found myself facing one reaction from the wider reading public and another from inside the Club. But it wasn't until Joe Morgan weighed in that I fully understood the discrepancy. Hall of Fame player, ESPN announcer, general man around baseball, Morgan was the closest thing to Club Social Chairman. And when Joe Morgan decided he needed to talk about *Moneyball*, the tone of the discourse went from weird to stark raving mad. In one of his mid-season ESPN chat sessions Morgan was asked what he thought of the book. Morgan wrote:

> It's typical if you write a book, you want to be the hero. That is apparently what Beane has done. According to what I read in the *Times* [the *New York Times* had excerpted *Moneyball*] Beane is smarter than anyone else. I don't think it will make him popular with the other GMs or the other people in baseball.

A number of people pointed out to Joe Morgan, in print, that Billy Beane hadn't written *Moneyball*. It had no effect. A week later, during another chat, someone else asked Morgan what he would do to improve the A's, if he were Billy Beane. To which, after summoning all of his wit, Joe replied, "I wouldn't be Billy Beane first of all! I wouldn't write the book *Moneyball*!"

Here was the nub of the problem: Joe Morgan hadn't read the book but he was certain Billy Beane had written it. Even people inside the Club who understood that some other human being had actually taken the trouble to scribble down the words in *Moneyball* took the book, at bottom, to be the work of Billy Beane. *Billy Beane was saying that there was some objective way to measure the performance of a baseball team, and that he was the best at it.* Even worse: *Billy Beane had written a book to say that a lot of things that Club members do and say is ludicrous.*

It was, in a way, an author's dream: the people most upset about his book were the ones unable to divine that he had written it. Meanwhile, outside the Club, the level of both interest and reading comprehension was as good as it gets. The Oakland front office had calls from a cross section of American business and sporting life: teams from the NHL, NFL, and NBA; Wall Street firms; Fortune 500 companies; Hollywood studios; college and high school baseball programs. There was even a fellow who ran a chain of hot dog stands who found a lesson for his business in the experiment occurring inside the Oakland front office. (Don't ask.) Every nook and cranny of American society, it seemed, held people similarly obsessed with finding and exploiting market inefficiencies—and the Oakland front office inspired them. The people most certain they had nothing to learn were other Major League Baseball teams.

But of course they didn't! They weren't a business, they were a Club. In a business, if someone comes along and exposes the trade secrets of your most efficient competitor, you're elated. Even if you have your doubts, you grab the book, peek inside, check it out. *Just to see.* Not in baseball. In baseball, they were furious. In the Club, there was no need to read it—baseball executives routinely *bragged* that they hadn't read it—because, well, it was offensive. *In poor taste,* was the absurd phrase actually used by Seattle GM and Grand Poo-Bah of the Raccoon Lodge, Pat Gillick.

What baseball did, instead, was cast about for reasons to dismiss what had happened in Oakland—and what was now happening in Toronto and Boston. If the nerve was so raw, it was because the idea of rational baseball management had already begun to spread. The Boston Red Sox, having failed in their attempt to hire Billy Beane, did the next best thing, and hired a very bright young man, Theo Epstein, who viewed Beane as his role model. The Toronto Blue Jays had already hired Beane's right-hand man, J. P. Ricciardi. Both Epstein and Ricciardi met with cultural resistance—though the Red Sox press is so reliably venomous that it was impossible to distinguish the poison directed at the new

regime from the poison they'd aimed at every other person who
had the temerity to pass through Fenway Park. What was interesting in Boston was the story that never got written, and the
question that never got asked: if we've been doing things more or
less the same way for eighty years, and we are hysterically angry
about the results, shouldn't we try something different? Might not
science offer an answer to the Curse of the Bambino?

Toronto was closer to a pure case study. Ricciardi, the new GM,
had done what every enlightened GM will eventually do: fire a lot
of scouts, hire someone comfortable with statistical analysis
(Keith Law from baseballprospectus—*a Web site, for cryin' out
loud*), and begin to trade for value, ruthlessly. He dumped as many
high-priced players as he could and replaced them with a lot of
lower-priced ones—and began to win more games. His biggest
problem was finding teams willing to take bloated stars off his
hands. (His best day all year, he told me, was when George Steinbrenner watched a Yankee right fielder drop a fly ball, blew a fuse,
and demanded the Yankees buy Raul Mondesi off the Jays.) He
slashed the Jays' payroll from $90 million to $55 million. In an
efficient market, if you cut your payroll by 40 percent, you would
expect to lose a lot more games. That's not what happened, of
course. What happened was that the Jays went, overnight, from
being a depressing group of highly paid underachievers to an excit-
ing team. They were younger, cheaper, *and* better.

For the most part, the city of Toronto appreciated the change.
But even there, in that gentle and decent place, was that noisome
sound—the miserable squeaks of protest from the Club's Women's
Auxiliary. One morning during the 2003 season, Toronto woke up
to a front-page story in the *Toronto Star* that raised alarming questions about the new Blue Jays. "The White Jays?" it was called.
The headline, along with the mug shots of the players, read: "In a
city of so many multicultural faces, Toronto's baseball team is the
whitest in the league. Why?" The baseball writer behind the article, Geoff Baker, had made his own little study. He'd found that

there were ten nonwhite players on the average big league twenty-five-man roster and that, after Ricciardi's wheeling and dealing, the new Jays had only six. The new GM seemed to be systematically trading for lower-priced *white guys*. How sad, how regrettable, in a city as famous for its diversity as Toronto, that the Blue Jays no longer represented it. "Ricciardi is at a loss to explain the numbers as anything beyond coincidence," wrote Baker, who was not similarly at a loss. He found an explanation in the way J. P. Ricciardi ran a baseball team.

It was an intriguing line of attack, but with a tactical weakness. By its very nature, it demanded a response from outside the Club. (That, in the end, is the Club's Achilles heel. It can never fully escape the larger culture that supports it.) Letters poured into the *Star*, the *Star's* ombudsman was called in to apologize for the package, and other newspapers took the piece to heart. The *National Post* ran a withering editorial that pointed out that the Jays' promotional campaign featured two players, Carlos Delgado and Vernon Wells, both black. That Toronto was 8 percent black and 2 percent Latino, its baseball team was 12 percent black and 12 percent Latino, and so, taken literally, the article made the case for *reducing* the number of racial minorities in Blue Jays' uniforms. That it was grotesque to make racial generalizations based on a couple of moves. Wrote the *Post*: "The story, shot through as it was with vague hints of racism, comprised a smear job on a baseball team with no other agenda than to win games and please its fans."

But where the anger climaxed was in the Blue Jays clubhouse: the players were ticked off. You see, they were laboring under the impression they'd been selected for their ability to play baseball, not their skin color. Carlos Delgado told the *Toronto Sun*, "It was the most stupid thing I've ever heard. It doesn't make any sense. You don't see anybody writing anything about the Maple Leafs not having a black guy or the Raptors having 90 percent black players. It [race] has nothing to do with it. We don't have any kind of problem in the clubhouse and we don't need that shit."

Enter, stage right, Richard Griffin, a second baseball writer on the *Toronto Star*. Griffin was another old baseball guy who had been on Ricciardi's case from the start. Relentless in his ire for the new regime, and their new methods, he never missed a chance to point out where they were going wrong. Now he explained patiently to the *Star*'s readers that they should not "shoot the messenger." His colleague's article hadn't been about racism, he said, but . . . well, what *was* it about? He cast about for a phrase and came up with: "The fluctuating racial mosaic of baseball." *Ah! So that's it*, the innocent Toronto newspaper reader must have thought, as he scratched his noggin. Then Griffin clarified his meaning: "Jays GM J. P. Ricciardi along with Oakland's Billy Beane and other new wavers," he wrote, "believe in building offence through patience at the plate and taking no chances on the bases. That's pre WW-2 style of play. Under those criteria, Jackie Robinson could not have played in the majors."

Well, if you want to steer the conversation away from racism there are safer examples to pick. It was the nearest thing baseball writing has seen to a Marx Brothers routine. Griffin was Harpo who, seeing his friend engulfed in flames, grabs the bucket of water, without noticing that it's marked KEROSENE. What made the whole episode doubly weird is that Jackie Robinson was exactly the sort of player the A's and the Jays salivate over. He had the stats they tended to stress—high on-base, plate discipline, great power for a second baseman, etc.—plus *he was undervalued*. Indeed, one way of looking at the revolution in baseball management is as a search for less dramatic versions of Jackie Robinson— players who, for one unfair reason or another, often because of their appearance, had been maligned and undervalued by the market.

Still, in one way these two Toronto baseball writers were right: no matter how artfully it tried to insinuate racism, their story wasn't about race. Race was merely a tool, a weapon in a bigger, more important struggle: the fight against people who didn't take

the scout or the sportswriter on faith. What had got under their
skin were all these . . . little nerds out there with their Web logs
and baseball stats and computers who thought they had something to say about building a baseball team. Pelted with rotten
fruit, Baker claimed that the response to his story was no more
than a conspiracy of these nerds. "We suspect," he wrote to me,
"that many of the e-mails and letters complaining about the story
were in part the result of an organized campaign started on baseball web logs and by other parties with an interest in refuting the
story." Those pesky outsiders!

The "White Jays," the uninformed rantings of baseball writers
too lazy to pick up a telephone, the snide asides on ESPN, the
knowing jokes about Billy Beane's "genius"—it was all of a piece.
To defend the Club against the new idea, the members had to distort the idea.

By the end of the 2003 baseball season I had learned something
from publishing *Moneyball.* I learned that if you look long enough
for an argument against reason you will find it. For six months,
inside the Club, there had been a palpable longing for the Oakland
A's to fail. At the start of the season, after the book came out,
there was some hope this might happen quickly. Scrambling to
ditch payroll, Billy Beane had traded his star closer, Billy Koch, to
the White Sox for a pitcher a lot of people had written off, Keith
Foulke. He'd lost his fourth starter, Cory Lidle, who'd also become
too dear. The A's, once again, were playing in a division with far
richer teams. Worst of all, the Red Sox and the Blue Jays were
making the market for baseball players more efficient. How on
earth could the A's continue to win?

Well, they did win. They won more regular season games than
anyone but the Giants, the Yankees, and the Braves. They then
won the first two games of the five-game playoff series against the
Red Sox. There was real joy in this—not just in watching David
beat Goliath but in watching people with an investment in

Goliath's lifestyle try to prepare for what appeared to be David's imminent victory. Every year for the previous three, after the Oakland A's had been bounced from the playoffs, the Club's Women's Auxiliary raised a chant: the A's can't win! Their dislike of the sacrifice bunt, the skepticism about the stolen base, their bizarre taste in players, their terrifying irreverence of old baseball wisdom—all these quirks that worked so well for them during the regular season somehow doomed the Oakland A's in the playoffs. Well, after Game Two, nobody—and I mean nobody—said, "Ah, the Oakland A's can't beat the Boston Red Sox. They might have taken the first two but by the very nature of their enterprise they cannot ever win a playoff series." What they did was cast about for an explanation to rationalize the horrible events about to transpire. A consensus of what that might be began to congeal:

Ramon Hernandez bunted!

The A's had won the first game of the Red Sox series when their molasses-footed catcher, with two outs, dropped a bunt down the third base line. The act itself triggered a chemical reaction in the minds of Club members.

Moneyball teams don't bunt! These . . . little nerds all say that smart managers don't trade outs for bases. Ha! Look! Okay, they won. But they've proven our point!

Never mind the absurdity of attributing the outcome of a game to the single event. Never mind that a single exception does no harm to the larger argument: that over the long haul it's a mistake to give away outs for bases. Never mind that the dislike of the sacrifice bunt is a trivial sliver of the new approach to baseball. *It wasn't a sacrifice bunt.* There were two outs! Ramon Hernandez wasn't trying to trade a base for an out. He was bunting for a base hit.

Well, thank God, the Oakland A's lost in five. (Though, surely, the case would be cleaner if they lost in three, no?) And when the Florida Marlins won the World Series, it was of course inevitable, the result of their true grit. The special something they possessed that only Club members could understand. *Baseball America* columnist Tracy Ringolsby—by far the loudest, most obsessed of Billy Beane's critics—was on the scene to pant all over Jack McKeon, the Marlins' manager, and pay him the ultimate compliment, that "he certainly doesn't buy into the theories of the book *Moneyball*, which proclaimed teams should draft only college players, particularly pitchers." Of course, it didn't matter what McKeon thought about drafting players, as he hadn't built the Marlins but was air-dropped into their midst in mid-season. This McKeon guy had that special something that Ringolsby understands—and that guys like Billy Beane never will. That piece of manhood that little nerds will never understand. The bracing thing that Ringolsby can feel in his bones and you, weak-chinned outsider, cannot. The special something that won championships.

That special something, or its absence, happens to be the other thing that, in Ringolsby's view, was instantly apparent in *Moneyball*. The problem wasn't just that Billy Beane's ego was out of control. It was that the author of *Moneyball* "has a limited knowledge of baseball and total infatuation with Billy Beane." *A limited knowledge of baseball*—it sounds damning enough, but what does it mean? What it surely does *not* mean is that Ringolsby has performed on a baseball field under pressure—or that I have not—for he has never come near the field of play. Nor does it mean that he has actually tried to understand what these people in Oakland are up to, for he's never bothered to interview them. Think of it! A guy who makes his living writing about baseball working himself up into a fine lather, year after year, about this radical experiment in Oakland and never once bothering to pick up the phone and ask Billy Beane to explain what he's up to. *A limited knowledge of baseball*: What it means, so far as I can tell, is that he's just another unathletic guy who's assigned himself the job of keeping people out of the game who, in his view, have no business inside. He's not a writer. He's a bouncer.

But he has his own moment, this fellow. When he sits down to write his column he knows in his heart that he speaks for a lot of people who work just off the field of play. He may only belong to the Women's Auxiliary, but his view of the game reflects those of actual Club members. A lot of people who make the decisions about building baseball teams think a lot like he does. That's why it's possible, on the field of play, for a team with no money to win so many games.

ACKNOWLEDGMENTS

I never could have written this book without the help and encouragement of the Oakland A's. Many people who work for the organization feature prominently in this story but a few who were important to me do not, and I would like to thank them here. The team's co-owner, Steve Schott, took me to a ball game and encouraged me to pursue my line of inquiry. The front office's first line of defense, Betty Shinoda, Wilona Perry, and Maggie Baptist, never made me feel anything but welcome. Jim Young and Debbie Gallas made my life easier than it should have been in the press box. Mickey Morabito, who had no interest in letting me anywhere near the team's plane, took me along for the ride. Keith Lieppman and Ted Polakowski, who must have wondered why I so longed to pester their minor league players, instead helped me to do it. Steve Vucinich might have asked what business I had in his clubhouse; instead he did everything to make me feel welcome short of steaming LEWIS on the back of an Oakland A uniform and sending me out to the mound. Jim Bloom introduced me to big league players and helped me to sell them on my project. Two of those players, Tim Hudson and Barry Zito, helped me far more than their brief appearances in this book suggest.

Several old friends read parts or all of the manuscript and saved me from myself: Tony Horwitz, Gerry Marzorati, Jacob Weisberg, and Chris Wiman. Several new friends combed through the first draft and helped to save me from baseball: Rob Neyer, Dan Okrent, and Doug Pappas. Dick Cramer and Pete Palmer offered invaluable counsel on both the theory and history of sabermetrics. Alan Schwarz provided assistance on the history of baseball statistics, which was remarkably generous, given that he is himself writing a book on the subject.

Roy Eisenhardt introduced me to Billy Beane, a fact that went a long way with Billy, with reason. Looking through my notes it's clear that the book arose from what amounts to a year long open-ended conversation with Billy Beane, Paul DePodesta, and David Forst. And yet not once did any of them seek to control or dilute what I might write. I will always be grateful to them for their generosity of spirit.

I am blessed to write for the publishing equivalent of the Oakland A's. Encouraging me to write about baseball was as bold as telling Scott Hatteberg to play first base. For this I am more than usually grateful to my editor, Starling Lawrence, and his assistant, Morgen Van Vorst. The Norton sales director, Bill Rusin, should have put a stop to this project before it began, but he at least pretended to approve of it. I am grateful to have had the chance to present the book to Oliver Gilliland, but it goes only a little way to alleviating the sorrow of knowing that it was the last time I ever will.

For help in just about every phase of this project I am grateful to my wife, Tabitha Soren. Her official stats, impressive as they are, still don't do justice to her performance.

INDEX